Other Running Books by Hal Higdon

On the Run from Dogs and People
Fitness After Forty

For Children

Heroes of the Olympics
The Electronic Olympics

Beginner's Running Guide

Beginner's Running Guide

by Hal Higdon

Recommended Reading:
Runner's World Magazine, 1400 Stierlin Road,
Mountain View, CA 94043; $9.50/year
Write for a free catalog of publications
and supplies for runners and other athletes.

Library of Congress #78-369
ISBN #0-89037-030-X

For Bob, Judy, Helen & Dolores

Contents

Introduction: Everybody Can Run 1

1

Part One: In the Beginning

1 Run Dick, Run 11
2 Closet Jogging 21
   Schedule: A Guide for Closet Joggers 26
3 Making Tracks 29
4 First Steps and Breaths 35
   Schedule: A Guide for Beginning Runners 43
5 Commitment 47

2

Part Two: Where, When, and in What

6 Running Out the Door 61
7 Running in Circles 71
8 Fitting It In 79
9 Finding the Right Shoes 89
10 Upward from the Foot Bone 113

3

Part Three: Coping

11 Battling the Elements 127
12 The Three D's 139
13 The Running Lifestyle 153

4

Part Four: Doing It

14 Looking Good 163
15 Textures in Training. 185
16 Putting It Together. 197
17 Perhaps You Need a Coach 209

5

Part Five: Competition

18 All About Racing 221
   Schedule: A Guide for Beginning Racers 233
19 Stalking the Wild Marathon. .237
   Schedule: A Guide for Beginning Marathoners 248
20 All About Tactics 253
21 Running Off the Road 267
22 Getting Hurt 279

6

Part Six: Running for Everybody

23 Women's Running 295
24 The Young and the Old 305

7

Part Seven: Running Hot and Cold

25 Hibernation. 315
26 Going All the Way. 323
   Schedule: A Guide for Elite Runners. 334

Index 338

Introduction
Everybody Can Run

How do you run? It sounds like a simple question, and strangely enough, the answer may be just as simple. In a seminar on running last year Don Kardong, fourth place finisher in the 1976 Olympic marathon, addressed the question of how you run this way: "First you place your right foot in front of your left foot. Then you put your left foot in front of your right foot. Then you alternate."

Don Kardong was joking, of course, but running is almost that simple. The only refinement that might be made of Don's definition is that at some point during this alternating process, you should get both feet off the ground—otherwise you are walking.

Unless inhibited by some physical handicap, anybody can run. You can run. While researching my previous book *Fitness After Forty*, I encountered one man who taught his 71-year-old, bedridden mother to run. Babies learn to run almost before they learn to walk. Their first tottering steps—when they hurl themselves forward off one foot to land and struggle for balance on the other—resembles running much more than it does walking. Only when they get older, often *much* older, do children abandon running as their preferred form of locomotion.

Watch any playground where younger children gather and you will see a group in almost perpetual motion. Young children run continuously while at play—never very fast, and with frequent pauses between running bursts—but almost continuously. That is why coaches who work with age-group teams seldom have to

1

waste much time on basic conditioning. Children come to them already in shape because of their normal activity.

When children become teenagers, they begin to move away from their youthful play activities. Partly through observing sedentary adults, they have gotten the idea that running isn't hip, running isn't cool, running is something for kids. Adults smoke and drink, they see, so that's what kids must do to be perceived as adults. (Coincidentally, this is when atherosclerotic plaques begin to form in the arteries of previously healthy young individuals during the teen years—but more on this subject later.) The point is that we learn to run early in life, then forget this lesson as we mature.

Our running ability remains part of our permanent motor skills, even though our muscles deteriorate from disuse. In *Fitness After Forty* I identified the four best sports for increasing physical fitness: swimming, cycling, cross-country skiing, and running. Regardless of the aesthetic value of each, only one of the four might be considered "natural." If you threw someone unfamiliar with swimming into a pool, there is a good chance that person would drown before figuring out the proper strokes. Similarly, imagine what would happen if you transported a bicycle several hundred years back into history, how long would it take an individual to learn to sit on the bicycle, balance, and pedal it. As for cross-country skiing, even people who know how others move with skis and poles often have difficulty mastering the tricky maneuvers.

Sedentary critics might claim that if God meant us to swim, cycle, or cross-country ski, he would have equipped us with gills, spokes and/or very long, narrow, flat feet. But God did equip us with legs suitable for running as well as walking, and everybody can run. You just do it. You run!

While doing research for this book, I decided to teach a course in running at the YMCA in Michigan City, Indiana. My own beginnings in running dated back 30 years, so although I knew all the mechanics of how one runs, I had a hard time remembering the problems, both physiological and psychological, of a beginning runner, someone without my continuous exposure to the running sport.

The first time I met my class, I made a few basic statements about running as an activity, then said: "Let's do some running around the gym."

And everybody ran. Some ran more gracefully than others and some ran longer than others (not necessarily the same ones), but everybody ran. I did not need to show them the running motions or hold their hands to balance them as I might a baby starting to walk. They simply did it. Running is a very simple act.

But it also can be a very complicated act, or I would not be sitting down to write a 26-chapter book on how to run. My well-worn *Webster's New World Dictionary* defines the word *run* as: "to go by moving the legs, rapidly, faster than in walking, and (in a two-legged animal) in such a way that for an instant both feet are off the ground."

Fair enough. And that is only the first definition. Immediately after are 29 additional definitions of the verb *run*. Then come 24 definitions of *run* used as a transitive verb, 29 definitions of the noun form, and 4 definitions of the adjective form. In fact, nearly two pages of the dictionary are monopolized by various variations of the word, including: a *run for one's money* (powerful competition); *runaway* (a fugitive); *runner* (a person, animal, or thing that runs, as a racer); *running gear* (the working parts of a machine); *running mate* (a horse that is a teammate for another horse); *run-of-the-mill* (ordinary); and *runway* (a way, as a channel, track, chute, groove, trought, etc., in, on, or along which something runs, or moves).

In contrast, *Webster* wastes precious little time with the word *jog*. We learn only that to jog is "to give a little shake, shove, or jerk to." Small wonder then that some runners are insulted if someone comes up to them at a party and asks: "Are you a jogger?" The question might be reinterpreted as "Are you a jerk?"

Joggers and Runners

The question, "What's the difference between jogging and running?" is one frequently asked me when I make appearances or give interviews for the media. Because there is no simple answer, I often respond facetiously, which usually permits us to move on to the next more important question. I say: "If your wife catches you jogging around with another woman, she probably won't get as mad."

Others have attempted to define the difference more precisely either through time (anyone who runs faster than eight-minute miles is a runner); through activity (if you enter races, you're a runner); or through attitude (if you think you're a runner, you're a runner. If you think you're a jogger, you're a jogger.).

I am willing to accept all the above definitions—plus one of my own. Three is the magic number. You convert from a jogger to a runner when you keep at it past the third month, start covering more than three miles in your workouts, and do it more often than three days a week. But even the most gifted Olympic runners also remain joggers and often make comments like: "Let's jog a few laps before taking a shower."

During National Running Week 1977, I visited the home of *Runner's World* publisher Bob Anderson for a post-race party following the New Year's Eve Midnight Run in Los Altos, California. Among those at the party were world-class athletes Bill Rodgers, Marty Liquori, and Jerome Drayton, along with a number of fitness runners who either were employees of World Publications or friends of Bob and his wife Rita. At one point during the festivities I wandered into the kitchen where Josh Kimeto, a Kenyan runner who attended Washington State, conversed with one of the fitness runners about his aches, his pains, his plans, his training. After Kimeto left, the fitness runner turned to me with a broad smile on his face and remarked: "You know, he sounds just like every other runner I've met."

And that is true. Olympic calibre athletes share a common activity and interest with the jogger who does a few miles, three times a week, around a YMCA track. The fact that the former group runs endless miles at a sub-5:00 pace and the latter group struggles to do one mile under 10:00 matters less than the fact that both run.

It is a shared experience.

You Are Not Alone

But this returns us to the basic question with which we began this chapter: "How do you run?" The beginning runner who poses that question to the instructor at the local YMCA, or to the marathoner who happens to live down the block, is not asking how to run. That person already *knows* how to run, in the Kardongian sense of moving the right foot, then the left foot, then alternating. That person is asking a series of more complicated questions:

What sort of shoes do I wear

How do I swing my arms when I run?

How do I breathe while running?

What can I do to get rid of this pain in my side?

How far should I run?

How fast should I run?

Where should I run?

How often should I run?

Should I race?

One final, very important question, which hopefully has led some already experienced runners to purchase this book, is: How do I run faster? In fact, that last question is one which even Frank Shorter would like to answer. If Frank could have answered that question in Montreal in 1976, he might have picked up a second Olympic marathon gold medal instead of a silver.

My purpose in writing this book is to produce a basic, instructional guide on the act (and art) of running that will provide everything that a beginning runner needs to know to get started, while not turning off the more experienced runner who wants to learn more about the refinements of the running sport. In fact, the beginning runner changes very rapidly into the experienced runner; the maturation process takes about three months.

The jogger—if you will permit me this expression just once— begins to have runner's experience the moment that person starts "placing his right foot in front of his left." The jogger experiences shortness of breath, fatigue, and most likely very stiff and sore muscles afterwards. The jogger needs someone to say that he or she is not the first person to have such feelings. When members of my running class first complained about their stiff calves, I assured them that when Frank Shorter runs too hard, he has stiff calves too.

In fact, I remember that particular noontime class because my legs ached more than theirs. I had run a hard 10,000-meter race the previous weekend over a course covered with ice and snow, which forced me, in order to maintain balance, into an unnatural flat-footed gait using different muscles than those I use normally. Since I was covering 90 miles per week preparing for the Boston Marathon, I had not taken the necessary rest afterward for my legs to recover. I had that familiar, stiff, deadwood feeling that competitive runners often have when they push themselves too hard in training.

So, beginning runners, when you get those aches and pains, remember: You are not alone.

Information Exchange

A story told to me by my cousin Bob Molinaro illustrates the importance for runners to exchange information on their running experiences.

Attracted by the publicity given the First Chicago Distance Classic in 1977 (5300 runners would eventually enter), Bob decided to attempt that race. Several days before the start, he called me for some last-minute advice. Fearful of the dangers of attempting too much, I tried to talk him out of racing. However, Bob explained to me that he had been running six miles a day on his lunch hour with 8- and 10-mile runs on the weekend. I reconsidered, commenting: "You're probably in better shape than I am."

He ran, finished, and three months later did 3:27 at the Mayor Daley Marathon, his first attempt at that distance. His wife Judy, a slim, attractive 29-year-old, took up the sport, completed a 10-miler I sponsored that fall in Beverly Shores near my home and later won her first merchandise prize (a pumpkin pie) in a Thanksgiving Day six-mile. Meanwhile, the wife of Bob's brother Johnny began to jog as did her sister and Judy's sister. After nearly 15 years of being the "odd one" at family gatherings, I suddenly was no longer alone.

Anyway, the story Bob told was about one of his coworkers (call him Jim) who also finished the Mayor Daley Marathon in a time ten or fifteen minutes faster. Bob and Jim saw each other several times at work in the days that followed, but Bob did not get a chance to speak to him until two weeks later. "How do you feel about the race now?" Bob Molinaro finally asked.

"Pretty good," Jim replied, "but I've been having trouble with my training."

"What's the matter?"

"I've been so tired that I've only trained three times in the two weeks since the race was over," said the worker, "and on one of those runs, I only got as far as 24 miles."

My cousin (who at least had received some preliminary advice from me) was stunned that anyone could believe that to run a 26-mile-385 yard race you had to run that far each day in practice. In fact, the raw ability of someone capable of doing that also stunned him.

Jim typifies the new breed of American runner—eager, but still getting his (or her) act together. In 1977, Farrah Fawcett-Majors appeared on the cover of *People* magazing jogging with her "bionic" husband and the Gallup Poll informed us that 18 million adult Americans jogged at least occasionally. A book on the sport (*The Complete Book of Running* by Jim Fixx) was not only the number one best-seller but stayed there until displaced by the latest post-Watergate confession. The size of many races was doubling, and even tripling, as the American public turned to running as its number one fitness activity.

Bob Molinaro eventually offered his fellow worker some advice, suggesting that he cover less distance during some of his workouts but at a faster pace. Jim accepted the suggestion and later reported that it seemed to improve his speed. He mentioned that he frequently passed, on his regular workouts along the Chicago lakefront, one of the top finishers from the Mayor Daley Marathon. But they were always going in opposite directions and passing each other too rapidly for an exchange of information.

Exchanging information is essential for runners, new and old, if they are not to repeat the mistakes that almost everybody makes when they start to run. That is why I decided to write *The Beginner's Running Guide*. Although I cannot promise that by reading it you will cut even 10 seconds from your marathon time, I hope that I can make running more enjoyable for you by giving my opinions—garnered from 30 years in the sport as runner, racer, lecturer, and writer—of how best to do it. And how *not* to do it.

Eight MPH

Of all the 18 books I have so far written on subjects as diverse as crime, business, and the Civil War, *The Beginner's Running*

Guide has been the most enjoyable to research. This is because I wrote it on the run. This book was composed at approximately eight miles per hour, my approximate training speed, at least during the winter when encumbered by extra clothes and over snowy surfaces. As I worked out each day—in fact, twice each day—I would meditate about my running and the running of others. Usually my best thoughts would come to me after I had gone about five miles, the 40-minute effect about which I'll be writing later in this book. When I returned home I often rushed upstairs, still dressed in my running gear, to type my ideas on index cards, before my post-workout shower washed them from my mind. I am staring at one of those index cards right now. It has "eight mph" written across the top of it.

But imagine the classic rationalization of being able to say to your wife as you run out the door en route to a 12-mile workout: "I'm going to do some research."

The results of that research follow.

Part 1
In the
Beginning

1

Run Dick, Run

The trick in learning to run
might be knowing when to stop

I do a lot of running on Lake Shore Drive in Long Beach, a suburban community outside Michigan City, Indiana. So do a lot of other people now, although when I first moved to town in April, 1964, I was pretty much The Lone Runner. I didn't have a Tonto to carry my silver bullets either.

I remained in that singular position for a number of years, but one by one, others began to run on the same road. Now Lake Shore Drive is like a superhighway for runners. Only last weekend I rose early and started my workout at 5:30. At that time on a Saturday morning, you normally would expect few creatures to be stirring, but I encountered two other runners before finishing my first mile.

One of the main advantages of roads paralleling lakes, rivers, or oceans—other than the view—is that there is no cross traffic. You only have to worry about being struck by a car from three directions instead of four. (More on that subject when I discuss defensive running in chapter 12.) Some of us who run on Lake Shore Drive facetiously refer to this street by its initials, LSD. To readers of *High Times* (which has nothing to do with the lack of quality of your last race performance), LSD is the name for a drug, also known as "acid," that became prevalent among youth in the 1960's.

A familiar form of training popularized by running-author Joe Henderson, also goes by those initials. To Joe Henderson and his disciples, LSD originally meant "Long Slow Distance"—although Joe later modified that term to "Long Steady Distance," so as not to offend runners who do not like their 7:00- or 8:00-per-mile pace identified as "slow."

The use of this term, and its drug connotations of "dropping acid," often caused a few double takes, a case in point being the time when Ralph Pidcock, the former United Fund director in Michigan City, commented one day in the bank: "Well, I guess I'll go take my LSD." *Flip, flip, flip* went all the secretaries' heads in his direction.

By LSD, of course, Ralph meant "Long Slow Distance"—as he quickly explained to the bank director who was about to pick up the telephone to have him fired. Moreover, Ralph added that he planned to take his LSD on LSD, the latter meaning Lake Shore Drive. If I was the Lone Runner, Ralph played the part of The Shadow: he liked to cloud men's minds. Eventually Ralph moved out of town to Chillicothe, Ohio. I haven't checked with him to see if that city, to keep up with current trends, might have a Cocaine Avenue.

Scout's Pace

Ralph also could have said, had it been his style, that he was going to take an IV injection. In this case he would not mean "intravenous," but rather "interval," a form of training on the track where runners alternate fast sprints with slow jogs. It is important for beginning runners to get the jargon down, even before you don the pair of training flats you purchased at the local sporting goods store for $39.95.

Anyway, one recent morning in the middle of winter I was out on LSD doing some LSD when I encountered someone taking their IV. Let me explain.

I was midway through a 16-mile workout, when I approached from behind a woman bundled up in a bright yellow sweatsuit running and walking along the road. I could tell she was a woman from the gait, and I could tell she was a novice because she ran on the right side of the road, bad positioning if you want to survive in traffic.

Her newness to the sport seemed apparent also from her running pattern: a measured number of steps running, followed by a like amount walking. This pattern of jog-walk-jog resembles the old "Scout's Pace" I learned years ago in the Boy Scouts.

Scout's Pace is 50 steps running followed by 50 steps walking, and you can cover a lot of ground in this manner. Most of the books and articles on how to run offer some form of advice, or schedule, similar to this jog-walk-jog system. It seemed obvious that she had read one of them, because she was beginning the proper way.

As I approached from behind, I planned to offer a few words of encouragement, as I do often to obvious newcomers I encounter on the road. ("Looking good!" is one typical remark, to which the reply sometimes comes: "Feeling bad.") But suddenly the woman turned, startled as she realized I was upon her. She looked as if I had caught her stepping out of the shower. Beginning runners are often self-conscious about how they look, not only to other runners, but also to non runners who may hurl cruel insults at them. When you are new at any activity, you often feel more vulnerable than you appear.

I smiled and shouted hello, and she helloed me back. We passed. Too quickly, because I wanted to at least tell her she was going about her running the right way. Beginning runners need all the encouragement they can get at first, because often their muscles hurt, and they wonder if they *ever* can cover a mile nonstop much less run it at a pace comparable to that run by a Bill Rodgers. As for the former achievement, probably yes; as to the latter one, probably no, but that does not mean that a beginner need not learn to enjoy the running sport at his or her appropriate level. The best piece of advice to give a new runner is to begin slow and take it easy. Sooner or later they will learn to run well, and enjoy their running.

Peeking Through the Fence

So before you get out in those LD-1000-V's, or Montreal II's, or SL 76's, drive someday to the local high school track, or cross-country course, or wherever it is that the fast, young athletes in your area train to race. You will have to go by car, because we haven't gotten you in good enough shape, *yet*, to run there. If it is spring, you will find these birds of competition flying around an all-weather 440-yard track. Stay outside the fence, because we do not want to contaminate you with too much early exposure to the sometimes hectic world of the competitive racers. Peek through the fence and see how they train.

See Dick run. See Jane run. Encourage them by your presence as a spectator. Run Dick, run. Run Jane, run. Observe them and their patterns.

Most likely they will be doing some form of interval training (the IV injections mentioned previously). Interval training was developed by the German physiologists Gerschler and Reindell, and it was very popular in the mid 1950's when I used to train with German runners while stationed in Stuttgart, Nurnberg, and Wurzburg. The methods of Gerschler and Reindell remain popular today, though modified greatly by new generations of athletes and coaches.

Interval running consists of hard, fast runs over relatively short distances punctuated by easy, slow runs often of the same length. A typical interval workout would be 10 x 440, 440 jog (10 fast 440-yard laps; 10 slow 440-yard jogs). The fast 440s (or "quarters") might be covered in 70 seconds; the slow 440s might be jogged in two minutes. The theory is that by resting briefly between fast runs, the runner can train longer at the pace at which he normally would race. A miler capable of 4:00, for example, might do that same workout at 60-second pace.

The term "interval" comes from the period (or interval) of relative rest between these fast runs. I often hear young runners talk about "doing my intervals," meaning they identify an interval as the fast portion of the workout, but they are mistaken. You already know more than they do. Hold your head high, beginning jogger!

Sometimes an interval workout may consist of 110s, 220s, 880s, miles, or any mixture of those and other distances. The interval jogged—or even walked—between can be any of the above distances as well, or it may be predicated on a time basis. Scientifically-oriented coaches sometimes measure pulse rate. When the athlete's pulse rate returns to a predetermined norm, he runs again. If you rest longer than about five minutes, some coaches say you are doing "repeats" rather than interval training, but let's not get into that yet. One favorite interval workout of mine, done in the mid-1960s, when I sometimes trained with indoor mile record holder Tom O'Hara, was to run 24 x 440 in 75 seconds with a 30-second break in between. To some that may seem incredible, but actually that was the workout we did on our "easy" days.

That probably is more than any beginning runner needs to

know about interval running at this point (although we will consider the subject in greater depth later in the book). A knowledge of this training method is important because interval training is the easiest, and most efficient, means by which any beginning jogger can start to get in shape. Of course, no YMCA instructor would begin the first session of his jogging class by telling the people gathered in front of him, some of them overweight, many of them smokers, or ex-smokers, that they were going to engage in the same style of interval training used by Olympic champions. He would frighten them, but nevertheless that is what they will do. Interval training is basic to beginning running, as the woman in the yellow sweatsuit knew, although she probably could not express it in those terms.

Consider these basic words of advice that I offered my class at the Michigan City YMCA on the first day I met them: *Run until you begin to get tired. Walk until you feel recovered. Then run some more.* In other words: jog-walk-jog. Run-jog-run. Interval training. However, don't let your Y instructor know you're on to him yet.

Slow Down

The most important thing you can tell a beginning runner is not to start too fast, not to do too much, not to establish unrealistic goals. In other words: *slow down.*

These are the most frequent words that I offer new runners, most recently to Paul Marshall, a freelance photographer who has taken the dust jacket photographs for several of my previous books. For a while Paul was complaining about various running-caused pains: in his lungs, in his knees, in his side. "Slow down, Paul," I said. On enrolling in my running class in January, he had given up cigarettes after 20 years of smoking. Among those moving in tight circles around the YMCA, Paul moved faster than all but one other individual. The class met three days weekly, and on the off-days Paul snuck outdoors to run.

Naturally slender, Paul Marshall actually began to gain weight when he started running. He had an obvious flair for running and seemed to sincerely enjoy it. After only six weeks, he was up to occasional runs of four to five miles—but he claimed to hurt. "Then slow down," I advised.

Paul looked at me as though I had uttered a heresy. On enrolling in my class, he had set his goal (aside from giving up
cigarettes forever): the completion of a 15-kilometer run to be
held in Michigan City in June. Bill Rodgers was coming in for
the race, and we expected more than 1000 participants. A
number of people in town were using the race as an excuse to
mount personal fitness programs. Only three months remained
before the race, yet Paul seemed to be acting out of panic, as
though he felt pressed for time. "Slow down, Paul," I kept
preaching.

I also would tell him: "It took you 35 years to get out of
shape, so how do you expect to get back in shape in only six
weeks?"

Actually, Paul Marshall is a poor example, because aside
from his chronic cigarette smoking, he had no other major obstacles standing between himself and what one book calls "total
fitness"—except he could never achieve that in the 10-minute-
per-day program advertised on its cover.

At least Paul was not grossly overweight, nor were any of the
others who enrolled in my class, indicating that some pre-selective
process goes on as to the type of people who decide to be
runners. I started my beginning runners with easy jogging and
walking, but John Joyce, who serves as director of cardiological
fitness and testing at the Leaning Tower YMCA near Chicago,
often recommends that people begin at an even lower level. "I
tell people to start walking first," he suggests. "Just loosen up
and get their legs used to carrying their weight around for 10-15
minutes."

Good advice. And slow down.

Magic of the Mile

The mile run is probably the most popular event in track and
field (although lately the marathon has surpassed it in popularity among road runners). People who have no idea what might
be a fast time for 100 meters, or even the marathon, can relate
to a 4:00 mile. They may even know that, back in the dim days
of antiquity (1954), Roger Bannister became the first mortal to
run faster than 4:00 for that distance.

So the first thing that an otherwise sedentary individual embarking on a running-based fitness program does (unless he has first bought this book) is to go out and see how fast he can cover a mile. He wants to measure himself against Roger Bannister, Herb Elliott, Peter Snell, Jim Ryun, and Jim Walker, and all the other fast milers. Notice that I said "he," and it was not from my usual "sexist" attitude of always using the masculine third-person singular even when describing both men and women. No woman yet has run a mile on a track as fast as Roger Bannister, so women feel less the need to measure themselves against men. Women, at least in this respect, are smarter than men. We will probably come to some other areas where women are dumber than men, but at least for the present let that statement stand.

The beginning runner who decides, on the first day, to see how fast he can run a mile is asking for trouble. If I laid off training for a year, I would have trouble running a mile at full speed despite my previous athletic background. The individual, male or female, who sets out to run a mile the first day will finish feeling considerably worse than when he started. The result may be sore muscles for a week. At the risk of frightening prospective runners, that person might kill himself by precipitating a heart attack. More likely, that person will not finish the mile, thereby discouraging him from any future efforts to modify his lifestyle with appropriate benefits to his health.

One friend of mine who was determined to run a mile on the first day was Bill Dixon, a 40-year-old insurance agent from Glens Falls, New York. A former pole vaulter in high school, Bill considered himself "in relatively good shape," despite being 50 pounds overweight, smoking three packs of cigarettes a day, and overindulging in alcohol several times weekly. When he decided one day to see how fast he could run a mile (four laps on an outdoor track), he made it only one-and-a-half laps. He was so stiff and exhausted from the effort that he literally had to crawl on his hands and knees up the stairs to his office. He was so sore he could not drive his car home.

When I met him several years later in Lake George, he had shed his excess weight, started a "No Smoking" rule in his office (because, having kicked his habit, he no longer could tolerate cigarette smoke), and was looking forward, some day soon, to running faster than three hours for the marathon, a time that would put him in the top 10% of the nation's runners. But for every Bill Dixon who makes it that far, many others quit running because they went at it too fast, too early, and decided that the activity was too difficult for them to succeed at. That's too many too's.

Stopping

One piece of advice that may help you is to stop. Don't stop running, just don't be afraid to stop *while* running. Forget the idea that to pause in the midst of your workout is to court failure. During the 1975 Boston Marathon, which he won, Bill Rodgers stopped on several occasions for drinks of water. If a world-class runner of his calibre can stop, not merely on a training run but in what probably was his most important race of the year, maybe of his career, what makes you think that you're superior?

By stopping, I don't mean that you should stop your workout that day and go into the showers. Stop before you have to and walk a while. When you feel recovered, do some more running. When you begin getting winded again, stop another time. Jog-walk-jog. Run Dick, run. See Dick run. See Jane run. See Dick and Jane run the sensible way, not the maniacal way that may land them in the hospital. Remember that you read it here first.

The trick in learning to run may be knowing when to stop, and doing so before you get so tired you won't get started again. This process might be compared to what happens when you walk away from leaving the headlights on. With the battery exhausted, you will be unable to restart the engine. If, however, somebody passes that automobile and alerts you about the still-burning headlights, you may be able to restart the car despite a low battery, allowing it to recharge. The same principle applies while beginning to run.

In fact, the same principle applies while *continuing* to run. Remember those fast, young, high school runners you spied through the fence on your first, clandestine visit to the track. If they run the first of their ten 440s too fast (something that happens frequently, young runners often making mistakes), they may be unable to finish all ten 440s, or finish them at the steady race pace that will do them the most good.

The best way to determine when to stop in the middle of a

run is when you begin to get out of breath. Some people must pause because of weak leg muscles, but in this cigarette-oriented society what usually halts a new runner is poor wind. The newcomer starts gasping for air, and his lungs begin to burn. It is best to start walking before reaching this point.

So slow down and don't be afraid to stop—as long as you start again.

2

Closet Jogging

Begin at home,
but don't be afraid to come out

Many people appear for their first YMCA jogging class, or spring through their front door sweatsuit-clad, to begin their running career without any preparation. This is a perfectly acceptable way to begin. A journey of 100 miles begins with one step. I forget who said that: most likely George Sheehan, but he probably was quoting someone else.

If you do enroll in a running class somewhere, you may be best off allowing the instructor to worry about how you should begin. After all, that is what you are paying for. But not everybody has the courage to reveal themselves as hopelessly unconditioned even to others at the same level.

The first word concerning my intention to teach a noontime running class at the Michigan City YMCA appeared in our local newspaper. The news item did not say *men's* running class, *women's* running class, or even men *and* women's running class. It just said: running class. Come enjoy! The first day approximately a dozen embroyonic joggers appeared, only one of them male. But sitting out in a car in the parking lot that first day, his sweatsuit on, a clean pair of tennis shoes on his feet, was a man who planned to sign up for the class. He never got out of the car. He sat there watching—and apparently counting. He came to the erroneous conclusion that the running class was all women. Not wishing to place himself in the embarrassing position of being the lone male, he turned the key in his ignition and headed home.

I learned about this several days later from my wife Rose, who knew his wife from the school where she taught. I asked Rose to relay the information a week later that the man would not be alone, that several other males, by now, had appeared. In addition to class members, an equal number of nonenrolled individuals, mostly men, jogged noons at the YMCA on their own.

Nevertheless, he did not reappear. Perhaps he feared he might look foolish. Perhaps he was overweight, or so far out of shape that he thought he might not be able to "compete" with the housewives he thought he would be running against. In running, particularly in the area of fitness jogging, you do not compete against others, but it is hard to get this message across to someone who gets no closer to your class than the parking lot. Perhaps the reluctant individual returned home and began a clandestine conditioning program so that by the time notice of the next running class appeared in the paper he would have more self-confidence.

The incident seems somewhat amusing, but all of us have gone through periods when we doubted our abilities to achieve. We remember the time, as teenagers, when we tried to work up enough courage to ask the girl across the floor to dance; then we finally did and got rejected. Or maybe we were that girl, wondering why nobody crossed the floor to ask us to dance.

If you have any fears of feeling foolish the first time you set rubber shoe to wooden floor in a YMCA gymnasium, don't worry about it. Because maybe what you need to bolster your courage is some preliminary activity before starting to run. My advice to you is first become a closet jogger. Run in place in your home where nobody can see you before revealing yourself to the world. Closet jogging is a perfectly acceptable means of getting in shape before getting in shape. Start this way and never more will you have to drive your car away from a YMCA parking lot feeling defeated and frustrated from fear of going in.

The Beautiful Body

I know several individuals who began running in place before beginning to run. Helen Molinaro (sister-in-law of Bob Molinaro mentioned earlier) jogged in place in her home for eight months before taking her first running step. She started doing it while watching an exercise program named "The Beautiful Machine" on WTTW, the public broadcasting channel in Chicago. The hostess began and ended each program running in place, suggesting to viewers that instead of sitting idly watching other TV shows, that they exercise while doing so. She recommended, as openers, running in place during commercials. Most standard commercial slots on prime-time TV last two minutes, so this would offer a reasonable beginning, although someone attempting to jog their way through a late-night movie might be more tired than if they ran the Boston Marathon.

Helen did as the exercise hostess suggested and soon progressed to running in place during an entire half-hour show. The thought that some programs might be better to jog to than others intrigued me. For instance, would you get a better workout watching "Starsky & Hutch" or "The Six-Million Dollar Man?" Maybe the frantic pace of "The Gong Show" would develop you cardiovascularly better than "The Waltons." No, Helen said, she ran in place during situation comedies: "The Jeffersons" and "All in the Family."

At least she did until her husband John objected: "Sit down. How can I watch TV with you running around like that." Which is true, since Helen has a very good figure. If I had a choice between watching TV and watching a lovely woman run in place, the TV set would not get much of my attention.

Eventually Helen switched to daytime soap operas, particularly "Another World," which was her favorite. Some people claim they're in another world while running. For Helen, at least, it was true. "Another World" lasts 60 minutes, but Helen refused to escalate her running to fill the entire hour: She continued to run a half hour, then sat down to watch the rest of the program.

After eight months she enrolled in an exercise program at the YMCA, and the first time she stepped on an indoor track ran three miles. I mentioned this one day to my group at the Michigan City YMCA, most of whom still were struggling toward goals at that distance after nearly several months, and they all groaned. What I failed to tell them was that Helen was 38 years old and had two children, because that really would have made them feel inferior. Not only that, but after the first three miles, Helen said she experienced no aches or pains.

The reason, of course, was all the running in place, not to mention additional exercises, she did in the eight previous months. Since then, Helen Molinaro has become more involved as a runner, moving some of her workouts outdoors and working up to runs of as much as nine miles in length. When I talked with her to get information for this chapter, she was looking forward to her first official competitive race: the Bonne Bell 10,000-meter run for women in Chicago. She still runs in place on alternate days, but now only about ten minutes at a time since she gets enough regular running outdoors.

Helen Molinaro's experience with running in place as a preparation for regular running seemed to contradict what I heard from several others. My wife Rose, who enjoys walking or cycling better than running, worked her way up to 10 or 15 minutes running in place one winter, which after a while became quite easy. She thought that much preparation would allow her to cover at least a mile comfortably, but found outdoor running twice as hard. Harriet Miller ran in place for several months before enrolling in my running class. One day, while I was discussing closet jogging, she kept shaking her head. When I asked her why, Harriet said: "It did absolutely no good. The first day I started to run I was utterly exhausted."

She admitted, however, that she only ran in place for a few minutes at a time. And she may have obtained more benefits from this preliminary training than she herself suspected. In her first two months in my class, she made what I felt was considerable improvement, particularly for someone who was an ex-smoker and had to reeducate her lungs to breathe fresh air. I also thought my wife's jogging ability improved after her winter of indoor work. But the answer, of course, is that you get back what you put in, and obviously Helen Molinaro's half-hour of running in place while watching "All in the Family" and other such shows gave her a better base than those who did less.

I don't recommend closet jogging for everybody, since many can move straight into a running program with little stress or strain, but for those looking for a very gradual introduction to fitness and the fun of outdoor running, running in place may be the way to start. Let me suggest a six-step approach.

Six Steps

1. *Go into a closet. Begin to jog in place.* You won't remain there very long. If nothing else, the smell of mothballs should drive you out into your bedroom, but at least you will have proved to yourself that you can lift one leg after another without falling on your face. In a closet, unless you have a very large wardrobe, there is no place to fall.

2. *Come out of the closet. Jog in place in a larger room.* Watch your form, which you can do by looking in a mirror. Keep your arms up about stomach high. Remain erect, chin high. Jog on the balls of your feet. In fact, one valuable point about beginning to run by jogging in place at home is that it is an activity that is almost impossible to do landing on the heels of your feet. Try it if you don't believe me. The ankle exercising and stretching you will get by jogging on the balls of your feet will be helpful when you later move outdoors.

3. *Keep track of your jogging by watching a clock.* Obviously you can't count miles, which is probably to your advantage. If you have been jogging in place for several days, or several weeks, take note of how long you last before getting out of breath. Establish that as your base line time for exercise. If the time period is five minutes, try and do at least that much each time you exercise. Every now and then, maybe once every second week, try to expand your base rate by pushing a bit beyond your previous limit. Don't flog yourself, or jog to exhaustion, but as you begin to get into condition you should find yourself capable of doing more. If you want to follow a definite schedule to gradually build your jogging ability consult "A Guide to Closet Jogging" accompanying this chapter.

4. *Begin to move around the room as you jog.* Even though you are jogging in place, no rule says it must always be in the same place. Move about the room, or move from room to room. Don't attempt to stride out like a quarter-miler or you may start knocking down furniture, but as you jog, move gradually in one direction. My wife developed a circuit on the second floor of our house: from the dressing area of our master bedroom, into the bedroom itself, then back out into the hallway past the rooms where our kids slept for a U-turn, then down the hall again and

into my office to circle the typewriter on which I am now typing, then back into our bedroom.

5. *Utilize any possible scheme to alleviate boredom.* Boredom is the ultimate enemy of the closet jogger. Jogging in place is simply not much fun, or at least I fail to find it so. If it was the only workout I would get that day, I could not jog in place for more than 30 seconds before climbing the wall, both literally and figuratively. But then I'm used to the sights and sounds of the road. Beginning joggers, however, seem to suffer less from cabin fever. Some of them watch television while they jog in place, which seemingly would alleviate the boredom problem, except I hate to think they are improving their body while destroying their minds. Others organize their thoughts for the day and plan projects, which is often what I do while running through the woods.

The ultimate form of indoor conditioning for a runner would be to purchase a treadmill similar to those used in human performance laboratories. A recent issue of *Runner's World* advertises one motorized treadmill for $989, but I suggest you wait until you've been jogging a few weeks before buying one.

6. *Come out of the closet.* Only when you move out of your house and into the world of the outdoors, can you experience the full pleasure of running. That is what the rest of this book is about.

A GUIDE FOR CLOSET JOGGERS

PHASE ONE

Establish a base line for yourself. Look at the second hand of a clock. Begin to jog in place. Jog until you *begin* to get out of breath, or until your legs become weak and too tired to comfortably continue. Don't push yourself too hard. Glance at the clock again when you stop. The number of seconds you lasted jogging in place becomes your base line time. If your base line time is more than 120 seconds or two minutes, go on to Phase Three.

PHASE TWO

Plan to jog in place three days a week, resting one day between each session, as follows:

Monday: 3 x base line time (as determined above), complete rest between. (During the rest intervals, you can use the time to do stretching exercises

to loosen your muscles. See chapter XX.)
Tuesday: Rest.
Wednesday: 3 x base line time, complete rest between.
Thursday: Rest.
Friday: 3 x base line time, complete rest.
Saturday or Sunday: Rest or go for a long, easy walk outdoors. (How long is "long" depends on your definition of that term.) At the end of two weeks retest your jogging ability and if you can go further without fatigue, increase your base line for future workouts. When you achieve the ability to jog in place for two minutes, go on to Phase Three.

PHASE THREE

Plan to jog in place four days a week, resting no more than one day · between each session, as follows:

Monday: 3 x 1:00 jog, complete rest between.
Tuesday: 2:00 jog.
Wednesday: Rest.
Thursday: 3 x 1:00 jog, complete rest between.
Friday: Rest.
Saturday: 2:00 jog. Slightly more if you're beginning to feel stronger.
Sunday: Rest or long walk outdoors.

At the end of two weeks retest your jogging ability and if you have improved, increase the length of your Monday and Thursday interval jogs to half your new base line time. (If you jog 3:00 in your test, do 3 x 1:30 on those days.) On Tuesday and Saturday try to equal your base line time. If you feel good on one of those days, say Saturday, · attempt to push on a bit further. When you achieve the ability to jog in place for five minutes, go on to Phase Four.

PHASE FOUR

Plan to jog in place five days a week, taking a day rest twice whenever it fits into your schedule, as follows:

Monday: 3 x 2:00, complete rest between.
Tuesday: 5:00 jog.
Wednesday: 2 x 3:00 jog, complete rest between.
Thursday: Rest.
Friday: 3 x 2:00, complete rest between.
Saturday: 5:00 jog, or more.
Sunday: Rest or long walk outdoors. When you think nobody is looking, jog a few steps and see how it feels. If it feels good, do some more short, easy jogging a bit further down the road.

At the end of two weeks, retest your jogging ability and adjust your workouts as you improve your base line ability. Feel free to experiment with different combinations of numbers of jogs, length of those jogs, and even perhaps the amount of time you take between. But keep the amount of time and/or effort about the same, and don't strain. When you achieve the ability to jog in place for 15 minutes go on to Phase Five.

PHASE FIVE

Plan to jog in place five or more days a week, taking a day off when you feel you need it as follows:

Monday: 15:00 jog.
Tuesday: 3 x 6:00, complete rest between.
Wednesday: 2 x 8:00, complete rest between.
Thursday: Rest, or a few minutes easy jogging in place, untimed.
Friday: 15:00 jog.
Saturday: 3 x 6:00 jog, complete rest between.
Sunday: Rest or long walk outdoors. On some flat, easy, secluded stretch start to jog at a slow pace and see how far you can go before getting tired.

At the end of two weeks, or at periodic intervals, retest your jogging ability and continue to adjust your workouts. Feel free to experiment with different combinations and try moving through the house if you have not already done so. Whenever you feel you are ready, go on to Phase Six.

PHASE SIX

Come out of the closet and begin a running program.

3
Making Tracks
Pick an interesting place
to do your running

The Michigan City YMCA opened in 1974; therefore, it has no running track.

Students of logic will realize that one more premise is needed to complete that syllogism. The missing premise is that nearly all YMCAs built between the late 1930s and the mid 1970s are planned without indoor running tracks. Almost all you need do is examine the date on the cornerstone of a YMCA before entering to determine whether or not you will find a track.

Many of the YMCAs built before that era have such tracks, usually suspended on a balcony over a basketball court. The West Side YMCA in New York, the Hyde Park YMCA in Chicago, and the YMCA in Benton Harbor, Michigan, come to mind. But some time during the Depression, apparently, such tracks fell out of fashion among community leaders who planned drives to construct new YMCAs. Maybe it was because during hard times, indoor tracks seemed an unnecessary, added expense. Most YMCA physical directors, who might have been *forced* to run when they went out for football or basketball, probably felt them, at best a luxury, at worst space-wasters. I can imagine the rationalization: "Nobody uses the damn things anyway."

And that was probably true, since running was not very fashionable in the 1940s, 1950s, and into the 1960s. In fact, soon after I moved to Michigan City in 1964, I learned that, although the YMCA in nearby La Porte contained an indoor track, it was being ripped out like some dangerous cancer. So it came as no surprise to me ten years later when the community leaders of Michigan City included in their plans for a new YMCA: two basketball courts, two handball/racquetball courts, a weightlifting room, and a swimming pool—but no area in which to run.

As a result, in the winter of 1978, when I decided to teach a running class at the Michigan City YMCA as a research project connected with this book, I found no ready-made track awaiting me. A few joggers did use the YMCA, but they had to circle the two basketball courts, which were half-size at that, giving them laps of maybe 60-70 yards. The effect was somewhat like being a squirrel in a cage—or so it seemed to me, since I do almost all my training for long-distance races on roads, golf courses, and cross-country trails, and find circling even a 440-yard outdoor track tedious. Joggers just coming out of their closets undoubtedly are troubled less by lack of wide expanses than those of us who run 50-100 miles a week, nevertheless I wanted to make running as easy and enjoyable for them as possible.

Carpet Joggers

I knew the layout of the Y building resembled a series of boxes connected in a "Maltese-cross" formation, the boxes containing handball/racquetball courts, the swimming pool, basketball courts, meeting rooms, and locker rooms. A carpeted corridor bordered the central box and a pair of double doors broke up the corridors. On the first day before I met with my class I talked with Gretchen Jone, program director. Her sport was swimming, but she planned to run with us. I told her: "We're going to open the doors."

Gretchen's eyes widened as though what I suggested smacked of heresy: "Why are you going to do that?"

"Because that way we can jog out the gym and into the corridors. We can double the size of our running track."

Gretchen's eyes grew still wider: "But nobody's ever done that before."

True, but also nobody said it could not be done—yet. Gretchen and I wedged the double doors open that day, and no word of complaint escaped the lips of the Y's executive director, Chuck Haynie. (Maybe, because I was teaching the class without salary, he figured he couldn't complain. That's one of the advantages of being a volunteer.) Later, he did comment about possible wear on the carpet, but by that time we had established precedent as carpet joggers. So our class began jogging the corridors as extensions of the inner gym. From closet joggers to carpet joggers in one easy lesson. The other joggers, who had been utilizing the gym regularly before my arrival, shunned us for a while, continuing to circle like squirrels around the basketball courts, but one by one they began to realize: maybe we were on to something. Pretty soon everybody who jogged in the YMCA utilized my course.

Democracy in Action

Five or six weeks after my class began, a reporter from a local publication, *Dunebeat*, visited the YMCA to do a feature story on the noontime joggers. I used the opportunity to air one of my pet peeves: the fact that three athletic facilities had been constructed in Michigan City since my arrival in 1964, and not one of them contained facilities for indoor track. The three included: (1) the YMCA, (2) a new high school with a 7000-seat basketball gym, and (3) an athletic building attached to the old high school.

Before construction of this last facility track coach Cabot Holmes and I thought we had the school board talked into including a 110-yard Tartan track. When I took my plea to one of the monthly school board meetings, the board president assured me that, yes, such a track was in their plans. Later, with the facility almost completed, I learned that the school board quietly changed those plans without telling me. In place of the Tartan surface would be a standard wooden basketball floor, even though it would save no money, Cabot Holmes informed me.

"Then why did they drop the track?" I asked him.

"The custodial staff complained," Cabot explained. "They say that a track would be more expensive to maintain than a basketball floor."

"So will a swimming pool be more expensive to maintain," I argued.

But my argument was not with Cabot, but with the school board. When the *Dunebeat* reporter came to interview me, I complained about the lack of indoor track facilities, stating arrogantly: "I'll register my displeasure at the next school board election." This took a great deal of courage on my part, since my wife Rose had returned to teaching four years before and was not eligible to obtain tenure for one more year. Maybe if she got fired, I no longer would have to make breakfast and do the grocery shopping.

When the next school board election occurred later that spring, only one of three incumbent members on the ballot had opposition. So much for democracy in action. By that time I began to realize that the running course I had designed might even be an improvement on the standard above-the-gym tracks built years ago.

Indoor Cross-country

Consider my course in the Michigan City YMCA. You begin in the lobby and start through the double doors and onto the edge of the basketball court. If a full-court game is in progress, you get to watch it. Then you may have to dodge around a pile of mats left from the last gymnastics class. Someone will be shooting baskets on the second court and as he misses the rim entirely, startled by your sudden presence, you get to catch the ball and return it to him. Two quick 90-degree turns at the end of the court and you head back toward the basketball game in progress where you probably have to maneuver around one of the players taking the ball out of bounds. When I began my noon running class I considered imposing a set of restrictions on use of the gym by the noon basketball players, which I could have done, but then figured: "What the hell, we'll just co-exist." I decided to maintain this attitude at least until one of my middle-aged female joggers got cold-cocked by some 200-pound player storming in for a driving layup. It hasn't happened yet.

You then exit the gym through the other double doors, where you have to detour around a tarpaulin and sawhorses because of a leak in the ceiling. Immediately you sidestep an equipment cage that juts out into the corridor. The woman who attends the cage has a television set inside so she can watch soap operas while working, so in passing you get a flash of "All My Children." Or you can focus your attention on the muscular men lifting heavy weights on the other side of the corridor.

A 90-degree turn brings you past the swimming pool where, through a glass wall, you can see other YMCA members doing laps during the noon swim. Joggers and swimmers mix about as readily as oil and water. Depending upon their body somatotype, people find one or the other activity more difficult than the other. Although I did a certain amount of long-distance swimming while a boy, I have so little body fat that I sink readily when I get in the water. I consider swimming equally as good a cardiovascular activity as running, but I no longer enjoy it as a regular activity. Most runners I know get bored quickly in the water for the same reasons that swimmers become bored jogging. Probably few swimmer-types would pick up a book titled *The Beginner's Running Guide*, although they would be attracted to a book titled, *The Beginner's Swimming Guide*. Executive director Chuck Hainey said that all of us were free to use the other facilities, including the pool, after our running class, but few did.

Reaching the end of the swimming pool corridor you turn left at 90 degrees again, being careful to dodge anyone using the water fountain at that point and come into what we called "Pollution Alley," the area by the front desk where for some reason I could never understand (in a building dedicated to health) people could smoke cigarettes. Sometimes we had to run through a cloud of smoke. With smokers present, I simply held my breath down that straightaway, although not all my class had as much pulmonary reserve. Several complained about the smokers, including individuals who until they joined the jogging class had been smokers themselves! The better physical condition you achieve, the less tolerance you have for the cigarette smoke of others.

Finishing one lap of this form of indoor cross country, you could continue for two, five, ten, or even 13½ laps, which I figured was about a mile, having paced it off one day. Or maybe it was 14½, depending on how tight you cut the corners. No matter: the people in the class more or less decided among themselves that 14 laps equalled a mile, and who was I to argue with them.

The more I thought about it, the more I realized that this obstacle course with its sights and sounds, including "All My Children," was preferable to the run-of-the-mill, banked-in-the-turns, YMCA track that simply went in circles. So much went on around them, my joggers could not waste too much time concentrating on their aches and pains or they might get hit in the head with a basketball or stumble over a small child wandering the corridors. Another nice aspect of that particular YMCA was that during the course of one lap we passed three wall clocks: one in the gymnasium, one in the equipment cage, and one in the lobby. None of them agreed on the time, so you couldn't even focus on how long you had been running unless you remembered which clock you started on.

I never could count laps either, although I would often try. By the time I reached three or four I would fall in with someone's pace, engage them in a conversation, and forget where I was. Certain class members apparently could keep count, because every now and then one would tell me how many laps they did on a particular day, or a certain number of miles they had run; except for a word of praise I tried not to emphasize distance covered. While the 90-degree turns might have bothered a competitive runner who wanted to do speed work, they seemed less bothersome to our slow joggers. If anyone ever hires me as a consultant to a YMCA under construction, I think I'll design their jogging track with lots of hazards—including "All My Children."

The distance of 130 or so yards per lap also was fortunate, since it was not so far that a brand new jogger could not make the distance, nor so short that covering it several times was not an accomplishment. It allowed the beginners to break their workouts into small, reasonable segments. Remember what I said earlier about peeking through the fence and interval training again.

If there is a message in all this, it is as follows: *When possible, pick an interesting place to do your running.* Let us take that subject up in more detail in a later chapter.

4

First Steps and Breaths

Your muscles and lungs
might ache at first...

The first thing you're going to worry about as a beginning runner is breathing. Don't ask me why, but the subject of pulmonary function seems to worry new runners the most. "How do I breathe?" the members of my class at the Michigan City YMCA would come up to me and ask, as though they had not been doing it for the last 20 or 30 or more years of their lives.

"Breathe naturally," I respond, assuring them that there is no particular trick to the way that runners breathe as opposed to ordinary people. I don't think about breathing when I run, nor do most experienced runners. It just happens. If you have to concentrate on your breathing it steals attention from the other biomechanical functions such as stride length and arm carry that maybe should worry you more. (And even these functions become automatic after a while.)

Maybe beginning runners focus on the act of breathing because that often is the first thing they notice when they start to run. They experience the phenomenon of "getting out of breath." They come face to face with the working of their own pulmonary apparatus. "My God," they think. "My lungs are running amok! What can I do to save them?"

If they are running in a group, and that group contains experienced runners, they may notice that these individuals seem to be having less difficulty breathing. If so, it must be because they possess some secret technique. If you play basketball, there is a way to let the ball roll off your fingertips to impart spin to

it. In tennis, you need to position yourself properly and step toward the net as you hit your forehand or you won't be able to
control it or hit hard enough.

There are some hints you can give a beginning runner about
form and style (which we will get to in a later section of this
book), but when it comes to breathing, you just breathe. When
I notice what I'm doing while running, which is not often, I
realize that I take two strides as I inhale and two strides as I
exhale. When I push myself to exhaustion at the end of a race,
my breathing may become more rapid, but hopefully you'll
never reach that point until after you have many training miles
behind you. So if you still are worried about breathing, simply
follow this advice: *two-in, two-out.* If your body doesn't work
that way, however, don't telephone or write. Work out your own
body rhythms.

The only one I ever heard admit to breathing somewhat differently was Frank Shorter. I hesitate mentioning this, because
everyone who reads this passage will say, "Aha, that's why he
won his gold medal," ignoring the fact that Frank also runs 140
miles a week. Frank Shorter appeared at a clinic I sponsored in
conjunction with the USTFF National Age Handicap Championship at Michigan City, Indiana, in April 1977. During the
question-and-answer period, the inevitable question about
breathing was raised by someone in the audience. Frank commented that he took three strides when he inhaled and three
strides when he exhaled.

It seemed as though there was an audible gasp from the audience as it suddenly dawned on all us two-in-two-out breathers
that maybe we had been doing it the wrong way for the last five,
10, or 20 years of our running careers and only now—too late
for true glory—had learned the secret of true greatness. I half
expected runners to pop out of their seats and start striding up
and down the aisle to see if Frank's breathing system really
worked, but everybody stayed cool. I know what everybody tried
in practice the next day: three-in-three-out. Then when no
golden halo appeared around their heads, they went back to
their old method of breathing.

We're all looking for hot tips, and so are you or you wouldn't
be reading this book. I tried the three-in-three-out method myself about a month later in the Revco-Western Reserve Marathon in Cleveland. It was my first marathon in five years, since I

mostly had been running shorter events in masters track and field since turning 40. Being more interested in finishing comfortably than in finishing fast, I decided to run the race at what might be described as a "float" pace rather than at top speed. In fact, you would be surprised how much more pleasant marathons can be if you run them 15-30 minutes slower than your actual capability, but that's another subject.

Unworried about final time or position, I could experiment with the way I ran, so I began the race using the Shorter three-in-three-out method, floating along at a comfortable 7:00-or-so-per-mile pace. It seemed not to affect my ability to run one way or another except I had to make a conscious effort to maintain that breathing pattern. After a while I became bored with conscious breathing and forgot about it. Near 12 miles, we came onto an extremely hilly stretch of course and I became more interested in seeing how fast I could fly up and down the hills. The hills lasted until the 18-mile point. By then I began to reach a level of fatigue, so I just worried about finishing at some semblance of good pace. I never did learn anything new about my breathing.

At National Running Week in California that year I attended a clinic session where one of the speakers was Marty Liquori, holder of the American 5000-meter record. During the question and answer period, I told Marty what Frank Shorter said about his breathing. Marty's reply was to the point: "Don't listen to anything Frank tells you. All runners lie when asked about training." The only problem is, I don't know if Marty was telling the truth.

One final comment about breathing as it applies to beginning runners. A sub-question of "How do I breathe?" is "Should I breathe through my mouth or my nose?"

I am asked that question frequently too, and the best response is one that New Zealand coach Arthur Lydiard gave when we appeared one evening together at a clinic at the Leaning Tower YMCA in suburban Chicago. In response to this standard question about mouth-breathing vs. nose-breathing, Arthur replied: "Breathe through your mouth. Breathe through your nose. Breathe through your ears if you can figure out how to do it. Suck the air in any way possible."

Alan Claremont, a runner and physiologist from Madison, Wisconsin, however, suggests that mouth-breathing is much

more efficient than nose-breathing. Al recalls one Madison runner who always sounded like a horse when he ran and, when
asked, responded that it was because he breathed only through
his nose, apparently a carryover from a previous boxing career.
Al suggested he try breathing through his mouth instead and
the following week the runner sliced two-and-a-half minutes off
his fastest time for five miles! Claremont advised: "Nose breathing works only if you have nostrils as large as a horse — or maybe
four legs."

Muscles

The first thing you will learn when you start to run is that you
have muscles. Forget what you've heard about skinny runners
not having any muscles; we have as many muscles as any defensive lineman playing in the National Football League. Ours
simply have adapted somewhat differently as a result of the specific training we do. Runners want muscles that function efficiently over long periods of time in a continuous, smooth, rhyth-
mical fashion. They want lean muscles so that they have less
weight to carry. A thin individual with a lower body mass to
body surface area ratio can more easily dissipate the heat that
develops as a result of the body's movements. Football players
need more short-term strength and speed, as well as bulk so as
to be able to resist assaults from heavy opponents. Heat dissipation is less critical since they can relax between plays.

But even sedentary individuals possess the same muscles; they
simply use them less. When untrained individuals start to run,
they discover their muscles very rapidly, because they begin to
hurt. This is why many people who exercise infrequently think
that running is more painful than it is. What they experience
are the painful effects of *excessive* running. And for someone
who has not run, even one lap around the gym might be considered excessive, the equivalent of a full-distance marathon for a
trained athlete like Bill Rodgers or Garry Bjorklund.

Usually the people in my class at the Michigan City YMCA
came up to me the second or third day after they began to run
and announced: "My calves hurt." Or maybe it was their thighs,
or their backs, or their stomachs. From the expression of their
voices, it was almost as though they had done something wrong
and were looking to me (the instructor) to correct them, as a

tennis pro might adjust a beginner's serve.

Actually, they had done nothing wrong—unless you consider beginning to run wrong. I can take the most athletic high school boy, send him running around a 440-yard track, and he will return the following day complaining of the same aches and pains experienced by my group of middle-aged beginning runners. I get sore legs. Bill Rodgers's calves ache when he runs or races too much. It comes with the territory. Any time you exercise to excess in any sport, you get sore. As well conditioned as I am, if I were to go out and play even an easy set of tennis, I would.be sore the next day, not from using different muscles but from using the same muscles different ways.

To understand what happens you might compare the human body to an automobile. The body burns oxygen in the same way an automobile burns fuel. But the result of this combustion is a number of harmful waste products: exhaust with the automobile. Physiologists still argue over which waste products contribute to cause decline in the human body. If you have an efficient exhaust system, you can remove the waste products, otherwise they remain lodged in your tissues causing stiffness and muscle aches. Beginning runners merely have inefficient exhaust (cardiovascular) systems, which is one reason why their muscles ache. But even well-conditioned athletes often push their bodies so hard that they override the efficiency of their exhaust systems. This causes them to tie up and slow down at the end of certain races, and it also causes them the same aches and pains the next day as experienced by the beginning runner.

So when beginning runners tell me they have sore calves, I simply tell them: "Welcome to the club." The best antidote for such a problem is, when you begin to run, relax, take it easy, and don't do too much the first few days. This advice is easier said than followed, however.

Drag Racing

The danger is not that you will have sore legs if you run too hard too fast, but that you may actually cause some more lasting injury. Runners learning to run, extending the automotive analogy further, operate like drivers who take their new cars to the drag strip. I have done several articles and books about automotive racing, including a biography of drag racer Don

Prudhomme, so know that the principle is the same.

When a new racer arrives at the drag strip with his stock automobile the first day, he floors the car and drives it full speed toward the finish line a quarter-mile away. Something will break, if not on that first trip then one or two trips later. Usually it is the clutch, so the drag racer visits his nearest automotive shop and pays $85 or more for a heavy-duty replacement clutch that will not fail again under pressure.

On the next visit to the drag strip with that same car, the clutch stays in one piece, but the transmission cannot take the strain. It costs another $100 or so to replace that damaged part with a heavy-duty one that will last under extreme stress. But on the driver's next trip to the drag strip, he tears up the axle, strips the gear shifter, or blows a piston out of the side of the engine.

One by one, by trial and error, the novice drag racer determines the weakest parts of his racing machine and replaces them with heavy-duty equipment. When he finishes, he has a smoking, stomping, honkin-machine capable of taking almost any kind of punishment and beating anyone else's machine at the strip—and he also will have spent several thousand dollars. Of course, it is a never-ending quest for perfection since even those heavy-duty parts will fail and need more and more expensive replacements.

The end of the line is the kind of car driven by Don Prudhomme, which costs $30,000, burns a special nitromethane fuel that costs $1.50 a gallon, but can propel Prudhomme through a quarter-mile in less than six seconds and win him a national championship. Prudhomme goes through engines the way some runners go through band-aids. I was sitting in his truck just ahead of the starting line at a track in Irvine, California, one day when his engine exploded in flames. Don had to react instantly and roll out the side window to save his life. For taking such risks Don Prudhomme earns more than $100,000 a year. To minimize those risks, he wears a flame-retardant suit, crash helmet, and gas mask. When you consider the hazards in certain other sports, chondromalacia (or "runner's knee") hardly seems like much of a problem.

Unless it happens to you. Then you would gladly jump through a burning hoop to cure it. If you don't believe me, talk to any podiatrist who treats running injuries. "Jump through a flaming hoop? Where do I stand to take off, Doc?"

One way to avoid flaming hoops, or flaming pains, particularly when you begin, is to start slow and to continue at a relatively easy progression. That way you avoid causing any unnecessary damage by excessive zeal. And although there probably is no way to avoid tight calves, or other little aches and pains when you begin to run, there also is no sense to convert them into *big* aches and pains by running too hard. People are so different in their running abilities, that I usually resist offering a definite schedule of what to do Monday - Tuesday - Wednesday for fear that what works for one person will not work for others. But I am including at the end of this chapter a guide for beginning runners, designed for those first few months when you begin to run. Use it judiciously though, and don't be afraid to modify its dictates to suit your own needs, talents, or schedule.

The Dreaded Stitch

No matter how easily you begin, however, there will be certain problems that some of you will be unable to avoid. One such problem is the dreaded, and classic, "stitch," which is simply a pain in the side. Denise Kniola, young, recently married, began running the summer of 1977 in Beverly Shores, just west of Michigan City. Sometimes Denise ran as far as six miles but she abandoned the sport when cold weather came. When she learned of the class I planned to teach at the YMCA, she joined so it would give her an excuse to start running again.

She was such an excellent runner, if a coach had discovered her a decade earlier she might have been converted into an Olympic middle-distance hopeful. Denise's only problem was she kept getting stitches when she ran. Stitches never bothered her the previous summer when she ran outdoors, only when we ran indoors in the YMCA so I wondered if the problem might be caused by the tight turns. "Which side is your stitch on?" I asked.

"The left side," said Denise.

So since we had been running counter-clockwise around the gym I had the class run clockwise the next time. "Still the left side?" I asked.

"Yep."

"Maybe it's your appendix," I offered encouragingly.

Denise thought a while about that, then felt her side gingerly. "My appendix is on my right side," she decided.

"You're right."

"That's what I said."

"No, I mean, you are right. Anyway, it's not your appendix."

"Thank goodness."

This diagnosis eliminated, I questioned Denise about her eating habits. I thought maybe she had been visiting Burger Chef a half hour before class. If so, I could have performed a miracle cure by having her stop. One cause of possible stomach problems in runners can be running too soon after eating. But her last previous meal was usually breakfast, four hours before.

It remained possible that she had some sort of lactose or gluten intolerance, since certain population groups cannot tolerate milk, or grains, or various other foods. For instance, 72 percent of adult Eskimos in Greenland cannot tolerate milk. But I hate to get involved in technical solutions best left for doctors.*

"Try belly breathing," I next recommended. Ron Gunn, the running coach at Southwestern Michigan College, once told me that he cured one of his athletes of a stitch problem by having him breathe with his diaphragm, like women do in natural childbirth classes. But belly breathing did not seem to help Denise.

"You're not pregnant are you?" I asked.

"Nope."

"That's probably why."

I searched through several dozen back issues of *Runner's World,* checking the columns by George Sheehan, M.D., the fountain of all running medical knowledge. He had a half-dozen solutions, all of which, and none of which, seemed to work. People kept writing him about their stitch problems and each time George had a new answer. George seemed to get as many letters about stitches as Ann Landers got about sex.

Finally through experimentation, Denise and I learned that if she started running faster her stitch sometimes went away, and if she started running slower, or even stopped to walk, it sometimes went away, so our cure was for her to do something. Just something different — anything. And maybe do some bent-knee

---

The Complete Diet Guide For Runners and Other Athletes, which I edited for World Publications, contains a chapter by George Sheehan, M.D. on dietary intolerances and includes lactose-free and gluten-free diets.

sit-ups under the theory that if we strengthened her stomach muscles, it might help. Certainly it couldn't hurt. Eventually we both quit trying, hoping that if we left her stitch alone, maybe it would go away by the time the weather warmed and she got outdoors on the trails she loved.

Every now and then during one of our classes, Denise would come running past me, saying, "I've got another stitch." But she always said it with such a smile on her face, that I stopped worrying about it, and so did she. So maybe that's the best advice I can give you as you begin to run: if you can smile while doing it, it must be good for you.

A GUIDE FOR BEGINNING RUNNERS

PHASE ONE

The principle in starting to run is similar to that outlined for closet jogging at the end of Chapter Two. Begin by establishing a base line for yourself. Start to jog at a slow pace and continue until you begin to get fatigued, or "out of breath." You will have to define this limit yourself, but be conservative: Do too little rather than too much. When you reach this first fatigue point, stop jogging and continue moving ahead at a walk. Take note of approximately how much ground you covered. That becomes your baseline distance. When you feel rested, start to jog again trying to cover approximately the same distance you did the first time. If you can't, don't worry about it. Continue jogging and walking until you cover one mile. If you can comfortably cover one mile jogging nonstop the first time, go on to Phase Three. Otherwise begin training at the Phase Two level.

PHASE TWO

Plan to run at least three days a week, resting one day between each session, as follows:

Monday: 3 x base line distance (as determined above), walking between until you are rested. After the third repeat, continue walking until you have covered at least a mile.
Tuesday: Rest.
Wednesday: One mile of easy jogging and walking. Whatever feels comfortable.
Thursday: Rest.
Friday: 3 x base line distance, walking between until you are rested. Finish the rest of the mile walking. Or retest.
Saturday or Sunday: Rest or go for a long, easy walk outdoors. (How long is "long" depends on *your* definition of that term.

At the end of two weeks, retest your jogging ability and if you can go further without fatigue, increase your base line distance for future workouts. When you achieve the ability to comfortably jog one mile nonstop, go on to Phase Three.

PHASE THREE

Plan to jog four days a week, resting no more than one day between each session, as follows:

Monday: 3 x half mile jog (Half your base line distance), walk between until rested.
Tuesday: One mile jog.
Wednesday: Rest.
Thursday: 3 x half mile jog, walk between until rested.
Friday: Rest.
Saturday: Two miles of easy jogging and walking, or retest.
Sunday: Rest or long walk outdoors.

At the end of two weeks retest your jogging ability. Increase the increments run on Monday and Thursday to half your new base line distance. (If you cover one-and-a-half miles in your test, your Monday workout should be 3 x ¾ mile.) Or for a variation, run 4 x half mile on Tuesday. When you achieve the ability to run nonstop for two miles, go on to Phase Four.

PHASE FOUR

Plan to run five days a week, taking a day of rest twice, whenever it fits into your schedule, as follows:

Monday: 3 x mile, walk between until rested.
Tuesday: Two mile jog.
Wednesday: Three miles of easy jogging and walking.
Thursday: Rest.
Friday: 4 x 880, walk between until rested.
Saturday: Three miles of easy jogging and walking, or retest.
Sunday: Rest or long walk outdoors.

At the end of two weeks, retest your jogging ability and adjust your workouts as you improve your base line ability. Feel free to experiment with different combinations of numbers of jogs, length of those jogs, and even perhaps the amount of time you take between. But keep the amount of time you spend on your workout about the same, and don't strain. If necessary, back up a bit on your schedule before going forward again. Don't be in a hurry to reach the final phase. When you achieve the ability to run nonstop for four miles, go on to Phase Five.

PHASE FIVE

Plan to run five or more days a week, taking a day off when you feel you need it, as follows:

Monday: Four mile run.
Tuesday: 4 x mile, walk between until rested.
Wednesday: Five miles of easy jogging and walking.
Thursday: Rest, or an easy mile or two jog.
Friday: 2 x two mile, walk between until rested.
Saturday: Four mile run, or retest.
Sunday: Rest or long walk outdoors.

At the end of two weeks, or at periodic intervals, retest your jogging ability and continue to adjust your workouts. Feel free to experiment with different combinations including shorter distances at faster speeds (6 x 220, walking between). Whenever you feel you are ready, go on to Phase Six.

PHASE SIX

Stop thinking of yourself as a jogger and consider yourself a runner. Get involved with some running group and go on occasional long runs with other people, following their pace and workouts rather than what your schedule says to do. Give some serious thought to entering a race. Don't worry about winning, but enter mainly to participate. If you - have fun, you can examine our *Guide for Beginning Racers* later in this book.

5

Commitment

If you're serious, learn the
physiology and psychology of running

My tax accountant Sidney Jarrow has a favorite saying: "For the man who doesn't know where he's going, any road will take him there."

I'm not sure what Sid was trying to tell me because I go into a state of shock when it comes time to consider numbers, particularly those related to income taxes, but I can see how the statement applies when it comes to running: you need a goal.

That was one of the important points that Don Kardong made during his seminar: There is no sense beginning a running program unless you commit yourself to it for at least six to eight weeks. Many people decide they will try running, plan to take one or two test workouts, discover running can be painful, decide therefore that they don't like it, and stop. This is a mistake. Learning to run is somewhat like developing a taste for oysters. You have to stick with them for a while to determine whether or not you enjoy the experience. Come to think of it, I don't like oysters, and maybe after you try running, you won't like it either—but at least give running a fair try.

"Two weeks is not enough," states Don Kardong. "The first two weeks of running for any beginner are the worst two weeks of his life. They are bad, painful, dull, boring. People get the idea that running is always painful, when it's not." Kardong feels that it takes at least six weeks to get over the first hump of pain, maybe eight. After new runners have conditioned themselves for that length of time, they begin to move into a new state of physical fitness where they can run pain-free—if they want.

I add "if they want," because what often happens is that having learned that they can cover one mile, or two miles non-stop in a workout without suffering pulmonary or cardiovascular collapse, beginning runners often decide to explore the outer regions of their new-found fitness. They push themselves on to three, four, five, maybe even more miles in a single workout. Or they begin to run, if not farther, then perhaps faster.

This is how it happened with my class at the Michigan City YMCA, and it occurred right around the sixth week after we started. I looked out at my class running around the gym one noon hour and thought to myself: "You know, they're pretty good." It was a completely subjective feeling on my part, because I was doing nothing to quantify their improved capacity for training, either by timing laps, counting laps, or measuring pulse rates (although we did some of that in the early stages). But they all looked like runners, every one of them. Not only that, but judging from their comments during and after class, they were beginning to feel like runners. I could have taken any one of them, deposited that person in the middle of any race or workout group in America, and they would be totally indistinguishable from those around them. They could even talk the jargon. They had been converted into runners, and no more would bullies at the beach be able to kick sand in their faces, or in the faces of their boy friends. They could run away and escape.

Converting to Running

Why are people like those in my class at the YMCA converted from ordinary non-run-of-the-mill citizens into extraordinary run-of-the-mill fitness athletes? And why, precisely at six to eight weeks? I can think of several reasons for the conversion.

1. Physiology. The scientists claim that once you begin an exercise program your body begins to adjust to the new demands being placed upon it, particularly the new demands placed on the cardiovascular system. Compare this to the way your automobile works. If you want your car to go faster, you have to give it more fuel. If you want your body to go faster (or farther), it must be fed more fuel in the form of oxygen carried by the blood to the muscles. The lungs suck more oxygen from the air and into the blood; the heart beats faster to pump that blood through the body.

The problem in an unconditioned person, of course, is that the network of arteries, veins, and capillaries—the river bed carrying the oxygen-rich blood to the muscles—is undeveloped. It cannot carry the increased flow of blood effectively. It takes maybe six to eight weeks for that network to develop, a phenomenon referred to as capillarization when new capillaries burst forth like blossoms within the human body allowing the muscle tissue to be drenched with an ever-increasing flow of fuel in the form of oxygen. When this capillarization occurs at six to eight weeks, running suddenly becomes much easier. Running suddenly feels good. This is why Don Kardong felt that if, as an instructor, he could get a beginning runner to push past the painful two-week period of muscle soreness to the six-to-eight week moment of capillarization, he would be more likely to have created a runner for life.

The lungs and heart develop also during this time and affect the total process, but the most spectacular reason for improvement comes because of capillarization.

2. Biomechanics. Running also becomes easier at the end of the six-to-eight week period, because the person doing it becomes mechanically more efficient. Anyone can run, as stated in an earlier chapter, but not everybody can run with style and grace the first time around a YMCA track. For that matter, from the look of the form of runners I see in long distance running races, *ten* years of running may not produce style and grace. Midway through the Maryland Marathon in 1977, a runner came past me whose form was so bad I thought he might come apart if he attempted to go any faster.

We all do things differently, but with practice you at least can be more stylish and more graceful than when you started. It is a matter of posture, arm-carry, stride-length, foot-fall, and the manner in which you learn to move more efficiently across the ground. Though basically a simple activity, running becomes easier when you adjust your movements for efficiency. (We will discuss running form in further detail in a later chapter.)

3. Psychology. This is the feeling of accomplishment you get when you recognize you are becoming a runner with all of its mythical and symbolic virtues and values. Competitive runners often measure their improvement in tenths of seconds, some-times from year to year, but beginning runners improve dramat-ically, and often day by day. A woman who in the early weeks struggles to go even one lap around a gym without getting hope-lessly out of breath or having to clutch her side finds herself at the end of several months piling up lap after lap, or mile after mile, without undue stress—and even feeling good about it.

This gets into the area of the runner's high, the 40-minute effect, which we also will discuss later. When you get your phys-iological and biomechanical act together, you find that you can run without concentrating every step on the act of running. As your body memorizes the movements, a subconscious control system takes over and running no longer requires mental effort. So it's easier.

4. Pride. Don't discount the feeling of elitism that comes when you succeed at running—and even to run is to succeed. "I run, therefore I live," states George Sheehan, M.D. We all come equipped with egos (some admittedly more expansive than in others) and want to feel that, in some small way, we are better than other people. And we *are* in the sense that we convert our bodies into more efficient machines for accomplishing a number of activities. At least until the time when 200 million Ameri-cans, instead of only 35 million, run at least one mile a year, the person in that latter group can consider himself or herself as having one leg up on those in the former.

In fact, two legs up, both of them in motion.

The Saga of O. J. Dubie

One of the individuals in my running class was a man named O. J. Dubie, 65 years old, who showed up the first day dressed in regular clothes and street shoes and asked a million questions, all of which seemed to be leading up to the point that he knew he should run, but perhaps he didn't want to do so. O.J. was no relation to the football player of the same initials, and as I learned later he went by the nickname Chet.

Apparently Chet's son on the East Coast was into running and was encouraging his father to take it up. Chet told me on our first meeting that his doctor once suggested that he not run. Apparently he had rheumatic fever as a boy. Chet said maybe he would ask the doctor about running the next time he saw him, except that he could not get an appointment for two more months.

Quite honestly, that first day Chet was a pain in the ass. I decided that he never would be back, particularly since he had not committed himself to entering the class by paying the $5 enrollment fee.

But at our second session two days later, Chet appeared at the YMCA carrying a pair of Adidas "Country" shoes under his arm and started to run. Well, maybe you couldn't call it a *run*, since what Chet did was more of a fast pad. When he wasn't padding, he did a lot of walking, which was all right with me because he told me about his childhood illness. I feared he might have a sudden heart attack in class, causing me, the fledgling running instructor, all sorts of embarrassment — not to mention what it would do to him. I began suggesting names of other doctors and fitness laboratories where he might get an exercise stress test. I even called one and learned that, as a favor to me, they would arrange an early appointment. This was rather radical on my part since I'm not a great believer in mandatory physical exams.

Chet never seemed to pad much faster, but he soon began to pad farther. During the early few weeks of the class we did some pulse-monitoring, everybody before and after running a few laps, so they would get some idea of what was happening inside them. I made no attempt to record pulses on wall charts like they do in some YMCA's and only introduced pulse-taking to the class to get their minds onto something else other than the fact that their calves and sides hurt. When Chet counted his pulse for 6 seconds immediately after running it was 12, which, multiplied by a factor of 10, gave him a standard pulse beat per minute of 120. After he walked a lap or so it bounced down to nine, or 90 for a minute. This satisfied me that he was tolerating the exercise well.

When after a couple of weeks he hadn't collapsed from a heart attack, I stopped worrying about O.J. Dubie. I noticed, however, that he always seemed to be running when I arrived at the YMCA for my class at 12:00, and soon learned it was because he arrived at 11:30 so he could get in some extra running. He was up to about four miles a day and looked like he could go forever. Several months into the class, Chet came up to me one day and announced: "Well, I finally had an appointment with my doctor."

"What did he tell you?" I asked.

"He said it was all right to start running," said Chet with a wicked smile. Apparently Chet failed to inform his doctor that he already had been running for several months. It made me feel better, however, because at least now Chet's doctor was on record that running might be good for his health. And if Chet suffered any problems, I could always say: "Gee, his doctor said it was okay to run." This is why people in charge of fitness programs want you to get physical exams. They're passing the buck.

Standing Still

One day Dick Gosswiller, a fellow freelance writer who publishes a weekly community publication called *Dunebeat*, came to the YMCA to do an article on our jogging class. The usual pattern for the class was to run for 15 minutes between 12:00 and 12:15, then break for 15 minutes until about 12:30. During this time I would talk about running or answer their questions, then have everybody do some stretching before returning to the gym at 12:30 for a final half-hour of running. The two running periods were open-ended, meaning that everybody could arrive or leave early or late depending on how much running they wanted to do. The period in the middle was planned partly to break their running in the middle — a form of interval training — so they could do more with less fatigue.

Sometimes I prepared an actual "lesson" on some aspect of running. On other occasions I would come unprepared, deciding on the spur of the moment what to talk about, often simply letting them decide for me by their questions. It was less a lecture than a talking-together period. On the day Dick Gosswiller arrived I was unprepared, so I simply asked the class: "Does anybody want to say something about how they feel about running?" The minute those words left my lips I realized what a dumb question it was. Nobody would say anything and I would be up there looking stupid while Dick was taking photos. Well, maybe we could do a few more stretching exercises to fill time.

Suddenly, and without warning, Chet spoke up and began talking about what running did to him. He really enjoyed it, he said, and felt better because of the physical activity. "I used to have periods where I'd feel very depressed," Chet explained. "I would feel very down about how things were going in my life, so to cure my depression I was taking two Valiums a day. But since I started running, I find that I no longer have those periods of depression any more. And I really look forward to the time of day when I go run." (By then Chet was running even on days when we didn't have classes. So were several others.)

Dick Gosswiller, showing the natural, and necessary, skepticism of the freelance writer, suggested: "Maybe, it's because running gives you something to do."

Chet refused to accept that explanation. "I was always active and went a lot of places," he explained. "It's just that running makes me feel better."

It was a rather extraordinary testimonial, because our class had not been meeting that long, but I understood exactly what was happening to Chet because I had just completed a two-part article on "Running and the Mind" for *Runner's World* (January-February 1978) that described the efforts of a select few psychiatrists and psychologists to use running as a means of curing forms of mental illness, including extreme depression. And they were achieving success as I learned at a conference I attended at the University of Nebraska in Lincoln in September, 1977.

Some researchers, particularly Dr. William P. Morgan of Arizona State University, suggested that the curative effects of running might be from a "time out" effect, the fact that running takes you away from the tensions and preoccupations of hectic, everyday, American life. There are no jangling telephones on jogging courses. Others, particularly Dr. William Brown of the University of Virginia, believed that running might actually produce a chemical change within the brain. Running therapist Dr. Thaddeus Kostrubala of San Diego (author of *The Joy of Running*) had even begun running with schizophrenics. Dr. Kostrubala discovered that he needed to be extremely aware of side-effects, because the effects of running on their bodies caused a shift of the amount of medication they required. They needed fewer drugs to control their mental illness while running regularly. Running also was providing a more efficient means of depression control for Chet than the two Valiums he had been taking previously. And one other female member of the class later confessed that she too no longer needed her anti-depressant pills.

One more note about O.J. Dubie: Each Wednesday a senior citizen's group met at the YMCA for lunch and at the same time we held our running class. After lunch they sometimes spilled out into our "running lobby" and sat in nearby chairs smoking cigarettes, which disturbed several members of the class. (I simply would hold my breath as I ran past the smokers.)

One day one of the senior citizens pointed at Chet as he circled the gym and said: "Look how slow that old guy is going."

I said nothing, but thought to myself: *Moving slow is faster than standing still.*

Will Running Cure Pimples?

The fact that Chet seemingly cured his depression may not necessarily serve as an excuse for you to begin a running program. You may not even have depression, and running may not necessarily cure it or whatever else ails you.

I refuse to promise you even one extra day of life. Running may improve the quality of your life, but I offer no guarantee there either. If you paid money for this book and, after reading it, you still have not been transformed from an ugly frog into a beautiful prince, forget it. Go find a princess to kiss you. You can't have your money back. I've already spent the royalties on a new warmup suit.

In addition, not every run you take will be a Beautiful Experience any more than every time you climb into bed with a man or woman is a Beautiful Experience. Most such experiences are good; some are better than others. Or maybe you just roll over and go to sleep without really trying. If such is the case, running will—no, I better not promise that either.

When it comes to running, at least you should try, even on those days when you don't feel the urge. One of the reasons for establishing a planned schedule for workouts, and maybe keeping a diary of your training, is that it forces you to run even on the days when you don't want to. If you have committed yourself to running three days a week, or at the other end of the scale, 100 miles a week, then go out and do it because you told yourself you would do it. And sometimes running turns out better than you thought.

One day in January, I spent some time chopping ice off my driveway before starting on my daily run, so by the time I moved out onto the road, I already felt fatigued. I had a bit of a sore throat. My muscles were sore from a race I had run over the weekend. Moreover, in trying to pull my basement door free of some ice that had been holding it, I broke the handle on the door, which made me mad.

As I began my run that day my entire concentration focused on how bad I felt, how much it hurt each step I took, how unpleasant it all was. "My God," I thought, "if beginning runners feel like this, no wonder they stop before they get past two weeks." But I decided to swing with it even though, instead of going a planned nine miles, I decided to run five. Maybe that helped, because about halfway through the workout I began feeling more relaxed. I made no attempt to speed up, but I found I no longer was wasting my concentration on my many injuries, real and imagined. My mind spun free and I was away into a million other thoughts. I finished more refreshed than when I started. Still not a Beautiful Experience, but a reasonably good day's run: If not four stars, maybe at least two.

Feedback

Don Kardong had suggested that the most important thing to do when starting a running program was to have some goal. That goal might be to cover two miles continuously at the end of a 10-week period. Or the goal could be to cover a certain total number of miles.

He also considered it important, in motivating people and in having people motivate themselves, to obtain some form of feedback, which might involve three areas:

1. **Weight loss.** Running burns calories and it is a simple fact of physiology that if you burn more calories than you ingest, you lose weight. Run one mile and you burn approximately 100 calories. Run 10, you burn 1000. You probably will not lose as much weight running as you hoped, however, since you may start to eat more. The best results come if, in addition to your exercise activity, you also control your food intake through diet.

2. **Pulse rate.** Running has a beneficial effect on the cardiovascular system, particularly when it comes to lowering previously high blood pressure, but you might never realize this unless you attempt to measure it. The simplest form of monitoring is to take your pulse, before, during, and after each exercise period and recording the numbers. Over a period of months, as your physical condition improves, your pulse rate should de-

cline, particularly after exercise. You will recover quickly, a sign
that your heart is becoming more efficient in pumping blood to
the muscles. But don't make the mistake of comparing your
pulse rate with that of your fellow joggers, since the fact that
theirs is either higher or lower than yours may be meaningless.
As Dr. Sheehan says: "Everybody is an experiment of one." For
what it is worth, my pulse rate at the moment I type this is 40,
and I have measured it in the 20s while horizontal. (At the same
time, my knees hurt and my legs are stiff because I am running
too many miles a day.)

   3. Mileage. The easiest and most common form of measurement, and accomplishment, is miles. The fact that you can run
one mile nonstop one week and two miles several weeks later
says something about your degree of development. Runners like
to record miles, and practically every diary and running calen-
dar designed for runners has some place where they can record
their daily, weekly, monthly, or even yearly mileage. Some runners even make a fetish of it and become mileage freaks. They
are not happy unless they run a certain, predetermined amount
of miles. For many competitive racers, the watermark seems to
be 100 miles a week. There is a feeling that unless you train at
that level you cannot compete at the top level. But even fitness
joggers have their own watermark. Recently I received a newspaper clipping from Ralph Pidcock, mentioned earlier, showing
him crossing a bridge in celebration of the 25,000th mile he ran
since beginning to run some 10 years previous. That mark was
significant, because it was the equivalent of one time around the
Earth. And now Ralph is out there on his second act of circum-
locomotion. For the astronauts, it takes about an hour and a
half to circle the globe. Ralph took 10 years, but since everything is relative, his accomplishment may equal theirs.

   4. Time. I hesitate mentioning the fact that you can, as a
fourth form of measurement, record the amount of time it takes
you to cover a certain distance, whether a mile, or more, or less.
I believe beginning joggers should stay away from stopwatches
as a form of motivation. If you stay in running long enough
there may come a point when the amount of time it takes you to
cover certain distances may become very important to you, but
now is not that point. Check back with me later when we reach
the part of this book that deals with competitive running.

AHA: FOUR STARS!

Although I said earlier that not every time you ran would result in a Beautiful Experience, sometimes it happens that way. Only a week or so after the day on which I had been chopping ice, my two star day, I rounded a corner coming out onto Lake Shore Drive about two miles north of my house and was suddenly struck by the sight before me. It was late on a clear afternoon and the sun had set, leaving the sky orange above the lake. From where I live we can look across 35 miles of Lake Michigan on certain days to see the lights of Chicago.

The lake at that time was covered with ice, piled near the shore in small mounds from the action of breaking waves. The spray freezes in the sub-zero air building up higher and higher. The blue shadows from these mounds contrasted against the stark whiteness of the ice itself, which in turn formed a sharp contrast to the orange left from the setting sun. It was one of those moments of incredible beauty that occur now and then. Four stars! Moments like these happen, and I try to enjoy them as I run.

Part 2
Where, When
and in What

6

Running Out the Door

Locating a running course
on or off the roads

One of running's main attractions is that you need little in the way of extra equipment and you can do it almost anywhere. So the simplest solution for a runner seeking a place to train is simply to run out the front door. Train in the area nearest your home. Some years ago while traveling through Canada I stopped at the home of runner Ron Wallingford in Hamilton, Ontario. Sitting in his living room, I recall looking out the window and seeing a long grassy expanse of park.

"You're lucky to live near a park," I commented.

"Luck had nothing to do with it," admitted Ron. "I chose this house *because* of its location."

I did precisely the same when I relocated my family in the mid-1960s. With three growing children plus a need for an office in which to write, my wife and I decided we needed to move out of our apartment and into a house. There were a number of factors on which we based our choice. One was proximity to good schools. Second came convenient shopping nearby. A third very important factor was the availability of adequate running areas. You can guess which member of the family was most concerned with *that* factor.

I simply did not want to climb into a car and drive somewhere every time I needed to run. I expected to be able to run out the front door and within a few minutes reach some comfortable running area. The first two apartments in which we lived during the early years of our marriage fulfilled that expec-

tation. We lived first in Hyde Park near the University of Chicago. In addition to being only a few blocks away from Jackson
Park and the Chicago lakefront with its miles of traffic-free sidewalks, it was only a mile run, a good warmup, before reaching
the University track. Our second apartment was in South Shore
with the park and lakefront equally convenient, although I now
had to drive 15 minutes to the track. In buying a home I wanted
it in an area equally as convenient.

Eventually we settled in Long Beach, a neighborhood of
Michigan City, Indiana, on the south shore of Lake Michigan,
a little more than an hour's drive from Chicago.

We chose an old house overlooking the lake in an ideal area
for a runner. I could cross the street and descend a stairway to
the beach and run along the shoreline four miles in one direction and seven in another. During the winter when ice jammed
the lake making the beach unrunnable, I could move to the
road paralleling the beach: Lake Shore Drive (mentioned earlier), a relatively low-traffic avenue. Many other back roads in
our neighborhood and other routes into the surrounding rural
countryside offered much variation.

Only a half-mile away was an 18-hole golf course belonging to
the Long Beach Country Club, and although I don't belong, the
course is relatively unfenced and no one chases runners away. I
run only when I will not be in the way of golfers, which usually
means during the spring or fall, or summers very early in the
morning. In almost every direction from my house I can find
wooded areas criss-crossed with trails—ideal cross-country
routes. And if I want to drive 20 minutes, I can be at the Dunes
National Lakeshore, one of the most scenic running areas in
America.

Michigan City proved deficient only in tracks. The city had
three cinder tracks when I first arrived in town: one of them
marginally adequate, another inadequate, and the third (at the
high school) a disaster in terms of surface, aesthetics, and shape
(it was square). Recently it has been replaced by a passable all-
weather track. I must drive to reach it, but since I do very little
track training, this poses only a minor inconvenience. Michigan
City has no indoor running facilities unless you count my soap
opera course at the Y.

The Roads

Although many runners begin to run on indoor or outdoor tracks, once they become involved in running as a lifestyle they usually look toward other horizons. This is because the more you run on a track the more boring it becomes. A track that is adequate for two or three mile runs becomes intolerable for three to ten mile runs seven days a week. Having to carry a counter to keep track of your laps and mileage seems unnecessary, particularly when other avenues beckon.

The most common is the road. People interested in covering a lot of distance sooner or later move their workouts to the roads. Only by running roads can you obtain long expanses of ground to cover. And in covering this ground running becomes more pleasurable, every workout a sightseeing tour into the outdoors. In fact, running the roads is one of the sport's most pleasurable experiences and one reason that many people stay in the sport long after they might have become mentally fatigued touring YMCA tracks.

There are definite hazards, of course, the most obvious one being that in moving to the roads the runner invades the domain of the automobile. In a head-on collision between runner and automobile, the one weighing 4000 pounds will suffer the least damage. Whenever possible, runners should avoid collisions with 4000-pound objects. I'll explore that subject further in a later chapter.

In selecting a road course, the easiest way is simply to start running out the front door and go with the flow. Run where your instincts tell you. This may not be entirely satisfactory if you live in a neighborhood crowded with people or traffic. You are best headed toward areas where you can find long stretches of highway not frequented by many automobiles. In the middle of a city like Chicago, finding this kind of running route may be difficult, if not impossible, but for those people such as myself who live near rural areas, county highways provide ideal running routes. The streets of a typical suburban subdivision may offer at least a semi-satisfactory place to run. But even the most populated city has areas where you can train satisfactorily if you know where to look.

One way to locate good running courses is simply to look for runners. I could not have made such a statement ten or even five years ago, but today there are runners everywhere who usually

discover the best places to run by trial and error. So if you
follow the crowds you probably can learn from them.

Scenic Running Routes

One good clue in locating a running course is to look for a
river, lake, or other body of water. On a recent trip to Minneapolis I had made arrangements to run with Olympic 10,000-
meter finalist Garry Bjorklund one afternoon, but I arrived late
from the airport. When I called Garry's apartment, nobody was
home, so instinctively I headed in my rental car for the Missis-
sippi River and parked on one of the side streets near the University of Minnesota. I found a series of sidewalks and roads
atop the bluff beside the river and managed a good 10-mile
workout. When I saw Garry later that night, he said that I had
stumbled onto a very popular running course.

Rivers, lakes, and other bodies of water are good places to
look for running courses, because they naturally block traffic
and often have scenic drives or walks along them. On a trip to
Galveston, Texas, for instance, I discovered that the sea wall
protecting the city from storms made an ideal course. It had a
sidewalk atop it, so there was no worrying about traffic. At each
end of the seawall, long stretches of beach offered a softer-
surfaced alternative.

Chicago has a series of sidewalks along its lakefront (the site
of the Mayor Daley Marathon) that provide nearly 20 miles of
uninterrupted (and very scenic) running. Runners in San Diego
can circle Mission Bay, site of another popular marathon. The
most popular road running area in New York City is Central
Park, which is closed to vehicular traffic at certain times of the
day and on weekends to permit runners free use of the roads.

Parks in general make good running locations for the simple
reason that they often have sidewalks that go both nowhere and
somewhere. Even when you must share a road with autos, park
traffic restrictions often force cars to slow down. Runners in
Denver meet often in Washington Park for late-afternoon workouts. In San Francisco, Golden Gate Park attracts many. Shaw-
nee Mission Park outside Kansas City is an example of an excellent running park, since it has a road circuit approximately five
miles long. The only disadvantage for beginners would be that
some of the hills on the circuit are monumental enough to bring
even well-conditioned runners almost to their knees.

With the popularity of cycling many cities have constructed special bike paths, which runners usually share. The nine-mile Calumet Trail made out of crushed gravel and located in the Dunes National Lakeshore was built with cyclists in mind, but has proved to be a more satisfactory surface for runners. With the popularity of running, many communities now are designating special jogging trails. Chicago has one on the north side in Lincoln Park.

Establishing a Course

When you first go out to run, your best bet is simply go do it. Run in whichever direction suits you, along whatever route is comfortable. Don't worry about the distance—at least at first. Make adjustments in the course from day to day as you discover the flaws. Later, you may want to drive over the course in your car to satisfy your own curiosity as to how far you're running.

This can prove dangerous to your morale if you have been timing yourself with a watch. Recently I received a telephone call from a young woman in town named Julie Scholl, whom I had been encouraging to train for a 10,000-meter run for women sponsored by Bonne Bell in Chicago. She sounded crushed, despondent, deflated. Julie had measured the three-mile course she had been running for the last several weeks and discovered it to be only 2.2 miles long! This meant her pace over the course was only about 9:00 per mile, much slower than Julie felt she should be running in preparation for her big race. Obviously it was going to take additional encouragement to repair her punctured psyche. A four-mile workout over one of my favorite courses, on which she managed near an 8:00 pace, repaired the damage.

Almost all runners overestimate the length of their courses. During National Running Week, I went for a workout with Dr. Steve Subotnick on the golf course across the street from Steve's podiatric office in Hayward, California. Afterwards, Steve identified it as his 12-mile course. Glancing at my watch, I estimated that we must have been running at a sub-6:00 pace, amazing considering the conversational level of our workout. But there is no sense making people feel bad when you learn they are fudging. I just very diplomatically called Dr. Subotnick a no-good, rotten, cheating liar.

Actually, I have a seven-mile course that I run regularly near my home that I know is at least a quarter-mile short of that distance. I never clock myself over it for that reason, but I always record it in my diary as seven. My rationalization is that because of several extremely severe hills on that course, it equals seven miles on a flatter course. Subotnick's excuse is that as a converted skier trying to break three hours for the marathon, he needs all the psychological help he can get.

After you have been running for several years, and competing in races, and timing yourself in workouts over accurately measured courses, you get an instinctive feel for how much mileage you cover. The clock becomes one form of measurement. If I come in after running an hour, I might credit myself with eight miles, figuring an average 7:30 pace. Possibly on some days I cheat myself out of some distance either way, but things average out. Everything is relative anyway, and it probably makes little difference to your actual physical condition whether you run 98 miles a week or 100. It may be of some psychological advantage to think you go farther, which is why I had to deflate Steve Subotnick. I didn't want him nudging me off my position as *Runner's World*'s fastest columnist.

Settling in

After a while most runners become comfortable with certain courses that they have established over a period of time. They know the landmarks for certain mileages and can check their pace as they pass them. The distance matters little since they can compare their times when they pass this tree or that bridge. They learn the danger spots whether traffic, people, or barking dogs. Most often they will have adjusted their course in its planning stages to avoid such hazards. They become comfortable because of this, and can run more relaxed.

Over a period of many months, or even years, they can watch flowers blossom, trees gradually shed their leaves, entire neighborhoods change, families grow up. One day while running along Lake Shore Drive I suddenly realized than an ancient, graffiti-covered plank garage that used to jut out onto the road at exactly the 2.5 mile mark from my house was suddenly gone. It was as though a hand had come from out of the sky, plucked it up, and carried it away to the resting ground of old garages. It was a garage I had passed hundreds of times over 14 years, had been timing myself by it, and suddenly it was no more. Perhaps the garage had vanished six months previous, but this was the first time I had taken notice. The city has a thousand stories, and we touch briefly on only a fraction of them as we run along our road courses.

After a while runners may become frozen on certain courses, becoming too comfortable. Beginning runners particularly are guilty of establishing a certain place and distance for their daily run and doing it day after day after day. Even when runners expand to several courses and distances, they sometimes run them with unvarying inflexibility as though following some schedule carved in concrete. Monday becomes a 10-mile run along the lakefront. Tuesday is the day they go to the track. Wednesday they do easy jogging on the golf course. It must be Thursday, because I just passed the red barn.

But life does not need to be a routine because it says so in a book, this book or any other. Moving to a new course is a threatening situation, but it must be faced if we are to grow. So experiment with where you run.

Getting off the Roads

According to Dr. Subotnick, "The foot has not caught up with man's progress. Genetically our body has lagged behind our ability to produce concrete." (See, sometimes even if you can't get accurate mileage reports from your friends, you can pick up a good quote.) Dr. Subotnick claims that if you train on golf courses, or on sawdust paths, or the equivalent, you will decrease your likelihood of injury by at least 50% compared to exclusive road training. He also suggests that even those who train on concrete surfaces have more problems than those who train on slightly more springy asphalt.

I believe him, because as I write this I am just getting over a knee injury that has been plaguing me for nearly a week. This injury comes at the end of a long winter, which saw record snows in the eastern half of the United States. The snow seemed fun at first, because it was white and clean and even though it forced me to slow down provided a soft, cushiony surface for many of my workouts on roads only partially cleared.

But that was January, and in February the snow changed to ice, and in March the melted ice collected in puddles. Snow blocked access to my usual cross-country routes, and I began to pray for winter to end so I could get away from the constant pounding on the same, unyielding roads. I could have cut my mileage down, which would have been the sensible thing to do, but when you are training in preparation for a major marathon, your senses sometimes leave you. And my knees started to ache to the point where finally I had to back off my training and take several days off.

But I run cross-country not merely to avoid injury; I do it because I enjoy the variety of vistas it affords and the opportunity to get back in the woods where cars and dogs can't chase me. Also, I feel it makes me tougher. A 10-mile workout on cross-country surfaces has greater degree of difficulty than a 10-mile workout on the road, because uneven surfaces force me to run harder.

It may also impose different levels of stress to a greater variety of muscles and thus may have more value for general conditioning. I have a favorite cross-country course that I credit in my diary as 13.5 miles, although after this book is published I don't intend to allow Subotnick near it with an odometer. Anyway, there is no convenient way Steve could measure it short of hiring a surveyor. Whether the distance is 13.5 miles or not is irrelevant, since it is worth that much in effort. On a flat-out time trial over the course in 1972, at a time when I was in peak condition, capable of a sub-2:30 marathon, I managed it in just under an hour and 15 minutes. That's the world record, because nobody ever races it besides me. That record will never fall, because the course changes from year to year, sometimes from week to week as owners of the property I cross block it wth logs and branches to discourage trail-riding motorcyclists who also use portions of it. (Nothing discourages motorcyclists for long, and the logs usually have been moved the next time I pass through.)

The course begins at my front door and follows Lake Shore Drive for a half-mile, then down onto the beach for three-quarters of a mile, up onto the roads again heading inland for another three-quarter-mile stretch including two serious hills, then along a loose bridle path for maybe a half mile before following another half mile of road that is part dirt, part asphalt, and part collection of potholes that have to be navigated with extreme caution. The German shepherd that screams at me at this point is always on a chain.

Then out onto a golf course. Through tall grass and dirt

paths around a swamp for maybe a mile-and-a-half, followed by a route through the woods that mounts steep sand dunes before coming down onto a long stretch of beach. The distances get fuzzy around here, because I am into areas I have never measured. How far I go on the beach depends in part on the level of the lake. When Lake Michigan was high several years ago, part of my course became lost to me and I had to improvise with different routes, some of which were easier, some more challenging.

Eventually I come up from the beach onto the streets of a subdivision of New Buffalo, Michigan, my run having carried me across a state border. I make a short loop past private homes before heading back into the woods, now returning in the direction I came although over a different route. Coming through the woods, I must exercise care because of snags and small stumps in the path. Once, many years ago after running this course in one direction, I reversed the way I ran, coming at this path from the other end and found myself tripping over snags I never noticed, but apparently had programmed into my subconscious to avoid.

Coming down a sand hill out of the woods I follow the Amtrak right-of-way for the train between Chicago and Detroit. This quarter-mile stretch is the worst part of the course, because the path beside the tracks is strewn with rocks and stones that can prove painful particularly if you wear light shoes.

Next I duck back into the woods near the entrance to a camp owned by the YWCA of Greater Chicago, past "No Trespassing" signs where a fat man once threatened my son and me with a shotgun if we didn't turn back. We politely did so—that one time. I've seen the fat man only once in hundreds of trips onto the property, so I run on, passing the hulk of a junk car that has been immobile so long that small trees now surround it, preventing it from being moved, an artifact of the twentieth century.

The next mile is along a narrow path, up and down over thick, wooded sand dunes. When I set the world record on this course, the path was dirt and firm, but now it is sandy and eroded from the trail bikes that also ignore the no trespassing signs, one reason why when a more slowly moving runner comes along he has a shotgun waved in his face. At about nine miles, this path intersects the path followed earlier, so I recross swamp, golf course, more roads, and bridle path to get home, usually skipping the last stretch of beach.

Some days I practice theme and variation, detouring up a steep dune overlooking the lake to return along different paths that bring me home after 10 miles of running. Or I begin the run with a loop around an inland lake that extends the workout to 17 miles. No matter what distance, the terrain and surface force me into constant changes of pace, different stride lengths, varying muscle usages, which offers great variety to my conditioning in addition to the mental stimulus of pleasant surroundings. I love it. Every runner has a favorite course and that is mine. If you look hard, perhaps you will find one equally enjoyable to run.

Running in Circles

An indoor or outdoor track
might be right for you

A recent television movie starring Joanne Woodward and titled "See How She Runs" told the tale of a 40-year-old schoolteacher who starts to jog as one means of reaffirming her identity and ends up running the Boston Marathon. Midway through the story, not wishing to run in the dark through the winter months, the schoolteacher decides to visit a nearby YMCA to run on its balcony track.

She sniffs the air, repelled by the smell of stale sweat, poises timorously on the edge of the track, then plunges into the maelstrom of runners relentlessly circling it. *Voom! Voom! Voom!* They zoom past her, darting into the turns like Richard Petty in the Daytona 500. A few laps later she staggers off the track, gasping, joggled, battered, while the surge of runners moves on undiminished in their quest for fitness. In fact, those particular "joggers" were moving so swiftly in the movie that it appeared that the director had hired candidates for the Villanova two-mile relay team as stand-ins for the YMCA joggers. At most YMCA's, they simply do not move that fast.

Yet, the beginning jogger, approaching any track on which organized (or disorganized) running occurs, probably perceives the action the way the director of "See How She Runs" showed it to us. I am willing to silence my criticism and give him credit for giving us at least the appearance of reality, if not reality itself. In fact, not long after the Joanne Woodward movie appeared, I received a letter from Diane Messina, a young runner who had run in a 10-mile race I sponsored the previous fall in nearby Beverly Shores. Diane sought advice. Recently she had joined the Chicago Health Club so as to be able to run on its 32-lap-per-mile track. "I am dizzy, bruised from being elbowed by my fellow joggers, and damned bored," wrote Diane. "What is your opinion about this?"

Well, my opinion was she should resign her membership in the Chicago Health Club, purchase a knit cap and a pair of snuggies, and run outside — which she did. But there does remain a place in the world of running for tracks, both of the indoor and outdoor variety. Certainly few beginning runners will take their first workout on a 10-degree day in the middle of a snowstorm, so if they begin during winter they often do so on indoor tracks. Many fitness joggers remain on indoor tracks, or switch to outdoor tracks, during the summer simply because of convenience. Competitive runners sometimes feel the necessity to do at least some of their workouts on tracks, because it provides them an exact measurement of their time and pace. Tracks also provide a more appropriate surface and atmosphere for doing the speed work necessary for high quality performances.

Most experienced runners have no qualms about going to a track, even one they never have visited before, to become part of the maelstrom. Novices, however, may feel a bit like Joanne Woodward when they first arrive at a track to see the sweep of superiorly conditioned athletes hurling their bodies around the turns and into the straightaways. Understandably, these novices don't want to get in the way of the thoroughbreds for fear of feeling foolish or even getting run over. Nevertheless, beginning runners are welcomed at most tracks as long as they learn and obey the rules. Let us consider what some of those rules might be, beginning with a discussion of indoor tracks.

Undercover Running

The most common place for indoor running is at your local YMCA, which even if it does not have a balcony track usually provides an area around a basketball court for joggers. Such tracks are good places to begin, particularly since the level of ability among those who utilize them usually is relatively low and the pace they run comfortably constant. But once joggers progress much beyond the two- or three-mile-a-day level, they begin to get cabin fever and look for ways to expand their horizons.

If this describes you and you are lucky, there may be an indoor track at a nearby high school or college, and if you are especially lucky that high school or college may even let you use it (no certainty). The best indoor facilities can be found in field houses of large universities. Most Big Ten track teams, for example, practice on Tartan (rubberized) tracks, 220 yards long with gradual turns.

Running on these tracks can be very pleasant, but getting to use them is another matter. It helps if you are a student, a faculty member, or are a close friend of the track coach. For many years, while living in Chicago, I competed for the University of Chicago Track Club and used their facilities. I maintained my ties with the UCTC even though I moved out of the area. Recently the University totally renovated its field house, eliminating the old dirt in favor of a Tartan one. I paid $30 this winter for the privilege of using this track, which, when you consider I trained on it only four times, seemed fairly expensive for each workout—although not much more than I would pay if I wanted to play racquetball somewhere.

On other occasions when I am in Chicago, I run at the police gym on the south side not far from Comiskey Park. Mayor Michael A. Bilandic is among the people who regularly use these facilities, sometimes running as much as 10 miles in a workout, or 80 laps around the approximately 220-yard track that is part board, part asphalt. I say "approximately," because it seems longer, but maybe that is because the tight turns affect your times. At any given time there might be as many as 50 runners circling the track, the building staying open 24 hours a day. There are certain members of the Chicago police department that burglars will have little success running away from. Police teams compete in many of the distance runs in that city.

Whenever you visit a track for the first time, particularly an indoor track that may be crowded, learn the traffic rules before you take your first running step. Each track has its own etiquette that permits runners moving at varying speeds to coexist without danger to each other. For example, the police gym seems to tolerate runners moving in the opposite direction more readily than does the field house where the training level of the runners, some of them world class athletes like Rick Wohlhuter, is much faster. Sometimes the rules and regulations are posted on signs near the track; if not, you may be able to figure out the code of running behavior simply by standing for a few minutes watching the traffic flow. If you have any questions, simply ask another runner. They would rather have you ask than run into you. If there is a track coach standing nearby, question him, although this is risky in some places since he may ask you to leave.

Traffic rules are particularly important where fast-striders mix with beginning runners. A speedy quarter-miler often will circle a track at a speed two to three times faster than that of a fitness jogger, and the speedster expects only one thing of the jogger: to stay out of his way.

This is not an unreasonable request since the jogger probably also wants to stay out of the way of the fast runner, partly out of fear for his life and partly out of politeness. And since there usually are four to six lanes on most indoor tracks, there is room for both types.

Traffic Rules

While traffic rules may vary from track to track, following are some basic ones.

1. Stay out of the inside lane if you are not running fast or against the stopwatch. This is a rule that usually applies when competitive runners share the same facilities with joggers; it may apply less on a track (often the same one at a different hour) used only by joggers. Move to one of the outside lanes to do your easy running. This may not always be easy since outside lanes may be blocked by hurdles or in use by sprinters on the straightaways, but at most tracks where runners go fast inside there is a flow of slower moving bodies outside. You usually can identify this flow and move into it.

2. When passing a slower runner do not yell "track!" and expect that person to get out of your way. Simply slide around to the outside; you will add only a short increment to the distance you run. Although that person may seem slow to you, he may be fighting his own personal battle against the stopwatch. Others have the right to the inside even if their standard of fast does not match your own.

3. As you finish a fast run against time (and "fast" could be considered almost any pace where you push yourself into the fatigue area), ease gradually out of the fast lane. Do not stop suddenly and stand gasping in place because someone may be coming up behind you. You would not halt your car in the middle of an expressway during rush hour, and many indoor tracks operate on similar traffic principles as on the highway.

4. *Do not cross the track without looking in all directions*. The same expressway traffic analogy applies here. Sometimes runners can come at you from all directions, and you do not want to end someone else's running career, or your own, by a step in the wrong direction. Even if you get off the track and into the infield, you may not be entirely safe because you may cross the path of a pole vaulter or move into the drop zone of a shot putter.

5. *When you see someone bearing down on you while you are standing in place, freeze rather than move or jump in his path as he goes around you*. Clasp your arms against your sides so the runner knows your intentions. If you are running and are about to be overtaken from behind, do not move wide thinking you are doing the other runner a favor by granting him the inner lane. You may cause a collision by moving too late.

6. *Almost always run in a counterclockwise direction*. Tradition dictates that all track competition occurs in this manner and so everybody practices this way. Fitness runners also follow the infield-on-the-left pattern of running, even when running alone on an otherwise empty track. I say *almost* always, because sometimes you see runners warming up in outside lanes in a clockwise direction. And on some tracks used by joggers, particularly in YMCAs, they often alternate directions every other day so as not to overdevelop one set of muscles, which happens if you always turn one way. At other tracks there may be a flow going in both directions, but if you're a newcomer to someone else's athletic facility you probably will not want to independently challenge ingrained traffic patterns.

7. *Respect the rights of others on the track*. This is probably the most important rule of all. If you are a fast runner do not expect everybody to clear the inside lane just so you can run a quarter mile against the stopwatch. But if you are a slow runner respect the need of fast runners occasionally to use that inside lane to get a precise time over an exact distance. If you get in somebody's way by mistake, apologize. Be polite. And don't anticipate problems, because more likely they will not occur.

Fast runners and joggers coexist very well at most tracks; after all, in their warmup or cool-down periods, runners turn into joggers.

Moving Outdoors

In general, the same traffic rules that apply indoors also apply outdoors. Even though there is more room on a 440-yard outdoor track than a 220-yard (or smaller) indoor track, the same flow patterns exist. If there are differences, it may be because the same fields used for track practice also have other areas for football, baseball, or other sports.

The greatest danger is not from the participants in those sports, but their coaches. Football coaches in particular sometimes take a proprietary interest in the purity of their grass. They sometimes frown on joggers using their field, or even the grassy area just inside the track circling their field. No matter that the first play from scrimmage next fall will do more grass damage than a whole summer of joggers, they'll chase runners away, and place locks on gates. This probably happens less now than it did 10 or 20 years ago if only because even football coaches now run and so have become more sympathetic to runners' needs.

Perhaps a word should be included about why one would want to run on a track, particularly an outdoor track, when the parks, roads, and beaches beckon. The world of many runners is transcribed entirely by a 440-yard oval. Mihaly Igloi, the Hungarian track coach who defected to the United States in the late 1950s, had his athletes follow a highly structured pattern of interval training always on the track, two workouts a day with seldom a run in open areas. Many Igloi disciples still train this way and train others this way. I prefer wide-open spaces, but there are times when I utilize an outdoor track, and there are good reasons why every beginning runner should at least consider the occasional use of one.

• **The track provides security.** It is a place where people go to perform a single activity: run. You are not on a golf course getting in the way of golfers, or in a park getting in the way of lovers, or on the roads getting in the way of automobiles. Dogs do not usually frequent running tracks. You can run safely without worry about outside interference.

• **The track forms a protective womb.** At a running track you are among the company of other runners, most of whom love what they are doing, and they will respect you for attempting it too, no matter how ineptly. For this reason a track may be a good place to get started if you are at all self-conscious about your own level of ability. If you desire it, you also can obtain help, advice, sympathy, encouragement, and even companionship from those you meet there. (I met my wife at a bowling alley when I joined a church league to which she belonged.) Without question, many romances today are kindled in the running areas of America. Whether you go to a running track seeking a future spouse or not, such a place is a comfortable place to run because that is what it was designed for.

• **The track provides an opportunity for measurement.** Most tracks come in 440-yard sizes or more recently in 400-meter sizes, thus are four laps to a mile. You can tell exactly how far you run each day, which may be important if you are following a progressive schedule similar to some of those outlined in this book. Not only can you tell how *far* you run, but you can also tell how *fast* you run by timing yourself. This may serve as another important motivational device by which you can measure your own improvement. If you are interested in competitive racing, you may find it necessary to spend a certain percentage of your training time running against a stopwatch. Even if you are not interested in competition, you may want to train on a track as a form of discipline. Being able to run 10 x 440 yards in a specified time becomes a form of achievement equal to time or places in standard races. I look back on certain workouts that I have accomplished with pride, and I know many other competitive runners do so too. Workouts on tracks usually are considered a means to an end, but they also can become an end in itself.

• **The track can serve as a substitute club.** Tracks usually come connected to other recreational facilities. (In Europe they often come connected to taverns and restaurants, but we haven't progressed that far yet in America.) Even if you do not run on the track, you may want to use the facilities as a starting point for runs into other areas.

• **The track offers an injury-free environment.** Aside from the fact that automobiles and dogs cannot get at you, tracks are smooth and devoid of potholes, branches, or soft spots that may cause you to twist an ankle. One common cause of injury among runners is running on hills, particularly going too fast downhill. Tracks do not have hills. You will be less likely to trip or fall while running on a track unless you become ambitious and start leaping over hurdles. Tracks were designed for running, thus are very efficient places to accomplish that activity.

I now do most of my serious running elsewhere—on the roads, across country—but I still enjoy a hard, disciplined workout on a track. And I also enjoy racing there.

8

Fitting It In

Morning, noon, or night
can be the right time for you

In addition to deciding where to run, the runner also has to decide *when*. Ignoring a moment time of day, I can say without equivocation that the best day of the year on which to run is Super Bowl Sunday. Since this game lasts nearly three hours, you can get in a nice long workout.

The reason I prefer these three hours for running out of a possible 8,760 during the year is that most other Americans are inside watching their television sets. During the playing of the Super Bowl in 1978 (whatever Roman numeral it was), I left my son David and a group of his friends, all of them athletes in various sports, sitting before the TV set and went for a run along my usual seven-mile course. Because most red-blooded Americans were watching the game, traffic was almost non-existent. About a hundred yards down the road from my home a lone automobile passed me. I ran nearly six miles before seeing another.

What I did see, as I glanced through windows along the way, were shadows of the Great Game flickering on the sets of my neighbors. I also saw white snowflakes falling around me, their crystals brilliant in the moonlight because Pete Rozelle in his infinite wisdom had decreed that "The Game" would be played at night, prime-time like they say on Madison Avenue. And I felt the delightful peace and quiet that comes from being alone when you are not alone. At one point in my run, along a desolate stretch of road, motivated by a feeling of perversity, I raised

one fist in the air, and shouted: "Fuck football!" But I regretted
it at once, because I have nothing against football *per se*, but
only against the way in which it turns many Americans into sedentary spectators, content to watch others perform instead of
performing themselves.

Actually, some of my best friends are football players.
Howard Mudd, former All-Pro guard with the San Francisco
49ers, whom I had gotten to know while covering pro football
during the 1960s, attended most sessions of National Running
Week in 1977. Howard has to cycle rather than run, because of
too many knee operations, but his wife Marie and children enjoy
running. At least a few football players now are into running.
Alan Page of the Minnesota Vikings reportedly runs seven miles
a day and even takes a run on Sunday morning before games.
Large men have discovered they can enjoy running too. At
Southwestern Michigan College, track coach Ron Gunn says the
main problem he has with his field event men during the fall is
that they all want Nike Waffle Trainers so they can run in the
woods instead of staying inside to work out in the weight room.

But back to the Super Bowl.

Anyway, if, after reading this book, you decide to emulate my
advice and go running during the Super Bowl next year, you
will know I am out there somewhere running with you, lifting
my fist, screaming obscenities into the empty night. That is,
unless the Chicago Bears make the finals. I consider myself a
Bears fan, so there are limits to my dedication as a runner.

Assuming that you run each year during the Super Bowl, you
still must worry about finding time to train 364 other days of the
year. Examine your daily schedule. Determine what time of day
would be most convenient for your daily workout, whether it be
morning, noon, or night. Decide how much time you want to
run — or can afford to run — and simply fit that time into your
schedule. Even if you only plan to run a half-hour a day, four
days a week, be consistent in that running pattern. If you decide
that a certain time of the day you are going to go out and run
no matter what gets in your way, you can do it.

You probably will need to give priority to your work and to
your family, but don't let lesser activities interfere. Other people
will respect you for your dedication. If you allow lesser activities
to interfere, you probably won't remain a runner very long. You
never hear of an alcoholic or a drug addict allowing anything to
interfere with their daily fix. Runners become the same way and

become addicted to their daily activity. They even suffer withdrawal symptoms if they fail to run, and not running eventually becomes such an unpleasant alternative, they are going to run each day one way or another. According to running author Joe Henderson: "When it hurts more not to run than to run, that's when you become a runner." A beginning runner whose level of dedication has not progressed to this point may find this difficult to believe, but sooner or later you may reach that level described in a book by William Glaser, M.D., as "positive addiction." Beware, you are hooked.

Until you slide into a definite pattern for your running, consider the different times of the day at which you might run.

Morning Running

Recently, I awoke early one morning and went for an easy two-mile run. In the closing stages of my run I encountered Roy Bradford, one of my neighbors. I greeted Roy as we neared each other. As he passed, a broad smile crossed his face. "Have a nice day," he said. And it was a nice day, partly because he said it.

Finding time to run in the morning is very easy. You simply set your alarm clock a half-hour earlier, or whatever length of time you need for your workout. However, this may only work if you are a "morning person," one whose energy is highest during that time of the day. The world seems to be divided between morning people and night people. I am one of the former, so I enjoy a morning run, although usually I save my toughest workouts for later in the day. I only run mornings when I am doing double workouts as part of an all-out effort to reach peak condition.

Some people should not run in the morning, since they may not enjoy that time of day. At National Running Week, podiatrist Richard Schuster commented that morning runners suffered more injuries than afternoon runners, maybe as much as 50% more. He speculated that one reason might be that people are in more of a rush to get moving in the morning, because they have to come in from their run, eat breakfast, and get off to work. As a result, they may be less likely to warm up properly. They may neglect to stretch before they run. If you are a morning runner with a history of injuries, consider Dr. Schuster's words. Either spend more time in preventive exercises, or find another time of day to run.

Mid-day Running

More and more runners seem to pick this time of day for their daily workouts, particularly as running becomes more popular and respectable at executive levels. It is no longer considered "suspicious" if an executive passes on a three-martini lunch in favor of a six-mile workout during the noon hour. In fact, any corporation president who measured the afternoon performance level of noontime joggers vs. noontime drinkers would quickly realize which type of person he would rather have on his staff. Perhaps as much business may be conducted on jogging trails as once supposedly occurred on the golf courses.

Following the 1976 Olympics, there was a lot of media talk about corporations becoming involved in sports as one way of combatting the super-organized programs of Iron Curtain countries, particularly East Germany. It was going to be an example of capitalism at its best, with corporations hiring world class athletes, giving them an opportunity to train and time-off, when necessary, to compete.

I had a hard time suppressing a yawn when I heard about this program, because I thought it was attacking the problem from the wrong end. If corporations provided sports facilities for *all* their employees, not just an elite few, and if they made it convenient and respectable for *everybody* to exercise and/or train for competition, no matter at what level, we would have healthier citizens, stronger athletes, and would win some Olympic gold medals too.

But back to the subject of mid-day running, it may be the best time of day to workout. Stanley Kowalski, Dave Hoen, and several executives from the Bethlehem Steel plant in nearby Burns Ditch, Indiana, work out on their lunch hour in the woods and dunes surrounding the plant and have begun to attract others to their group. Housewives find running at this time attractive, particularly if they have children in school. Since more and more women have begun to run, more and more people will be doing it in the middle of the day.

This includes the select group of "professional" long distance runners in this country, who now find they can make a living from the sport, either by accepting appearance money from races or working in spin-off running businesses such as selling equipment, particularly shoes. This allows them to choose their own hours, and several I know now take their hardest workout at 11:00 AM with a second workout at 5:00 PM designed as an easy relaxed run. New Zealand coach Arthur Lydiard suggests this may be a better training program than an early morning, easy run, followed by an all-out effort late in the day. The second, late-afternoon workout, if done at a relaxed pace, allows you to partially repair the damage done during your hard, late morning run and permits you to train hard again the next day. During the winter I often run mid-day, because it is warmest then and I can run in daylight rather than dark.

One advantage of running on your lunch hour is that if you are interested in losing weight, substituting a calorie-burning workout for a calorie-increasing lunch may be the quickest way to do it. If you feel the need for some food to carry you through the day, a cup of yogurt, some slices of cheese, or a piece of fruit taken after showering may suffice. You'll be healthier for following that kind of diet. A few runners eat, then run. While attending Albany Law School, Barry Brown used to eat a full dinner, then, 30 minutes later, run hard intervals on the track. This form of "gut training" later proved to his advantage. In 1968, he went to the semifinal Olympic Trials not expecting to run, because he had not yet run a qualifying time. Less than an hour before the start of the 3,000 meter steeplechase, Barry was sitting in the stands enjoying a foot-long hot dog and a chocolate milk shake when track coach Bob Giegengack appeared and said he had obtained permission for Barry to run. Despite the food in his stomach, Barry Brown ran his fastest time of the year.

On a few occasions (the most recent being when I wanted to watch the Joanne Woodward TV-movie, "See How She Runs"), I have eaten dinner before a workout. On that particular occasion I ate tuna fish and soup, then did four miles in 34 minutes on snow-covered roads before coming in to watch the movie. You can train your stomach to accept stress just as you can train the muscles of your legs, but running immediately after meals certainly is not a regimen I would recommend for Joanne Woodward or for any other beginning runner.

Afternoon Running

This is the most convenient time of day for most runners. Colleges and high schools schedule their track practices around

4:00 in the afternoon. If you like company when you workout on a track, you will be most likely to find it at this time. Several executives I know sneak away from their desks at 4:00 so they can get an early workout while it is still light.

One big advantage to running at this time of day is that a workout after work serves as a tranquilizer to combat the day's stresses or a pep pill to alleviate the "logy" feeling that comes from doing a repetitive task. Running affects different people different ways.

Frequently we become fatigued not from the energy expended during work, but merely from standing in one place, or sitting in one place, and performing the same activities over and over. Even being forced to think and make decisions causes mental fatigue, which then masquerades as physical fatigue. It's that tired-all-over feeling that you hear about in TV commercials, but running works as a better antidote than any product advertised. Frequently I begin a late-afternoon run exhausted from a day at the typewriter or on the phone, wondering how I can survive more than a few miles. Somehow when I complete those few miles I feel renewed and invigorated and press on at an ever increasing pace. Most simply stated: Running makes you feel good.

It can also serve as an appetite-depressant, since immediately after a workout you probably will not feel like having a big meal. If you are on a diet trying to lose weight, plan to run immediately before the day's biggest meal for this reason. Some people use food as a form of tranquilizer to block out the stresses of the day. They come home and reach into the refrigerator as a form of therapy, or they imbibe several calorie-rich martinis to unwind. When you unwind by running, you lose weight, not gain it.

One hazard for late-afternoon runners, however, is that if they extend their workout too long they may return to a cold dinner and an even colder wife. Some businessmen work overtime rather than come home and face the stresses of dealing with their family life, and undoubtedly some use running as a similar excuse. I know several marriages that have floundered because of one partner's devotion to running, but undoubtedly running has improved the quality of other marriages, perhaps because the tranquilized running partner becomes easier to live with. I make no judgment as to whether running, in the afternoon or any other time of day, is good or bad for the institution of marriage. I only offer as evidence the fact that I've managed to stay happily married for 20 years.

Nighttime Running

People who do their running later than 8:00 in the evening probably are in the minority, but they do exist. One time or another I have run at all hours of the day and night. *Runner's World* sponsors a Midnight Run in Los Altos, California on New Year's Eve, and a major international race occurs at that same time in Sao Paulo, Brazil. I have run in the wee hours of the morning—after getting up early and sometimes after getting in late. I don't make a habit of night running, because I prefer seeing where I am going, but it does provide an option now and then.

Recently while writing an article for *Runner's World* on the aerobics program at Oral Roberts University, where reportedly 90% of the student body runs, I drove onto campus at 11:30 pm and came across a group of seven runners. The $2 million O.R.U. Aerobics Center with its six-lap-to-the-mile indoor track stays open from 6:00 am to 1:30 am, and many people find it convenient to run just before going to bed. When I competed for the University of Chicago Track Club, I borrowed a key from coach Ted Haydon so I could get into the Stagg Field track for late-evening interval workouts in the heat of summer. The University recently remodeled its field house, which now stays open until 10:00 pm, mostly for joggers using the indoor track.

Night-running outdoors, however, can be dangerous if you run on roads where automobile drivers may come on you suddenly. Indiana University miler Steve Heidenreich nearly lost his life after being struck by a hit-and-run driver while taking a late-night workout on some back roads near his apartment. I'll discuss the dangers of auto traffic in a later chapter, but I now run with a glow-in-the-dark belt to make sure that drivers see me during evening runs.

If nighttime is the only time you can fit a run into your schedule, you can adjust to this schedule. While stationed in Stuttgart, Germany, with the U.S. Army in 1956, I got off duty at 5:00 pm. Mess call was 6:00 pm, and the Army was not understanding as a wife might be and refused to hold dinner for me. Since I was training for the Olympics, I needed more than an hour, but on a private first class's salary, I could not afford to eat every night elsewhere. I usually waited until 9:00 or later to work out, running often through the nearby forests, which were criss-crossed with dirt roads and paths. The forest floor also had a soft, springy surface pretty much uncluttered with underbrush and branches. On all but the darkest nights, the moonlight was enough to run through the forest without fear of falling. After running awhile in this manner, your eyes adapt to the darkness and your instincts react to any hazards under foot. I remember these nighttime runs as among the most pleasant in my career.

There are hazards for runners in the modern city, however, that have nothing to do with branches underfoot. Most runners carry little of value worth stealing except perhaps a watch, but not all potential muggers are smart enough to know that. I try to avoid areas of possible conflict when I run, and I would suspect that most runners, particularly female ones, should think twice about where they train, particularly in the dark.

Flexible Running

The best answer to the question of when to run may not be one of the above, but all of the above. While it is important for a beginner to set a definite time and place and be consistent about it, someone who adopts running as a lifestyle will run daily even if it means missing a meal or losing two hours of sleep. Dedicated runners let their choice of workout times fall in place, fitting workouts into their schedules whenever it seems convenient that particular day.

Valerie Brady stopped by the house one day recently to deliver the transcripts of an interview for this book. We began talking about her running, which she has been doing for a year or so, managing to trim a half-inch from her thighs. Valerie explained her running course; I had no idea from her course description how far she was going, and neither did she—which probably was for the better. When she first went out she found herself coming back 10 minutes later, decided this was not long enough, so now stays out about 20 minutes. She predicates her workouts on time rather than distance, which is something that Joe Henderson recommends. I told her that if she enjoyed being outdoors, she might want to run a little slower and extend the length of her walks between running as a way to remain outside a longer period of time. When she began running, she ran as hard as she could for as long as she could, and she didn't enjoy it until I convinced her she should slow down and not worry about how far she goes.

The point she made about running, however, was that she liked it because of its flexibility. It was simple to do and didn't require any planning. If she failed to run in the morning, she wasn't locked into a schedule and could run later in the day. "This isn't true about swimming or playing tennis," Valerie said. "If I missed either one, it was gone. I would have to wait until the next day."

For her it was simply a matter of fitting a run somewhere into her schedule. And if you want to run badly enough, you can always find a way to fit it in.

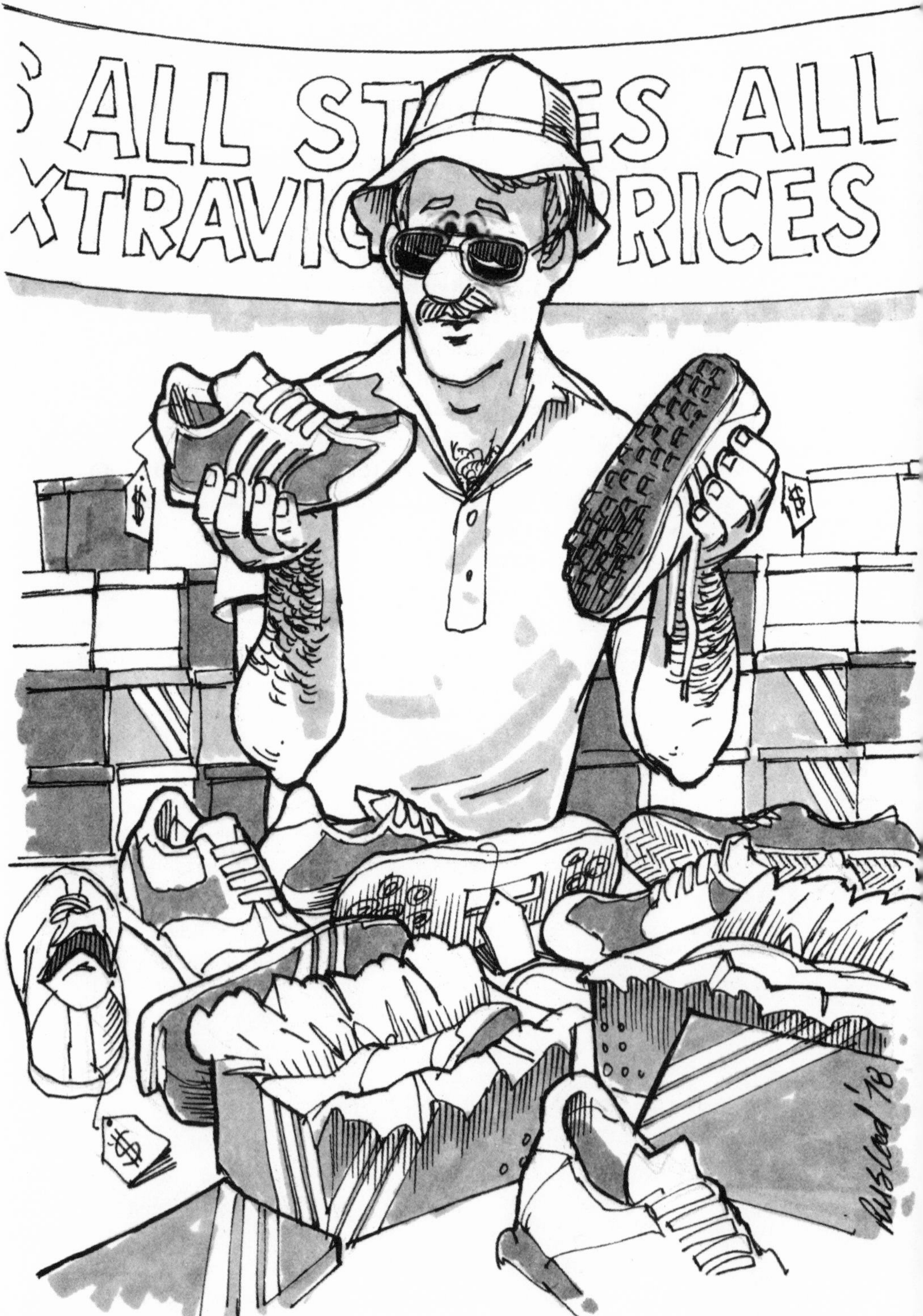

9

Finding the Right Shoes

Why, when, and
which brand of shoe

Craig Harms is a runner from Oxford, Ohio, notable for having run 100 marathons faster than three hours before reaching the age of 26. In his frenzy to accomplish this goal, Craig occasionally ran what is known in long distance circles as back-to-back marathons; that is, one 26 mile 385 yard race on Saturday followed by a second 26 mile 385 yard race the next day. My legs ache just thinking about it.

He also publishes a small-circulation, dittoed, running newsletter known as the *Miami Marathon Club Newsletter*, consisting mostly of entry blanks and results but also carrying Craig's opinions on a variety of subjects from shoes to nuts. It was in this former area that some of Craig's subscribers recently thought he was the latter. Craig decided in one issue to summarize his personal ideas on what were the best running shoes, sort of a miniaturized version of the annual special issue rating running shoes that *Runner's World* produces each fall.

The results were almost predictable for anyone who knows much about runners and their shoes. "Your ideas are 180 degrees off mine as to what is and what isn't a good shoe," wrote one subscriber. "You do your readers a disservice by trying to handle in two or three pages what *Runner's World* so miserably failed at in an entire issue," grumbled another. The marketing director of one shoe company, whose product Craig panned, wrote a caustic letter pointing out that, "Bill Rogers [sic] trains in our shoes." (Maybe so, but the Bill Rodgers who beat Frank

Shorter in six out of seven enounters the previous year wears shoes from another manufacturer.)

I was the irate reader whose views on shoes were 180 degrees off those of Craig Harms, but as I also pointed out to him: "This doesn't mean that either of us is wrong or right; we simply have different feet. The message is that runners shouldn't heed what is said by C. G. Harms, Hal Higdon, or *Runner's World*, but should learn to evaluate products that fit their individual needs."

Easier said than done, as I realized even when I wrote him. Craig boasts having covered 35,000 miles in training during his running career. Although I don't keep count, I probably have run farther during my 30 years on the road. Neither of us could adequately sample a fraction of the many running shoes now on the market. For its annual shoe issue in October, 1977, *Runner's World* employed ten consultants to examine shoes and had extensive testing done at Penn State University's Biomechanics Laboratory under the direction of Peter Cavanagh, but could at best make only an educated guess as to what ranked as the year's best running shoe — as that magazine's publisher Bob Anderson would be the first to admit. A very well-educated guess, but an educated guess nevertheless.

The problem is compounded by the massive number of both brands of shoes and styles of shoes available in a multimillion dollar running shoe market that is expanding as fast as the sport of running. In 1977 nearly 7 million quality running shoes were sold in the United States at a retail cost of $200 million. By *quality* running shoe, I mean a shoe that sells for approximately $20 or more, mostly more, and is meant to be run in, not merely looks like it can be run in. Numerous other "cosmetic" shoes (most of them cheap, some of them higher priced) merely have the appearance of running shoes without good quality or proper design. These include all the models available at many discount stores and most of the models sold at ordinary shoe stores, as opposed to athletic shoe stores, which are multiplying faster than McDonald's franchises in neighborhood shopping malls. People who begin a running program should make sure they buy running shoes and not merely shoes that look like running shoes.

Why You Need a Running Shoe

The simplest answer to that question is: because it makes your feet feel better. Running shoes are designed specifically for running — a straight-ahead action — as opposed to tennis, bowling, or basketball shoes, which are designed for the specific actions in those sports.

Few of the individuals who enrolled in my class at the Michigan City YMCA had done any running before appearing for their first session. Most arrived wearing something other than running shoes, what could most politely be described as "sneakers." A few, unfortunately, had visited shoe stores at our local shopping mall and purchased "look-alikes," figuring they were saving some money by buying a shoe that cost only $10 or $15. This was about half the price of the better running shoes at The Athlete's Corner, a specialty store which had opened only a few months before in the same mall.

Unless asked, I said nothing about shoes those first few sessions. I simply had my students walk and jog at an easy pace. At this stage in the class, most were doing more walking than jogging. A few asked about footwear and I tried to offer some basic advice without necessarily encouraging them to spend $37.95 for one of the shoes that *Runner's World* ranked in its top three.

After the course had gone several weeks, and my running students were past their initial aches and pains and looked as though they might last the entire three months, I invited Tim Topa, manager of The Athlete's Corner in the mall, to visit our class and bring along some of the shoes he sold. (Tim, a former high school baseball player, has been running about a year.) I also dug into my collection of running shoes which at last count consisted of 18 pairs, and there may be some tucked away in a far corner that I've forgotten about.

Tim and I showed our various shoes, told something about the features of each, and fielded questions. The most pointed one came from a middle-aged housewife who asked: "Why do I need a pair of running shoes?"

Tim seemed a bit embarrassed at first, as though not knowing what to say, then finally responded: "Because it feels so good when you run in them."

That remark was understandably greeted with skepticism by my students — understandably, because it sounded as though some Madison Avenue account executive had coined it—but it was the answer I might have given myself. One by one, over a period of about a month, my students would visit The Athlete's Corner and appear at the next class wearing new Brooks, Tiger, or Nike shoes. And they would each come to me afterward and say: "You know, he was right."

They also now were spoiled, because once you wear your first pair of quality running shoes, you never will buy the "cosmetic" running shoes again, even if they are cheaper. What also happened was that my students started going back to purchase second and third pairs of running shoes to wear around the house and for other leisure activities. This is another reason sales of running shoes have soared during recent years.

When You Need to Buy Running Shoes

I don't necessarily recommend that everyone buy a pair immediately. If you are a beginning jogger just signing up for a class at your local YMCA, you might as well start in whatever you have around the house that feels comfortable. Sneakers are acceptable. One woman arrived at class clad in canvas shoes smeared with paint from an interior decorating project. As long as you're only doing a mile or so, not more than three days a week, you can probably wear anything soft. If you're outdoors running on soft ground you can even jog in combat boots; for someone who is heavy, this may even be preferable.

At the end of two weeks, buy a good pair of shoes. By now you should be past the first aches-and-pains stage, the point at which many beginning runners quit. You'll probably last at least as long as the three-month class at the YMCA you signed up for and may get up to around two or three miles a session. That may involve around 100 miles of running, so why not treat yourself to a pair of comfortable shoes.

At the end of three months, buy a second pair of shoes even if you have not yet worn out the first pair. Having lasted three months you probably are hooked on running, maybe running alone on off days between classes and even be up to five or six miles. You owe yourself a second pair of shoes.

There also is a practical reason for having more than one pair. In his best-selling book, *The Complete Book of Running*, Jim Fixx recommended buying a second pair just before wearing out the first pair. This was so the second pair could be broken in gradually, a good idea, but he misunderstands the reasons for owning more than one pair of running shoes:

• If you run a lot, you may develop blisters and minor irritations from even the most comfortable pair of well-worn shoes. By switching shoes from one workout to the next, you can rotate sore spots and prevent major problems from developing.

• Your feet sweat when you run, so alternating shoes allows them to dry between workouts. This is particularly important during the summer when many runners, for reasons of comfort and lightness, do not wear socks. A pair of feet has about 150,000 sweat glands, or ducts, which pour nearly two quarts of perspiration into a pair of shoes each week. Only about 40% of the moisture in a pair of leather shoes will evaporate overnight. These figures are for normal street shoes worn daily, but runners undoubtedly pour a great deal of sweat into their shoes each time they run.

• You need different shoes for different surfaces. The shoe that works best on the roads may not be ideal for running cross country, on the golf course, or on cinder tracks. If you run a lot in different areas, you may want to use the best shoe for each area.

• You need to experiment with different models and different brands to see what works best for you. If you stay with the same type of shoe you begin with, no matter how comfortable, you may never discover that there may be other shoes more suitable for your foot.

• If you race, you may want a lightweight pair for competition. Many experts, including George Sheehan, M.D., medical editor of *Runner's World*, suggest that participation racers should avoid racing shoes, which might cause leg injury because of lack of cushioning, and race in their more protective training shoes.

• If you are an executive who works in an office every day, you probably have more than one pair of shoes to go with your Brooks Brothers suits. The same reasoning applies to running. As more and more people become involved in the sport at the fitness rather than competitive level, the sport has become social. You may want a special pair of color-coordinated shoes to match your new Jelinka warmup suit. I own several pairs of running shoes that I rarely run in, but wear only for leisure.

This includes one pair of Korean shoes I bought for $9.95 at a discount store mainly because they matched my denim trousers. But I would never run in the damn things: they would break my feet apart.

Watching Your Footfall

After you have been running in a new pair of shoes for a while you should become aware of wear patterns on the sole, partly because you want to see that your shoes remain in good condition, but also you want any clues that may help you avoid injury as you escalate your mileage from 5 toward 100 miles a week. Most running injuries are foot-related, so you may be able to prevent those injuries by knowing what your foot is doing each time it hits the ground.

Many people today have the misconception that runners land on their heels: and if you run some other way you may be going at it the wrong way. Maybe the heel does touch first, but the most efficient stride used by top Olympic runners features a landing on the ball of the foot, followed by a touchdown onto the heel, followed by a pushoff on the toe. Despite what some people think, the point of contact does not vary much between sprinters and marathon runners. Try and concentrate on your feet during your next workout. You may discover that they are doing something other than what you think. If you are landing heel first, you may be overstriding in a mistaken belief that a long stride equals fast times. (We'll discuss this subject more in a later chapter.)

The heel contacts on the outer edge of the heel along the outside of the shoe in an efficient stride (right side on your right foot, left side on your left foot). Several individuals in my running class came to me, worried because their heels were being worn down on the outside instead of in the rear which they assumed was more natural, but I told them that this was a normal wear pattern for a runner. To prove it I pulled off my shoes and let them examine its wear pattern.

The next point of most wear is across the ball of the foot in the middle of the sole, then to the inside of the toe (left side on a right shoe; right side on a left shoe). Draw a line from right-rear to left-front of the sole of your running shoe, and that is the way your shoe should wear.

If your shoe shows a different wear pattern it may be a warning of future problems, due to some structural defect that causes you to land off balance. This may cause no problems for a fitness jogger, but if that same person moves into a more ambitious, high-mileage competitive program, such injuries as chondromalacia, otherwise known as "runner's knee," may result. Don't panic; there are cures for such problems which we will discuss in the chapter on injuries.

While visiting a morning exercise class at the Leaning Tower YMCA recently in suburban Niles, Illinois, I noticed a young woman running around the gym. She seemingly had good form and was running very comfortably. Nevertheless, I asked the Y's John Joyce: "Has she ever had any leg injuries?"

"Not that I know of," he replied. "Why?"

I pointed at the woman's footfall. She was landing on the inside instead of the outside of her foot. You would never notice it from the smooth way she ran unless you glanced at her feet. Having just recently completed an article about feet for *Runner's World*, I was at least temporarily an expert on that part of the human anatomy.

I warned John not to say anything to her, because she might run comfortably without problems for years. If she became competitive, increased her weekly miles, and began to race, however, she might run the risk of injury. I suggested that she be told not to waste her time with ointments and whirlpool baths, but instead consult a podiatrist who could construct a pair of orthotics to be placed inside her shoe to compensate for the imbalance.

One way of staying away from the podiatrist, however, is to make sure that your shoes remain in good repair. Even if you do not have the type of footfall that will lead to injury, you may be injured if you allow your shoes to wear down to where they no longer give you support in the right places. One way to obtain long shoe life is to resole them, an expensive proposition if you go to a shoe store or utilize the various services that will redo your shoes, complete with new soles, for about $10. If your shoes are comfortable, however, any price is worth saving them. They become like old friends. Runners have love affairs with their shoes. Many high-mileage runners solve the wear problem by purchasing repair compounds such as "Goo," that comes in a tube, or by obtaining a glue gun, which allows them to resurface their bottoms efficiently.

I have what in the podiatric trade is referred to as a "neutral foot." It contacts the ground evenly, so I need no orthotics for correction. While at National Running Week in California this winter, I went for a workout one noon with Steven Subotnik, D.P.M., author of *The Running Foot Doctor* and a sports podiatrist in Hayward, California. At a clinic on feet later that day, he mentioned that I was a "perfect runner." While it bolstered my ego, his definition of someone who is perfect is one whose foot contacts the ground properly. I do have other flaws.

My oldest son Kevin, who runs for Southwestern Michigan College, is slightly bow-legged, however, which causes excessive wear on the outside of his heels. He rarely has an injury despite running 80 miles a week, but he must continually maintain his shoes with a glue gun. I never borrow his gun; because of my footfall, my shoes are just as likely to wear out on top as on the bottom. Most runners I tell this to tell me they hate me. That's one reason I have 18 pairs of shoes; none of them wear out very fast.

The Good, the Bad, and the Ugly

Despite this slow-wear pattern, I have had an opportunity to try practically every brand of shoe, although obviously not every style of each brand. I would have to be a centipede to do that.

During the writing of this book I went to Dallas to lecture at a running clinic and compete in a 20-kilometer run. I happened to be wearing a pair of Etonic Street Fighters, a new model that placed fifth in the most recent *Runner's World* survey, and during a break in the clinic someone in the audience asked how I liked the shoe. I told him that it was as comfortable a running shoe as I ever had worn. He agreed with me, so we spent several minutes gushing over what a great job the manufacturers had done on design.

An hour later during a second break, another runner approached me, also asking about shoes. He groaned after my response and said they were the most *un*comfortable pair of shoes he ever had worn. What this amounts to is: different strokes for different folks.

Nevertheless, I am going to give you my thoughts on different brands of shoes, but in doing so I am reminded of a comment once made by Daniel Patrick Moynihan, former Harvard professor and United Nations Ambassador and currently the United States Senator from New York. Someone at a lecture asked him a particularly difficult question. Moynihan responded: "I know absolutely nothing about the subject, but as a Harvard professor, I feel obligated to answer anyway."

So as the Editor-at-Large for *Runner's World* writing a book for beginning runners, I feel obligated to tell you what I know about shoes. Let us consider some of the major brands—in alphabetical order rather than in any numerical ranking:

Adidas

In the mid-50s, when I was in Nuremberg, Germany, with the U.S. Army training for an international track meet, I visited the Adidas factory with a group of several Olympic athletes including Tom Courtney (800 meters) and Ira Murchison (4 x 100 meter relay) who won gold medals in Melbourne. I understand that security at the Adidas Factory now is tight, precluding such visits, but back then, *die Marke mit den drei Riemen* (the Adidas slogan, "the brand with the three stripes") was just beginning to attract attention, pioneering a style of shoes that were colorful and flashy rather than solid black.

The name of the company came from its founder Adolph (nicknamed "Adi") Dassler; I still find myself referring to the shoes with the accent on the first syllable (*Odd*-ee-doss) instead of the more Americanized Uh-*dee*-duss.

Adidas shoes were much cheaper, as well as much better than American shoes, when they entered the running shoe market in the 1950s, partly because of the favorable exchange rate of dollar and German deutschmark. The value of American dollars relative to other currencies abroad is one reason for the present high cost of German shoes. (Puma and E. B. Lydiard shoes are also expensive for the same reason.) Although other shoes, particularly American, could not approach German shoes in design or quality, those gaps have now been closed. Despite their high price, Adidas remained the best selling running shoe in the United States until 1977.

In the 1950s, when I was wearing Adidas spikes in track meets, I never felt that the company gave as much attention to their flat shoes. They made flats that you looked good in while warming up before 50,000 people in an outdoor stadium, but not the kind that you would want to run 26 miles 385 yards in—

or even wear to train for that distance. In the last 20 years the
company has devoted more and more of its energy toward
making flats rather than spikes, but never has quite had the
lead in flats as in the spikes that 95% of the medal winners at
any Olympic games will be wearing.

One of the best racing flats ever made was the Adidas "Marathon," developed around 1970. The shoe had a white kangaroo
leather upper with black stripes and a smooth, black sole. I
found the shoe extremely comfortable for racing, but left my
pair in a locker after the Petaluma Marathon in 1971. Despite
pleas by mail to everyone from the track coach at the high
school where we dressed to the head of the custodial service, the
shoes were not found.

Adidas later redesigned its racing flat under that name. I find
the current Marathon shoe unsatisfactory for my particular
needs. In fact, I recently purchased a pair of Adidas field event
shoes, designed primarily for hammer and discus throwers who
spin on a concrete circle because they more closely resembled
the old Marathon model. I didn't realize this when I picked
them out. When I went to pay for the shoes in Gainesville, Florida, the clerk told me what they were designed for, but I
shrugged and took them anyway. I've worn them in numerous
races with good results.

I also own a pair of Adidas TRX shoes, apparently marketed
to compete with the Nike Waffle Trainers. The rubber-studded
sole, though, designed for longer wear than the softer Nike
bottoms, is too stiff and unyielding. I do not take many long
road workouts in TRX shoes. I find them excellent for running
on ice and snow in the winter, however, as well as through mud
during the spring.

Two Adidas shoes that became a favorite of many distance
runners were the SL-72 and SL-76 models, very highly ranked
by the *Runner's World* survey when they first appeared on the
market. I never have owned a pair. Adidas shoes maintain their
reputation for high quality and good comfort, but, barring
some future devaluation in the deutschmark permitting their
price to drop, they may find it increasingly difficult to compete
with improving American running shoes, at least in flats. Their
spikes continue to set the standard despite high price.

Brooks

Although I have never run in a pair of Brooks shoes, I have

been responsible for a number of sales of this brand to others. The reason is that when recommending shoes for my running class at the Michigan City YMCA, I visited the Athlete's Corner in our nearby shopping mall, and it appeared as though the Brooks Villanova (priced at $18.95) was the best buy for the money among the relatively limited number of running shoes available at that store. I had bought my daughter Laura a pair of Brooks shoes a year earlier and she found them to be very comfortable, so I recommended that my class follow suit. As they began to appear in their new Brooks shoes, I began to ask about the shoes and heard nothing but praise. Maybe as they get more into running, my students may drift toward more expensive shoes, but until then the Brooks Villanova seemed a good model to start running in.

There are two complaints that you hear most frequently about Brooks shoes: that they're impossible to buy and that they are of poor quality. As for the scarcity of the shoe, that was caused by high rankings for Brooks shoes several recent years in the annual *Runner's World* survey. Everybody apparently wants to wear the "number one" shoe, and when Brooks Vantage model won that honor in 1977, demand far exceeded supply.

As for the rap about poor quality, I have heard this from several individuals who sell shoes and get feedback from their customers about how well those shoes wear. I have heard stories of Brooks shoes coming apart after only two or three weeks' wear, but when I mentioned this to one of the members of my club, Hunter Goin, he became offended. "I've had a lot of good wear out of my Brooks shoes," he insisted. When you insult a runner's favorite brand of shoes, it is like insulting his wife. Hunter was ready to fight.

The latest word on Brooks shoes is that if there, indeed, was a problem of quality control with shoes being turned out by that company's Puerto Rican factory, that problem has been solved. None of my YMCA runners have yet made any complaints about the shoes I suggested they buy.

And in the meantime, I tried my first pair of Brooks shoes, their Vantage model, which I bought from a mail-order firm. Although I ordered my normal size nine, the shoes were too tight. I tried ripping out the insole, but the shoes still felt uncomfortable. I talked to one of my students who also obtained a pair of Brooks Vantage shoes; he said he had to get a pair a

half-size larger than normal. So I am reordering to see if that
helps, although it may be possible that Brooks and I are incom-
patible because of my particular foot. That does not mean I
won't continue to recommend the shoe for others. In fact, I gave
the original pair to my wife whose foot is slightly smaller than
mine. She found them to be very comfortable.

Converse

When I first started running cross country in the early 50s,
everybody in the United States wore Converse flats, because they
were practically the only flat running shoe on the market. They
were solid black, made of canvas, and were shaped like spiked
shoes with a narrow heel. They also had two round rubber pads
on the bottom: one under the forefoot, one under the heel.
Their main virtue was that they were cheap: about $5 a pair
then. Their main flaw was that they were always too tight when
first worn, and not until worn enough so the little toe wore a
hole in the side did they feel halfway good. Some runners I knew
cut holes in their Converse flats when they bought them to
shorten the process.

I went out for pizza one night in Minneapolis with world class
runner Garry Bjorklund, who is a couple of decades younger
than I, and reminisced about my old canvas Converse shoes,
then added: "You probably never had a pair."

Garry smiled: "The first pair of running flats I ever owned
were Converse, and I bought them second-hand."

Converse, one of the world's largest manufacturers of basketball shoes, may have continued to manufacture running shoes
for youngsters who bought them at the age Garry and I did, but
with the ascent of German (and later Japanese) shoes, no serious
runners paid much attention to the company. With the recent
tremendous expansion of running, however, Converse has begun
to give more attention to marketing its running flats, taking out
two-page, four-color ads to promote its new models.

While Converse's marketing division is in full gear, its design
department lags behind — at least in areas important to runners'
comfort. I own a pair of Converse World Class Trainers. They
are white, yellow, and black with the company's trademark of a
star prominently displayed on the side. If you were a youngster
who never owned anything and broke into a sporting goods
store, those shoes are the ones you would steal.

They also are comfortable on your feet—in fact, extremely comfortable. When I first tried on a pair, I couldn't understand why several world-class runner friends of mine had complained so much about the current Converse shoes. Then I tried to run with them and found out why. The sole is thin, unyielding, and offers little forefront cushioning. If I try to flex the sole with the shoe off, it bends all right, but right under the arch. (The sole should flex under the ball of the foot, which is where my foot bends.) And they are noisy when I run in them. I can hear the sole slapping the ground, which rarely happens in the other shoes I wear.

So Converse has a way to come to match, in running shoes, the reputation it earned making basketball shoes. The company certainly has the expertise to manufacture an excellent shoe if it has the desire. Sentimentally, however, I still miss my old canvas Converse shoes with the little toes sticking out the sides.

Etonic

This shoe manufactured by the Charles A. Eaton Company of Massachusetts which also makes Fred Perry tennis shoes, entered the running shoe business only recently. I never had worn any Etonic shoes until I met their marketing vice-president John Larsen at the Boston Marathon in 1977 where he asked me if I would like to try a pair and give him my opinion. Later, I reported that I found the shoes very comfortable for training (although I never would race in them because of their heavy, cushioned sole). My only complaint, which seems almost picky, is that the shoes have a distinct odor.

The reason, I guess, is that because of the built-in arch supports, the shoe contains a lot of material that causes your foot to perspire more than it normally would in lighter shoes. And because I wore no socks in the summer, my Etonic shoes began to take on the quality of an old unwashed sweatshirt. My wife would pass my shoe collection en route to her washing machine in the basement, and remark: "Pheewwww!" I think it was mostly my two pairs of Etonic shoes that she was smelling. I tried to alleviate the problem by dusting the shoes with foot powder, but that served only as a temporary disguise. I guess a better solution would be for me to wear socks when I donned my Etonics, since that would soak up the sweat. Another solution, which I recommended to the factory, although they have not yet taken my advice, would be to use a more porous form of material that would allow the shoes to breathe, or to include ventilation holes similar to those in some of the Reebok models.

The second runner who approached me in Dallas complaining about Etonics admitted he wore orthotics in his shoes. (Orthotics are plastic or foam-rubber supports to compensate for some foot imbalance.) I suspect that because of the built-in arch supports designed by podiatrist Rob Roy McGregor, there is not much room inside an Etonic shoe for supplementary support. This also could be true with recent Brooks models which have supports designed by podiatrist Steve Subotnick. If you need orthotics in your shoe, you should always carry them with you when trying on new models in a shoe store. But if you have orthotics you may not need a shoe that has interior support.

Two days after talking to the pro and con Etonic owners in Dallas, I went to another clinic in Chicago. A third Etonic owner approached me to ask about my Street Fighters. He was a lover of Etonic shoes, apparently, until they came out with their new models. He had tried on six different pairs but not one felt right on his feet. He said there was a ridge under the ball of his foot that he thought was a "flaw." He sounded heartbroken, as if he had just received a "Dear John" letter from his childhood sweetheart.

I suggested the shoe store might have received a bad shipment that did contain flawed shoes, and he should try another store. More likely the company in redesigning its shoe, "improving the breed," had removed all features that the runner had found so comfortable. "Shoe companies are always doing this to us," I said. "Just when you get a model you like, they go and change it." I mentioned my experience with the Adidas Marathon and suggested that when a runner finds a shoe he feels entirely comfortable, he probably should buy two dozen pair and store most of them in vacuum-proof polyethylene bags, like the mothball fleets of the U.S. Navy, so he can run in that model the rest of his life.

Previous Etonic shoes closely resembled Brooks shoes, because until 1977 Etonic subcontracted its shoe production to Brooks. Etonic now has a factory in Lewiston, Maine. I have a lot of shoes, and shift from one pair to another from day to day. I often choose my Etonics when I am going to run slow on hard surfaces because of the cushioning support they provide, particularly toward the heel. (Believe it or not, you actually need more cushioning when you are running slowly that when you are running fast, and skimming the surface.)

When I begin to have knee problems—and what runner does not at one time or another experience knee problems—I often switch to my Etonics for several days until the knee problems go away. Maybe this would happen anyway, but when a treatment works you don't ask why it works, you accept it. I have recommended this particular brand of shoe to others bothered by their knees or, for that matter, others looking simply for comfortable footwear. If you take this to mean that I consider Etonic a therapeutic shoe, you may be correct. I suppose if Adidas is the Cadillac of running shoes, maybe Etonic ranks as some form of ambulance with its red light flashing. But the Etonic Street Fighter is a racier name than the Etonic Ambulance, so don't expect any sudden name changes.

New Balance

To continue the automotive analogy, maybe New Balance should be described as the Mack truck. I don't mean that as an insult, but as a tribute to the durability of this brand. I once owned a pair of New Balance 305s, which I wore in training for several reasons, and they never seemed to wear out. The uppers became scarred and discolored from salt and water during winter workouts and the leather plate over my toe shriveled, pinching my feet, so I chucked the shoes into a wastebasket, but there still was a lot of mileage left on the soles. I don't know how much mileage I put on them, but it was a lot.

For years New Balance was the only American running shoe company that seemed competitive or even interested in competing with the Germans and Japanese. The New Balance Company manufactured funny-looking, box-like shoes, their most popular model being one with a ripple sole. The only people who seemed to own New Balance shoes were runners in New England who were logging 150 miles a week and found they offered a lot of protection and wore forever. Then in 1976 *Runner's World* anointed one of the New Balance models with its number one ranking and everybody wanted a pair. Other manufacturers then began designing funny-looking, box-like shoes to compete.

In the meantime, New Balance began to design "chic-ier" looking shoes, integrating an "N" into its side support, choosing orange for some of its models, and adding a lightweight racing shoe. The ripple sole still persists for purists who feel it offers the most cushioning. Perhaps one of the most important features of New Balance models, which other manufacturers only recently have begun to emulate, has been the availabilty of different widths in recognition that not every foot is a perfect size. If you have trouble getting a good fit in running shoes, because your foot is too narrow or too wide, you probably should look at New Balance.

Recently I obtained a pair of New Balance Trail shoes, a version of the studded-shoe, or waffle, model that has become increasingly popular. The shoes seemed well designed and very comfortable. Incredibly, that same pair of shoes had placed only 24th in the most recent *Runner's World* survey! This is not to criticize that magazine's rankings, but to point out that the quality of almost all styles of major-brand running shoes is very high today compared with what runners put on their feet as recently as five years ago. Part of the reason for the improvement in quality has been that *Runner's World* rankings may help to improve the breed. A few favorite styles fall by the wayside, but the general direction is up, up, up. The runner has benefited greatly in the competition for the runner's shoe dollar.

Nike

My biggest criticism about Nike shoes is that their shoelaces always seem to come untied. Usually I double-knot my shoelaces before I start out on a long run, but every now and then I have to retie a lace. This seems to occur invariably when I am wearing Nike shoes. This morning I went for an easy three-mile run before breakfast, I had to stop and retie the same shoe twice. I was wearing Nike Waffle Trainers.

Shoelaces aside, in 1977 Nike reportedly edged aside Adidas from its longtime position as the number one selling running flat in the United States. The main reason has probably been the popularity of the waffle design that Nike pioneered. Bill Bowerman, former University of Oregon track coach, began resoling shoes using his wife's waffle iron and the result was the most popular shoe design innovation in running history. Waffle shoes were originally designed for cross-country, particularly on courses that included some asphalt with dirt and grass. But runners soon began moving out into hard pavements with the shoes and found that the waffle-bottom apparently offered superior cushioning (even if it did wear out faster). Some top racers use the waffle-bottom Nike Elite model for running marathons with great success.

Nike began as the American distributor for Tiger shoes under the name Blue Ribbon Sports. Phil Knight, just graduated from Stanford Business School, appeared one day in the early 1960s at the Onitsuka factory in Japan and, when asked the name of his company, gave the first name that came to his mind: blue ribbon equating with the award usually given for first place. When a split developed over shoe distribution in the United States, Blue Ribbon Sports continued to distribute shoes under a new brand: Nike, from the Greek winged goddess of victory. People new to running sometimes pronounce the name as one syllable as in the old campaign slogan "I like Ike." But people familiar with the sport know the brand name is pronounced with two syllables as in: ni-key.

Tiger shoes first were marketed when German shoes led in popularity so their exterior design imitated both the Adidas three-stripe and the Puma single band. When it came along, Nike developed a boomerang-shaped stripe referred to as the "swoosh." A more important difference, however, is that Tiger makes narrow shoes whereas Nike makes wide shoes. Reportedly, Tiger used American Olympian Kenny Moore's foot as model for its early designs; Nike modeled their shoes off the wider foot of Steve Prefontaine. As a result, your decision whether to buy Nike or Tiger shoes may depend on the relative width of your feet. When selecting shoes: Forget the rankings and what everyone else says and wear what fits and feels comfortable!

One criticism of Nike shoes, more important than their shoelaces, has been a relative heel instability in certain models, which causes the heel to collapse. (A loose heel may result in shin splints.) I have not suffered any problems with numerous Nike shoes I have owned over the years, but my son Kevin had early trouble with his, particularly the leather Nike Cortez. Being slightly bow-legged, he lands farther on the outside of the heel, so when the heel shifted, he began to wear through the shoe on the side instead of bottom. We switched him to a Puma shoe that featured a round-backed heel, and this wear problem stopped. Since then, he has used several pairs of Nike Waffle Trainers, which have a more rounded heel without excessive side wear.

One compliment I hear about Nike shoes comes from people who sell shoes to runners and that relates to quality: Nike scores very high in quality control. Originally manufactured almost exclusively outside the United States, Nike recently has begun to switch more and more of its production to plants in Exeter, New Hampshire, and Saco, Maine.

Puma

This company was founded by Horstt Dassler, brother of Adi Dassler (founder of Adidas shoes). Although I never checked to determine if it was true or only rumored for public relations purposes, there supposedly was bad blood between the two. This surfaced most noticeably at Mexico City in the 1968 Olympics when the two companies competed with each other in signing up potential gold medal winners to wear their shoes. The shoe controversy made the cover of *Sports Illustrated.*

All controversy aside, Puma makes excellent shoes. If brother Adi's shoes are Cadillacs, maybe his brother Horstt's are Lincolns. Although Adidas has held the lead in running shoes in the United States, Puma has been more competitive in shoes for other sports such as soccer or basketball. At a time when the demand for running shoes is expanding, Puma seems to lack the marketplace visibility that it had a few years ago. Perhaps the new American shoes are making more inroads into Puma's share of the market than the more established Adidas line. If anything, Adidas seemed able to market its three vertical stripes better than did Puma its single horizontal stripe.

I always found Puma shoes slightly more adaptable to my feet than those from Adidas, not only in flats but also in spikes. I have a well-worn pair of Puma 9290's which were among the top-rated shoes by *Runner's World* several years ago. They are coming apart at the seams and are badly stretched out of shape, but are so comfortable that I know if some newer shoe causes me a blister problem, I can switch back into those old Pumas to repair my feet, duplicating the success I had in placing my son in Pumas after his wear problems with the Nike Cortez.

Unfortunately, the once high-ranked Puma 9190 has dropped in the rankings; in 1977 it dropped out of the top 25 as more highly cushioned waffle-bottom shoes moved up. This is unfortunate because it still is basically a well-designed, comfortable shoe. A loss in popularity may cause its discontinuance. *Runner's World*'s annual ranking has had a positive effect in the area of shoe design, forcing shoe companies to continually up-grade and improve their products. One negative result, however, is that sound, old shoe designs may be made obsolete because of the appearance of flashier models. But there was a place in the market for the Volkswagen long after its appear-ance, so maybe a few comfortable old shoes will also survive. The Puma 9190 deserves to be one of them.

Tiger

I like to think that I wore the first pair of Tiger shoes in a race in America. That may not be true, but I like to think so. Back in the early 1960s, Fred Wilt used to supervise my train-ing. Fred had access to people involved in track and field throughout the world. He once obtained a pair of Russian flats for me that were bulky and ugly, but very comfortable and which eliminated a problem I had with blisters in races longer than one mile on indoor board tracks. Soon after he obtained what he claimed was an even better pair of shoes made by Onit-suka, Ltd., a small Japanese firm that nobody had heard of at that time. The way I obtained the shoes was unique; I drew a pattern of my feet on paper, then someone in Japan custom-made a pair for me. I obtained several pair at no cost because they wanted fast runners to compete in their shoes.

One time a pair arrived from Japan and I wrote my name in block letters across the backs of the shoes. (Doing so once enabled me to recover a pair stolen from my locker at the Uni-versity of Chicago field house.) Then I realized the shoes didn't quite fit. Several days later Fred called and explained why. My order had been confused with another and he asked that I return them to him. The right shoes eventually arrived. Several months later while lining up in the front line for the start of the 1964 Boston Marathon, I looked at the back of the shoes of another runner, Ron Wallingford of Canada. I saw my name staring up at me. "Ron, you didn't steal those shoes out of my locker, did you?" No, his were the shoes that had been confused with mine. I saw my own shoes finish two places ahead of me that day. If I only had not sent them back!

After I went into semi-retirement the following year I continued to buy shoes from Japan, sending my foot tracings each time. The cost was extremely high: $5.00 for custom shoes airmailed to my home. Then one day the pair delivered was two sizes too small. I figured that some new worker in Japan had looked at the foot tracing and figured the outside of the sole, not the inside of the shoe, should conform to it. Mass production had arrived at my little Japanese shoe factory. At about the same time the shoe became available through regular channels in America, at higher prices and under the brand name Tiger. Tiger soon became one of the most popular race shoes among American marathoners.

Even though Blue Ribbon Sports, the American company that first began distributing Tiger shoes in this country, switched to Nike, the shoe retains a high level of popularity. Although Tiger began by copying German shoes, the Japanese soon offered innovations of their own, including all-nylon uppers. Tiger's racing shoes have ranked higher on recent *Runner's World* polls than have their training models, but I always felt the Tiger Montreal was a good, basic running shoe. I have bought several pairs for my wife as well as for myself. I also recommended the Tigress (similar to the "Montreal" but designed for female runners) to several in my running class.

Recently I ordered a pair of Tiger "Jayhawk," the company's best racing flat, through the mail, specifying my size as nine. Whereas that size in the Brooks Vantage was too small, that size in the Tiger Jayhawk was too large. I had to send the shoes back in exchange for a size eight-and-a-half. This emphasizes the necessity of trying on shoes before you buy them, unless you are experienced enough in ordering shoes by mail to know exactly what you want.

Other Shoes

Many other shoe companies manufacture excellent shoes for runners. Just because they do not receive prominence here, or in *Runner's World*, that does not mean you should avoid them. My favorite racing shoes are the featherweight Reebok World Ten, manufactured in Great Britain and they are difficult to find. I once searched all over London for a store that sold them and failed. I bought my current pair from a mail order house in Michigan.

Supply also is a factor with the shoes designed by Arthur Lydiard and produced by Eugen Brutting in West Germany. Brutting seems content to manufacture a limited number of shoes and has made only a slight attempt to penetrate the American market. A chain of athletic stores called the Footlocker sells E. B. Lydiard shoes, but unless you have one of those stores nearby or want to order by mail (always a chancy proposition unless you have sampled shoes in advance and know what size to order) you may have difficulty buying any. I own one very comfortable pair.

Karhu also makes excellent shoes, but this Finnish company also does not mass distribute in the United States. I owned a pair in the early 1960s when their lightness and design put Karhu far ahead of anything other companies offered to marathoners. On a trip to Helsinki several years ago, I tried on a pair of their brightly-colored yellow racing flats, but even in that country the price was more than I wanted to pay. Karhu no longer bothers to enter its shoes in the *Runner's World* annual sweepstakes, but if you can find a source for them you might want to give them a try. The same is true with other European models seen infrequently in this country.

Brand X

As to otherwise unnamed American shoe companies, the current running explosion in this country is attracting more and more of them, and some of these companies eventually will learn to make what runners want in a shoe.

I hope one of these companies is the one that distributes what I will call Brand *X*. While gathering information for this chapter, I debated whether or not to identify this particular shoe manufacturer, which made its name selling basketball and soccer shoes and only recently has become interested in running flats. The problem is that this company came out relatively poorly in the 1977 *Runner's World* rankings and felt their shoes had been unjustly scored. They claimed to have entered identical shoes, differing only in color, which for some reason received different lab scores. These lab scores were relatively high, but the independent panel downgraded the shoes. Then to compound this company's problem, apparently someone at the magazine added the scores incorrectly, causing them to sink still lower in the rankings. I hate to heap further scorn on this company; they have suffered enough abuse already, so I'm not going to identify them. But they succeeded in manufacturing what I consider to be the most uncomfortable shoe in my collection. As a matter of fact the *three* most uncomfortable shoes. I'll explain.

The main problem is a hard, inflexible sole. Their $24 model is what I call a "Foot Buster." You might as well have a steel plate on the bottom of your feet. In fact, this is a characteristic of most of the cosmetic shoes I find at nonathletic shoe stores, particularly discount houses that market low-cost shoes from Taiwan and Korea. You can't bend the soles. The $9.95 shoes I bought at a discount store only because they matched my jeans have similar inflexible soles. That pair came from Korea, and Brand X obtains its shoes from Korea. The two shoes seem similar in so many aspects of design and construction (even stitching) that they may have come from the same factory. But one shoe costs $14 more than the other.

I will not identify Brand X, however, because they only recently have entered the running shoe business and may improve their product by the time you read this. Some of the other manufacturers whose models I have so lavishly praised in the preceding pages also did not make top-notch shoes their first few years in the business, and all of the good companies continue to produce occasional lemons. Nike made an excessively wide-heeled shoe several years ago (the LD-1000) that nobody seemed to like; their next-year version with the heel shaved (the LD-1000-V) met with almost instant approval among runners.

Anyway, when I told a representative from Brand X about the problems I had with his company's shoe, he said they already had made major revisions in their latest models and would send me two new pair. I sincerely wanted to write something nice about them.

Alas, I went for a workout in the first pair and returned three miles later with a bad blister on the back of my heel caused by a too-tight heel counter. The other pair has a leather strip across the toe that I know is going to give my second toe on my left foot trouble, because that toe curls up slightly and I always have problems with shoes made that way. That is why I brand Brand X as responsible for the three most uncomfortable shoes in my collection. The company advertises that it makes an unending scientific study of the anatomy of runners' feet and utilizes intensive computer biomechanical analyses to make our feet comfortable. As far as I am concerned, they failed.

Recently, a Brand X representative told me they had a new improved model they wanted me to try. Among other improvements, they were using softer rubber on the sole. The shoe arrived a few days later by United Parcel Service and, by gosh, it did feel more comfortable. The heel counter didn't bind as much, although that might have been a result of their having sent me a shoe a half-size larger. Although still not what I considered an ideal shoe for my feet, at least it was better. This emphasizes my feeling that you should not worry about what someone else tells you about shoes, because their information may either be biased or outdated, but try them on yourself.

But these are only one man's opinions. Remember my comment earlier in this chapter that runners not heed what is said by C. G. Harms, Hal Higdon, or *Runner's World*, but learn to evaluate products for their own needs. Recently, I read an article in another running publication by someone I shall call Writer *Y*. He lavished Brand *X* with praise, so that company's shoe matched well with his feet. All this means is that if you have a foot like Writer *Y*, buy Brand *X*, but don't expect to see this statement quoted in any shoe advertisement.

10

Upwards from the Foot Bone

How to buy socks, inner soles, warmup
suits, wristwatches, etc.

Ted Haydon, track coach at the University of Chicago, provides the best answer I know to the question of why people run
long distance races, particularly marathons. Haydon claims that
pathologists at the University's medical school recently performed an autopsy on a champion marathon runner. They discovered that the foot bone was connected to the leg bone, the
leg bone was connected to the hip bone, the hip bone was connected to the back bone, and the back bone was connected to
the neck bone. But apparently the neck bone was *not* connected
to the head bone—and that's why people run marathons.

Some runners were insulted when they heard Haydon's comments (quoted in *Sports Illustrated*, among other physiological
journals). They wrote angry letters pointing out that a *Runner's
World* survey determined that 31% of its its readers graduated
from colleges, another 38% had advanced degrees.* These figures are impressive but don't necessarily prove that runners have
brains; they merely have degrees.

I tell a similar story on the subject. It seems that while Dr.
Frankenstein was gathering parts to construct his monster, he
visited the Transylvania Body Shop in search of a brain. The
shop owner first showed him a brain that once belonged to a
world-famous educator, on sale for only $250. Next the owner
let him examine the brain of a respected biologist, a special at
$500. Finally he led Dr. Frankenstein into a side room where he
had on display the brain of a marathoner. It cost $10,000.

*According to 1976 survey.

Dr. Frankenstein was astounded. "If an educator's brain costs only $250 and a biologist's $500," he reasoned, "why should the brain of a marathoner cost $10,000?"

"Because," declared the Body Shop owner, "it hasn't been used."

Back to the subject of running equipment, because that was what Ted Haydon's story about foot bones was meant to introduce. Everyone agrees that the most important item of running equipment is the shoe. It is the essential item of wearing apparel for all runners. They spend an inordinate amount of time, as they probably should, seeing that they are well shod. But you need more than shoes to run. Although a newspaper recently quoted someone proposing a nude marathon (Olympians in ancient Greece ran unencumbered by clothes), most modern runners use at least a few other items of equipment besides shoes. With the exception of women's special equipment and cold weather items (discussed in later chapters), let's consider those other items following Ted Haydon's organizational pattern of moving upward from the foot bone.

Socks

Normally I don't wear socks on my feet while running, at least during the warm-weather months. I have the mistaken belief that I am saving weight, thus allowing myself to run faster. The weight difference is negligible, so any benefits are probably psychological. It feels better to be "one" with your running shoes. Most running shoes, particularly those used for racing, are designed to fit almost like socks.

Probably a better reason, particularly in races where you are liable to be running faster and longer than in training, is that by not wearing socks you remove one less item that can result in trouble. Socks may bunch up in your shoes and cause blisters. Unless it is fairly cold (near freezing), you won't need socks for warmth, so you probably can do without them—if your shoes fit properly.

A few runners I know use half-socks as sort of a compromise between regular socks and none; women, more often than men, go this route, because they sometimes wear such items with their regular street shoes.

One important function of socks, apart from comfort or warmth, is to soak up sweat and offer some protection for your shoes against what might be called "runner's stink." You can douse your running shoes with foot powder to absorb moisture and make them smell better, but wearing clean socks and changing them daily may be a more practical solution. (Excessive perspiration soaking into your footwear can shorten shoe life.) Cotton socks probably are better than nylon socks, although I prefer the latter.

One thing you probably don't need, as a runner, are tube socks, the kind with stripes across the top, favored by teenagers who play basketball, or who want to look like they play basketball. There is no great necessity to keep your calves warm, which is probably tube socks' main function other than looking spiffy. If the socks are too tight above the calves, they could impair circulation, and if they are too loose, they might come down around your ankles. Unless you want to look like a teenager, you are best not wearing them. Actually, I am trying to think of all kinds of reasons not to wear tube socks, simply because I don't think they look cool on runners.

Panty hose are another matter. (I'm talking about panty hose for men, not just women.) I recall Frank Shorter appearing at the National AAU cross country championship on a cold November day in Chicago one year wearing panty hose for warmth. (This was long before Joe Namath appeared in the famous panty hose TV commercial.) Shorter at least had a practical reason for donning panty hose; Namath did it only for money.

Inner Soles

I have used inner soles for years, particularly in my competition shoes, which provide inadequate protection on the inside. Usually I would go to the drug store and for about 85 cents buy a pair of Dr. Scholl's footpads. I usually bought women's sizes, because they are narrower and thus fit more easily into narrow spiked shoes. Even still, I usually had to take a scissors and trim the pad to fit.

There are three reasons why you might want to purchase inner soles for your shoes. First, they provide you with additional cushioning and shock absorption, which may be especially important if you do most of your training on hard surfaces. Most of today's running shoes, however, have better built-in inner soles than those of five years ago, so usually I only replace them when they wear out.

A second good reason is that inner soles can protect your foot from blisters and irritations. Higdon's first foot care rule is that whenever something bad happens to your foot, such as a blister, look inside your shoe. You can probably spot the cause by matching your blister with a contact point inside. You would be surprised how many runners ignore this bit of common sense and continue to suffer similar blister problems run after run, race after race. If your blisters come on the bottom of your feet, the easiest cure may be to rip out the factory-installed inner sole (which may be worn) and replace it with a new one.

A third and related factor is that inner soles will help absorb the moisture that pours off your feet and into your shoes, particularly during warm weather. This will protect your shoes from deterioration.

Pro Comfort manufactures one style of inner soles out of a material known as Poron, which has unique shock-absorbing facilities. When I stopped by the office of Terry Mather at Arno Adhesive Tapes, Inc., which markets Pro Comfort Products and sponsors one of our local races, he demonstrated how you could drop a golf ball onto one of their inner soles and it would not bounce. The ball sort of goes *bloooomp*, and lies there quivering on the inner sole. "Frank Shorter stopped by our booth at the equipment show in Houston recently," Terry explained, "and he was fascinated by the fact that our inner soles absorbed a golf ball's bounce."

So that opens up entertainment possibilities when you have parties for your running friends. If you run out of conversation, you can pull out your inner soles and spend the evening dropping golf balls on them.

One word of caution. Another manufacturer at about this same time also gave me some inner soles asking that I try them in my shoes, which I did—too faithfully. I began wearing inner soles in all my running shoes, some of which didn't need them. As a result they pushed my foot too far up in one shoe tearing a hole in the top of my second toe. This eventually formed into a corn causing considerable pain. I still use inner soles in my shoes, but am selectful of how I use them, as you should be too.

Warmup Suits

I use the term "warmup suits" rather than "sweat suits," because some suits simply were not meant to be sweated in. On a recent trip to San Diego, I was invited to a runner's brunch that followed that city's regular Sunday morning Marathon Clinic. Everybody at the party arrived looking as though they had stepped out of a Bonwit Teller catalog. Running had become very trendy since my last trip to that city and obviously you and your wife aren't going to make it in society unless you own matching sweat—whoops, warmup—suits with the proper number of stripes. Before the 1977 Mayor Daley Marathon, one prominent socialite jogger had her French designer design a special warmup suit with cape motif.

On my return home I figured I would never be able to show my face in public again in my grey, cotton, baggy-bottomed sweat pants bought at Sears, so I blew $52.95 on a velvety smooth blue and yellow Jelenk warmup suit with stripes and zippered pockets and all sorts of creature comforts. The only problem is that I'm afraid to run in it. You know you're in trouble when you return from a long distance race and your dry cleaning bill costs you more than your entry fee.

You can run in warmup suits. After a while, however, you may find that the zipper in the pants legs no longer zips, so you flap when you run. The elastic in the waist no longer snaps, so your pants start sliding down around your hips. Also, since bottoms seem to wear out twice as fast as tops, you may end up with a wardrobe filled with matching warmup shirts that don't match anything. It may be enough to send you back to Sears for your equipment needs.

Probably the most important item in repairing worn warmup suits is the safety pin. Safety pins can be used to keep your pants legs from flapping and your waist from drooping. Safety pins also cost nothing, since you simply save those used to attach the competitor's number at the last race you ran.

Athletic Supporters

Men get "jock itch" because they wear the same jock several days in a row, and it becomes sweaty, then stiff, then chafes and rubs. So if for some reason, cultural or imagined, you feel you need the extra support offered by an athletic supporter, at least buy more than one and wash them regularly.

I don't think men need extra support. Men who feel they need to wear jock straps may be suffering from bra envy. I stopped wearing jock straps when I first ran in Europe in the mid-50s and discovered that most of the track athletes either wore shorts with loose, built-in support or wore briefs, a tight-fitting style of nylon underwear with no fly. Since none of them suffered from hernias, I switched. Almost immediately my time in the 5000

meters improved by nearly a full minute. It may not entirely
have been related to the equipment change, however, since I
also increased my weekly mileage from about 50 miles to 100
miles in two workouts daily. Perhaps some research physiologist
might consider a study on whether changing underwear affects
performance over 5000 meters.

I decided that briefs felt more comfortable than built-ins, so
continued to wear them on returning to the United States.
Locating briefs in the stores became a problem at first and for
several years I used to order a dozen at a time from Marshall
Field. Eventually some manufacturer decided to convince the
public that it was jet-settish to wear European underwear, and
briefs became popular in this country too. For a while they were
being promoted with shocking colors and leopard spots, but
thank God, that fad ended. You now can buy briefs at almost
any clothing store.

I also use them as underwear under my regular street clothes,
leave them on when I go run, and change after I shower. Thus I
have banned jock itch from my life.

Shorts

Track shorts used to be distinguished from ordinary shorts in
that they have a slit in the side to provide freedom of motion.
But as running became trendy by the summer of 1977, bathing
suit manufacturers adopted the slit style for their trunks. The
pair of track shorts with the highest slit are those manufactured
by Ron Hill Sports, Ltd. of Great Britain. Whether wearing
these shorts will allow you to run 2:10 and win the Boston Marathon as Ron did in 1970 is questionable, but the shorts·are comfortable, come in shocking colors and designs (including the
Union Jack and the American flag), and I wear them. They also
cost in the vicinity of $7.50 a pair, which means that if you are
interested in coverage rather than style you may want to shop
elsewhere. European-style shorts with built-in support—sometimes described as "unisex"—also can be relatively expensive.

Cost, however, is not the only criterion to consider when
selecting track shorts. Many of the shorts on sale at various
sporting goods stores—some of them running, some of them
not—are unsuitable for running long distances. One problem
with the design of many is too low a cuff. Some runners have
thigh muscles that bulge inward an inch or two below the

crotch, so if your shorts hang down into this area they can cause chafing. My New Jersey friend Don Higdon recommends that one way to minimize chafing is to buy different brands (and styles) of shorts so that you don't chafe the same part of your legs every day. This is similar to my reason for changing shoes from day to day to rotate blisters. It may be that Don has thicker thighs than I do, which cause chafing (I never have such problems), or it may be that instead of alternating brands he should find the *right* brand. Maybe I need to introduce him to Ron Hill.

What works best in shorts is what feels comfortable on you. Your individual preference will determine whether you want shorts that are cotton, nylon, or some other material.

Vests

Vests are what the British call running tops similar in style to the type of upper underwear with shoulder straps that used to be popular in this country until a few decades ago when everybody switched to t-shirts. Later this form of wearing apparel became popular worn as a regular shirt in warm weather under the name tank top. Regardless of nomenclature, it is what you probably want to wear in a race. Strap-topped shirts have been the standard racing uniform for track athletes for years.

Some running vests are cut low in the neck and armpits, which seems like a good idea until during a race the straps start shifting and coming down. Runners are rarely known for broad shoulders.

Only recently have sports manufacturers given some attention to the design of such vests. The main innovation has been to punch holes in them, the theory being that it allows more air to circulate and thus will help keep you cool during hot-weather races. The only problem is that the most popularly designed ventilated vests are made of nylon that is much less porous than cotton or other lightweight materials. Even with holes I find such shirts hot.

Before the manufacturers caught on, runners had been cutting holes in their shirts for years. I recall arriving at the Boston Marathon years ago on a Sunday when the temperature was in the 70s and sitting up that night using a toenail clipper to snip dollar-sized holes out of the front of a t-shirt. I also cut out the entire back. I was well prepared except that the next day it snowed. Fortunately, I also brought along a turtle-neck jersey, which on cold days I wear under a regular competition vest. When travelling to races, particularly in the spring or autumn when weather conditions vary, it is often important to be prepared for various temperatures.

I presently wear a vest available from Starting Line Sports that has a nylon top-piece and a tapered net lower, available in two colors. I do it as much for style as for its ventilating ability. Ron Hill Sports, Ltd. manufactures all-net vests, which is the next best thing to going bare, and at least you have somewhere to hang your number.

The most comfortable running vest I own is a soft cotton one that I once got in a trade with an Australian steeplechaser. But I tired of going to races with a kangaroo on my chest.

If the day is warm and the race is small, you may want to simply shed your shirt (if you are male) and run bare-chested, but many race directors expect runners to wear shirts on which numbers can be more easily displayed. Runners also may want to wear a specific shirt for stylistic reasons, as a means of club identity without being tattooed.

T-Shirts

Where would long distance runners be without t-shirts? I have collected so many t-shirts at races that I rarely buy undershirts at the store. It is embarrassing to be seen at parties wearing a Brooks Brothers three-piece suit, Gucci loafers, silk tie, gold pin, the whole bit, and have "Road Runner Track Club" visible under your shirt. If you ever hear of any races where they give plain white t-shirts for prizes, mail me an entry blank. I attempted to combat the garish t-shirt problem in my small way when I sponsored a 10-mile race last fall and ordered t-shirts with all the lettering on the back and the front bare. That way you could at least wear them under a low-neck sweater. This innovation will never catch on with true runners who want to bare their last accomplishment to the world, even at receptions for United Nations ambassadors on the White House lawn.

The t-shirt glut continues to be one of the major problems in the Higdon household, particularly since I not only win t-shirts at races in which I run, but manufacturers and club directors keep pressing other t-shirts upon me. It's like being a member of a "T-shirt of the Month Club," where if you fail to send back the card checked indicating "no shirt," you get inundated. My only salvation is that about once or twice a year either I or Steve Kearney from nearby Chesterton sponsor a low-key race where instead of trophies we give away used t-shirts for prizes. Nobody seems to mind that the t-shirts may be slightly worn since, to quote Don Kardong: "A runner would run through a wall for a t-shirt." So keep watching the race schedule for races in Northwest Indiana and you too may be the recipient of a frayed shirt advertising the Riis Park Striders or the LaPorte County Blueberry Festival.

Wristwatches

Recently I purchased a new digital wristwatch. It has four buttons. The button on the bottom left shifts it back and forth from time of day to stopwatch display. The button on the bottom right starts and stops the stopwatch display. The button on the upper right permits me to halt the stopwatch display while the watch continues to run, and I also can use it to show me the day of the week. I'm not certain what the button in the upper left does; maybe it starts World War III.

While I occasionally use this watch to tell me how late I am for some appointment, the main reason I bought it was for use while running, specifically to time myself in races. Last weekend I was at the age handicap race in Chicago mentioned previously. It attracted 1700 runners, which made life difficult for officials, who not only had to time the runners as they crossed the finish line, but also had to determine their actual time by subtracting the handicap. Even with the help of a computer, race officials still had not sorted out the times by the award ceremonies an hour later. People were wandering around the gym worrying when and if they would receive their time, but I already had mine displayed on my wristwatch.

The watch is practical and may even be a necessity for competitive racers, particularly in this era of races with 5000 or more competitors where race sponsors may not be able to provide every finisher with his or her time five minutes after crossing the line. Runners need to assume some obligation for recording their own performances either by bringing a friend with a stopwatch or timing themselves. In huge fields it often takes a runner back in the pack several minutes to even cross the starting line after the gun goes off, and this permits you to compensate for this built-in handicap—at least for your own records.

Another practical use for stopwatches is in timing your workouts, particularly if you do interval running on a track where the precise time of every segment run can be very important. Runners who go for long distance runs can also time themselves in this manner, often measuring their performance en route against different landmarks or mileage markers if they know the course.

I don't recommend that beginning runners time themselves in this manner. Until you have been running for at least three months and can comfortably cover several miles, you should not worry about how fast you run. My general rule in this regard is not to mix time and distance. It is all right to time yourself, as long as you do not know how far you run. Likewise, it is all right to know how far you run, as long as you do not time yourself. In other words, if you know that a certain course (or so many laps around a track or gym) is two miles, then do not look at the time. But you could run for a half-hour around that same track or gym as long as you do not bother to count laps. Or you could go for a half-hour run anywhere without regard to distance. Many running programs (including those offered by Joe Henderson in his book *Jog Run Race*) are predicated on time rather than distance.

Experienced runners often use watches during workouts to give themselves an indication as to how much mileage they cover. After you have been running several years, particularly if you do any racing or running against the stopwatch in practice, you can sense the speed at which you train. You know you are running 7:00 per mile, because that's what 7:00 pace felt like when you timed yourself over certain known courses previously. So if you come in from a workout that lasted 70 minutes, you can write down 10 miles in your diary with some assurance of accuracy. Frank Shorter once told a reporter from the *New York Times Magazine* that he could tell within a few seconds exactly the speed he was running in practice or races. The reporter was incredulous at this ability, and Frank may be better than most at sensing speed, but most experienced runners (as opposed to merely fast runners) probably have similar abilities. Soon after the start of a recent distance race, I realized that I had not seen the one mile mark. (As it turned out, there was none.) I punched the button on my watch and it said 5:25.

Considering my eventual finishing time, I probably hit the mile mark right on.

Wristwatches with stopwatch capacity usually cost more and they are delicate, but you can help extend their life by throwing away the band that comes with the watch and replacing it with a sweat band. This will help protect the watch from excessive moisture.

I have owned various wrist-stopwatches with sweep second hands over the years and sooner or later you punch a button too hard or they simply just wear out. Throw your watch away. My experience has been that they cost too much to repair and the repairs rarely last long before something else goes wrong with the watch. This includes regular stopwatches as well. Unless the watch is very expensive, or you have a warranty guaranteeing repairs, you may be better off investing your money in a new watch rather than repairing the old one. This relates only to sweepsecond watches, since the digital watch I currently own is my first. But the principle probably is the same.

Part 3
Coping

11

Battling the Elements

Secrets of running through all kinds of weather

One morning while runing on a brisk, fall day with a group of other runners, I noticed that Len Afremow of Northbrook, Illinois, wore only one mitten. At first, I thought maybe he lost the other one.

"No," Afremow responded to a query. "Today's only a one-glove day."

"What's a one-glove day?" I asked.

Afremow explained that he wore the mitten on one hand until the bare hand became cold. Then he switched back.

"Why not wear gloves on both hands?" I asked.

"Because then my hands would get too hot," he said with singular logic. Presumably, should the temperature dip another 10 or 20 degrees, it would become a "two-glove-day," and Afremow would don one more mitten for his workouts.

Len Afremow is a runner totally in balance with his environment. When the temperature grows colder, he dons extra pieces of clothing in precise, preordained amounts to protect him from the elements. He balances body temperature against environmental temperature. When the weather warms, he strips away his protective shell with similar preciseness. Len Afremow has learned the first lesson of how to run during cold weather: wear enough clothing to stay warm but no more.

Among the questions I get asked most frequently, particularly by non-runners: "How can you run in weather like this?" It is usually asked during sub-zero temperatures, although it is a popular question during heat spells too. My reply is simply that you can run in any kind of weather if you use common sense and wear the proper clothing. Battling the elements is part of the challenge of being a runner.

If you are a beginning runner, however, you probably do not want your first workout in January with four feet of snow on the ground and more in the air, when the temperature has dipped below zero for the 17th consecutive day, when the wind is howling out of the northwest at gale force, and when the wind-chill factor is so low it cracks the tube on your TV set when the weatherman announces it. Pick a day like that and you probably won't get as far as the mailbox.

Beginners should start in the spring, or at least at a time of year when they have at least several months of relatively good weather ahead. Start jogging on some indoor track where weather is irrelevant—at least until you climb into your car to drive home and find the engine frozen.

Yet the true runner, one who has become addicted to a daily diet of exercise, runs in every kind of weather. In fact, that person thrives in all conditions, may actually derive masochistic pleasure from so running. And that person might even be the same person who only a year before would *not* have made it to the mailbox. If you are a true runner, you run slower when threatened by the elements, or with more clothes on, or sometimes in different areas—but you run.

Learning to run in cold or even bad weather does take some adaptation, which can occur as the seasons move through their normal cycle from summer to fall to winter—and it does require special but not necessarily expensive equipment in most instances. Let us consider some of the problems of running year round.

Secrets of Cold Weather Running

Beginning runners often worry about the possible dangers of winter distance running. One of the most frequently asked questions when I lecture at fitness clinics in northern states is: "Will the cold air damage my lungs?" Questioners also worry about the possibilities of getting colds because of exposure.

Fear not. No damage will result. For the last 25 years,* I have run outdoors in severest weather conditions, rarely have missed

---

*If you compare this number with that used elsewhere in this book, you may sense a contradiction. I started running more than 30 years ago, but for the first five of those years, I either did not run in the winter or ran only indoors.

a day, and never have experienced the slightest lung or bron-
chial distress from my running. As for getting colds, I think my
cold-weather training increases my resistance to them. I get
colds more often during the summer.

The reason cold air won't damage your lungs is the adapta-
bility of and protective devices built into the human organism.
Any air taken in through the mouth is warmed in the throat
long before it reaches the lungs. I do admit to some lung discomfort years ago while running in college and working all
winter on an indoor track. Each spring after we first moved outside, I felt a "burning" sensation in my lungs for the first few
days. I assumed this to be because of breathing cold air; I
realize now it was the shift from breathing very *humid* air
indoors to very *dry* air outdoors. If you remain outdoors all
winter, you never experience this sensation.

When I talked about winter running at a lecture I gave not
long ago before the Coronary Club at Swedish Covenant Hospital, Dr. Noel D. Nequin suggested that perhaps individuals recovering from heart attacks who were into jogging programs
should be cautious about running outdoors, particularly if cold-
weather running caused them chest pains. Note that Noel did
not tell them *not* to run outdoors; he simply told them to be
cautious, which probably is sound medical advice for any jogger, whether post-coronary or not. Chest pains are more the
result of the extra stress caused by cold-weather running than
any cold-air effect on the lungs.

But the extra stress a runner faces in cold weather makes running more enjoyable — and more valuable in some respects for
conditioning purposes. Rick Wohlhuter, the Olympic 800-meter
bronze medalist from Chicago, agrees with me. When I interviewed him several years ago for an article in *Runner's World*,
he admitted that he could have fled the midwest for Southern
California, as many track runners have, but he thought that
working outdoors midwinter on the Chicago lakefront with the
cold midwinter wind blowing out of the north made him
tougher. And New Zealand's Olympic triple-gold medalist Peter
Snell once said: "I enjoy bad weather, because I know that while
I'm outside suffering, all of the rivals I'll race next summer are
indoors doing nothing."

One of the appeals of cold-weather workouts to many long
distance runners is the it-feels-so-good-when-I-stop motivational
attitude that keeps them running anyway. Only a few of the

most talented individuals score victories in races, but regardless
of our skills, most of us achieve personal victories by simply per-
severing. One of the magnetic attractions of the marathon is the
perseverance it requires to reach the finish line. In winter, the
elements become simply another foe to be conquered. I can
recall coming in from a workout in zero weather, half frozen,
totally exhausted, yet feeling fully exhilarated after bucking a
fierce wind, on snow-covered roads where I was barely able to
better a 10:00-per-mile pace. I had won. Winter had given me
its best shot and failed to conquer me!

Most runners who have continued their regimens outdoors
more than one season eventually learn by trial and error how to
cope with the elements. One afternoon in the fall of 1977, I
worked out with Chicago Mayor Michael Bilandic and Wendy
Miller, one of the organizers of the Mayor Daley Marathon. It
was a bleak, cold, gusty day.

We arrived late at the Mayor's dressing room near the Navy
Pier. The Mayor, on a tight schedule that evening, had started
ahead of us on a six-mile run. We had to run hard to catch
him, although running seemed effortless for some reason. I
realized why when we made the turn at three miles to head
back. We had been running with the wind; but now we had to
fight our way home against it, all the way back to Navy Pier. It
was a cold, chilling experience.

Back in the locker room, the Mayor stumped on a bench, a
smile on his face. "Next time," he said, "I think we'll run into
the wind going *out*, rather than coming back."

Balancing Heat and Cold

The Mayor had learned from experience one of the cardinal
rules of winter running: head into the wind the minute you get
outdoors. This makes finishing the workout much easier. In
winter, you try to finish faster than you began, avoiding the
chills that are possible if you overheat too early. You don't want
to finish your workout soaked with sweat and so fatigued that
you move slowly and fail to maintain body heat.

I have heard at least one clinic speaker suggest the opposite —
that you start with the wind at your back and *warm up* for the
cold trek back later. This same individual has been running
only a few years and does much of his running indoors. All I can

say is that you should try my way and his to see which one *you* like.

One important secret for winter runners is: Do not overdress. As Len Afremow does on his one-glove days, wear enough clothing to keep warm, but not so much as to overheat. Heat exhaustion and accompanying dehydration can sometimes be problems in winter as well as in summer, particularly because you will probably be less inclined to drink water before and during a winter workout.

The most efficient way to balance heat and cold—as almost any experienced skier will tell you—is to dress in layers. When the weather gets warmer I shed one layer; if it gets colder I put it back on. Unlike the skier, of course, the long-distance runner cannot drop items of clothing in the lodge between runs up and down the mountain, so testing the weather is important *before* starting out on a run. In this respect, what my body tells me is more important than what the weatherman tells me—particularly since that weatherman, or his equipment, may be many miles from my running course. I step outside and feel how cold it is.

When the fall winds start to blow, I begin layering by adding a cotton, turtleneck pullover atop my t-shirt. The turtleneck is important, particularly later on, because it prevents cold wind from getting down your back and traps warm air within. Trapping warm air between layers of clothing is the secret of effective insulation.

If the weather gets colder, I wear a sweat shirt over my turtleneck. If the temperature continues to drop, I add a lightweight nylon parka, hooded for maximum protection, although I raise it only during the most severe weather. I sometimes wear the parka, instead of the sweatshirt, over the turtleneck. A nylon parka also is very effective at shedding rain or snow.

I similarly layer my legs, although I normally use less clothing than on the upper part of my body because my legs are in continuous motion. I begin with the grey, cotton, totally unglamorous sweat bottoms from Sears. In extremely cold weather, I wear tight-fitting nylon sweat pants on the inside. Some runners use long underwear, leotards, or even panty hose. If you are male, unless your parka is long enough, you may want to don an extra pair of shorts to avoid the condition sometimes described as "frozen popsicle."

I commented once in print that I considered those inexpensive Sears sweatsuits perfectly appropriate winter wear. Soon I received a contradictory opinion from Jim Cavindess of Noblesville, Indiana, who wrote that the salty slush he enountered on his winter runs stained the bottoms of such sweats and caused them to deteriorate rapidly. They became wet, heavy, and uncomfortable in rain storms. He thought that nylon sheds slush and rain better than cotton. His choice of material probably was particularly important where he lived because a snowstorm in northern Indiana might be simply a cold rain farther south.

But Jim raised an even more important point when he talked about visibility, particularly because during the winter many runners find themselves running in the dark before or after work when days are short. One winter morning he was driving away from home when he encountered his wife returning from a three-mile jog. As Jim described it, "She sort of appeared in my headlights." The next day he went to a sporting goods store and bought her a more luminous Adidas warmup suit. "I can see her now, and so can other drivers."

Jim Cavindess also bought a Frank Shorter bright yellow rain suit for himself. Such suits are fairly expensive, but so are medical bills if you should get hit by a driver who cannot see you. Following Jim's lead, I also invested in a yellow and orange Shorter suit. My ego was thoroughly demolished while visiting my sister-in-law in Chicago, I appeared so clad in her kitchen before a run. "You look just like a candle," she said.

Covering the Extremities

Even if you are wearing a highly visible warm suit, you may be cold if you don't cover your arms and legs. Protecting the head is extremely important, because most of the body's heat-loss occurs through the top of the scalp. Begin the winter with earbands, instead of earmuffs, layering over them with a wool cap. The best type of cap converts to a face mask for days with extremely low wind-chill factors and accompanying danger from frostbite.

Frostbite should not be a problem if you maintain your body temperature even if your face is exposed. I recall hearing of only one case of frostbite during a race when the runner probably shed too much clothing in an attempt to be competitive. Winter racing is most enjoyable if you relax and do not worry about setting records.

Probably the biggest key to comfort is keeping your hands warm. Mittens are superior to gloves with fingers because they don't allow cold air to circulate. A wool mitten covered by a loosely fitting leather shell will keep your hands warm even in the coldest temperature. I am fortunate in that Michigan City has a glove factory where I can buy slightly marred "seconds" at very low cost. On medium cold days, some runners prefer cheap, white, cotton painter's gloves. They use them in races, sometimes discarding them when their hands warm after a few miles. Bill Rodgers won the New York City Marathon in 1976 wearing painter's gloves.

That leaves only the feet to be covered. My feet rarely get cold when I run, and I usually find that one pair of cotton socks is sufficient protection. Occasionally I wear a second pair of nylon socks. Because I rarely wear socks during warm weather, I usually choose winter shoes a half-size larger to accommodate the extra protection.

One important factor in selecting winter footwear is the sole, because a shoe with some tread may provide better gripping ability on snow and ice. I have found the Puma 9190, though it has slipped from the top 25 of shoes rated by *Runner's World*, an excellent winter shoe for this reason. The Nike Waffle Trainer and its many stud-bottomed imitators are good snow shoes. Among the several such shoes I own, the Adidas TRX seemed particularly satisfactory on snow and ice, because its inflexible rubber bottom works almost like a football shoe would in mud. For this same reason, however, I don't like the TRX in good weather.

Shoes with leather toeplates that cross the top of the foot are unsatisfactory because continued exposure to moisture shrinks the leather toe plate making the shoes uncomfortable. Nylon shoes seem superior to leather shoes for this reason, but leather shoes have almost vanished from the market. I have coped with the footing problems caused by packed snow on the streets by donning a pair of track spikes. I won a race on an icy road recently so clad. The second-place runner also wore spikes.

Thus clad, I can face the worst weather winter can throw at me. I see no need for the extreme tactics employed by Minneapolis marathoner Ron Daws, who constructed a treadmill in his basement to avoid going outside on zero days.

Of course, nonrunners fail to understand motivations that cause runners to battle the elements. During one extreme cold spell during the winter of 1976-77, my son's high school team continued to train outdoors every day despite the objections of one mother who feared her son might suffer lung damage, frostbite, or some other malady. The coach tried to reassure her by pointing out that Hal Higdon had been running outdoors for years with no problems. "Yes," said the mother, "but he's nuts anyway."

True, but there is an increasing number of other nuts who have found that cold weather need not limit their fitness regimen.

Secrets of Warm Weather Running

Hot weather should not prevent you from making your daily runs. I have run under a hot sun in Phoenix, Arizona, when the temperature was 112 degrees and the streets radiated so much heat you could have fried eggs on them. I didn't run very far or very fast, but I ran.

Less can be said about hot weather equipment than cold. When the temperature and humidity rise, I simply strip to the barest minimum. Some people suggest that a t-shirt that retains moisture may be cooler than bare skin, but I prefer bare skin. If you sunburn easily, you may want to protect yourself with clothing, but most runners who run outside year-round develop protective tans. My upper body burns more easily in races than in training runs. Excessive sweat and salt loss must magnify the rays of the sun, or maybe I run so fast that I get windburn in addition to the sunburn.

During the winter, I shift the entire focus of my training and concentrate on long, easy running at a slow pace, because that is all conditions sometimes permit. The same is true during the summer when a hot day may make fast continuous running not merely uncomfortable but also dangerous. So if I do go for long runs, I take them at an easy pace and choose a course that will take me along shade-covered roads. In winter I run at noon to seek the sun, and in summer I run at the beginning or end of the day to avoid it.

I can do little fast speed-work during the winter, but summer becomes the ideal time for such training. I do flat-out repeats on the track or sprints on the golf course, making certain I am well rested and cooled-down between each. I also drink liquid mid-workout, sometimes carrying it with me to the track. The Midwest where I live has variable weather and though we might have a week of 100-degree temperatures, the wind can shift quickly, resulting in a rainy day with temperatures in the 60s or lower. On those days, when the beach-goers are inside pouting, I run my hardest. I love running in the warm summer rain, feeling the drops splattering my face, the moisture trickling down my nose and chin. When lightning appears, however, I scatter for cover. I may be masochistic but I am not fatalistic.

By making adjustments in my own training regimen, and remaining flexible, I have learned to survive the summer as well as the winter. I would consider Gainesville, Florida with its combination of high temperature and high humidity to be one of the least desirable training areas in America, yet world-class athletes such as Marty Liquori, Barry Brown, Jack Bacheler, and Frank Shorter have thrived while living there. You can run anywhere and still enjoy it.

Racing in the Heat

Racing, however, is another matter. While you can adjust your workouts in terms of time, distance, speed, and verve to account for a sudden heat spell, you can do little about a race whose variables have been established a year in advance. You can avoid the race, in effect boycott it: but most runners who plan their training schedules and competition days, weeks, or even months ahead are reluctant to do this. When they have committed themselves mentally to a specific event, they race regardless of weather. Some runners, myself included, look on high temperature as another form of challenge along with high hills and (in the case of cross-country) uneven ground.

The danger in racing in high temperature—and high humidity—is the possibility of dehydration and accompanying heat prostration, which can kill. I hate to scare anybody, particularly beginning runners, but caution is required when running in hot races. Consider the following advice:

• *Dress in light clothing.* I described some of the items available in the previous chapter. Wear a net shirt, cut holes in an old shirt, or wear no shirt at all. Consider also wearing a hat to keep the sun off your head, but make sure it is ventilated or it may actually increase your body temperature. As mentioned in the section on cold, a great deal of the body's heat loss is through the scalp.

• *Drink copiously before and during the race.* Your body will lose liquid through perspiration much faster than you can replace it by drinking, but you want to prevent dehydration as much as possible. Water is the best drink during hot races, because it will be assimilated most rapidly. Various electrolyte solutions advertised as replacing chemicals lost in sweat will not speed liquid into your system, although they at best will not retard absorption if diluted enough. Certain drinks that have relatively heavy sugar concentrations—such as Gatorade unless it is diluted—actually may slow liquid absorption by your system. Drink high-sugar liquids before a hot race, or after you have finished and cooled down, but not during.

One other important point: I drink large quantities of water in practice, sometimes on the run, so I can do so in competition. If you trust only your instincts, you won't take enough.

• *Any extra water you can grab should be poured over you to provide a cooling effect.* Grab one cup to drink and one cup to pour. Duck your head and pour the water over the back of your neck, letting the excess cascade down your back. If people are standing beside the course sprinkling runners, tell them to let you have it right in the face, or chest. Run as close to them as possible, or they may miss. Water that drips into your shoes may cause you to start slip-sliding away for a while, but they will dry eventually. Getting your feet wet may cause blisters; another good reason to have well-fitting shoes properly maintained. Take anything else spectators hand you, towels, sponges, ice. Carry the ice with you and rub it around your body and under your armpits.

• *Beware the symptoms of dehydration.* The fastest runners, the elite who win all the prizes in big races, often succeed because of superior physiological ability combined with maximum training effort, but they also often have a greater capacity to concentrate on their own body signals. They "read" their body. Beginning racers should learn to do the same, which sometimes means you slow down before being forced to. If you suddenly stop perspiring, your body has depleted itself of its liquid reserves and you're in trouble. This may cause a sudden rise in body temperature. I recall running the National AAU 15-kilometer run in Detroit one year on a course that was up and back about a mile each stretch with 180-degree turns between. A strong wind blew in one direction. Running into the wind was relatively cool, but as soon as I turned and put the wind at my back it was like stepping out of an air-conditioned room into an oven. I slowed or speeded accordingly each time I turned and placed second, which was not winning, but was the next best thing.

Running near the front in the 1964 Olympic trials marathon in 96-degree weather, however, my ears suddenly began to ring. When I slowed the ringing went away; when I speeded up the ringing returned. I quit the race. There is no shame in accepting defeat if you have tried your best. That is a rationalization maybe, but one of the runners who passed me spent the next week in the hospital.

• *Train in the heat.* I suspect that the people most susceptible to heat injury are the ones least prepared for it because of lack of sufficient training. A beginning runner might particularly be vulnerable to problems during hot weather. There is a saying among beginning runners that if you train regularly at a certain distance (say three miles) you probably can cover twice that distance (say six miles) in a race, because the competition will spur you on. This is a reasonable assumption only if you run the six miles at a pace slower than you run three. Following such a two-for-one strategy can cause problems in hot weather. Don't overextend yourself. I sometimes train at high noon on hot days as a form of heat acclimatization, but I don't necessarily recommend this regimen for beginners, who more often are racing to participate rather than racing to win.

• *Start slowly.* You can sometimes get away with overpacing yourself during the early part of the race in cool weather, then slowing down. I sometimes run the first few miles of a race faster than I should as a form of test, or for tactical reasons. You never know how good you can run unless you extend yourself. Starting fast may force your rivals to give up. But the problem during hot weather is that such an early burst may raise your temperature so high you may never recover. I have taken part in several dehydration tests at the Human Performance Laboratory at Ball State University in Muncie, Indiana, running on a treadmill. Although I have stabilized my temperature in the middle of a treadmill run, I have never seen it drop unless I slowed significantly or stopped. It is better to underpace rather than overpace, particularly if you are a beginner.

All of this makes it appear that warm weather running is dangerous and nobody should ever race if the temperature rises above 75 degrees. Some physicians would just as soon abolish all such races, and maybe they have a point. If you are a beginning runner, perhaps you should avoid hot races and ease your training until cool weather comes. But if you want to run year round there is no reason why you cannot do so, if you battle the elements with intelligence.

12

The Three D's

Dogs, drivers, and doctors—
runners beware!

George Sheehan has identified the three natural enemies of long distance runners. All start with the letter D: dogs, drivers and doctors. I would like to add: not necessarily in that order.

Let us consider, one by one, these three D's and the reasons why runners have trouble with them.

On the Run from Dogs

Dogs bite. They also like to chase moving objects: automobiles, bicyclists, intercontinental ballistic missiles, runners. Again: not necessarily in that order. If you intend to become a long distance runner and plan to utilize any running venue other than the cloistered sanctuary of an indoor or outdoor track, you are going to encounter dogs and their owners, the latter often being more your enemy than the former.

If dogs were like any other wild animal, runners would not need to deal with them because they would be off in the wilderness somewhere like deer, mountain lions, or yaks. When was the last time you got chased by a yak? The problem is that owners first domesticated dogs, then let them loose in areas where runners were likely to pass. If dogs bother you, it is because the owners of those dogs allow them to do so.

If we confined our running to tracks we would rarely encounter dogs. Most dogs acknowledge tracks as runners' territory and don't intrude on them. (Now and then a dog will wander in and lift its leg to a high jump standard, but let the high jumpers

139

worry about that.) So if they don't invade our territory, why, dogs wonder, do we have the nerve to threaten their territory by running past it every morning at 6:00 a.m.? That's why they bark and why they sometimes bite.

I don't know the size of the dog population in the United States, but I suspect it has not grown appreciably in the last decade. I notice neither no more nor no less dogs when I make my daily rounds of our neighborhood. I do notice more runners, significantly more runners—and that has caused dogs great concern. They realize that they are losing the numerical battle for supremacy in this country. Runners soon may outnumber them and when that happens, bye, bye, Fido. They're being forced out of the neighborhood. Back to the wilderness with the yaks.

I have not suffered a dog bite in nearly ten years. I say this with some fear, knowing that I am tempting fate, but it is true. One of the reasons is that in 1971 I published a book entitled *On the Run from Dogs and People*, which became somewhat of a classic among running books. When someone approaches me at a race and says, "I enjoyed your book," I know they mean that one even though I have written 17 others.

The book included a chapter on dogs and runners entitled "Dogfood," and in that chapter I described how I extorted $200 from the insurance company of a neighbor whose dog had bitten me. When that incident occurred, the word spread rapidly through the canine population of my neighborhood. One dog told another: "Stay away from Higdon. He'll sue your owner and get you in trouble."

"Not only that," the other dog replied. "He doesn't even taste good."

That cleared a path for me among the dog population in my neighborhood. When that incident was related in *On the Run from Dogs and People*, it sent a message to dogs all over the country that they better not mess with marathon runners, because marathon runners were mean. The dog population of America became quite concerned, because there was hardly anybody left to chase. Postmen stopped walking long ago; they now deliver mail by truck. Automobiles travel on sequestered expressways at speeds too fast for dogs. One dog was overheard saying to another: "We could go after bicyclists."

"Naw," the other dog would reply. "They all carry Mace."

"You're right. Aw the hell with it. Let's stay in and watch TV."

The trouble is that *Lassie* no longer appears even on reruns, so they were stuck watching *Welcome Back Kotter* and *Charlie's Angels*. Pity the poor dog in America, particularly after Farrah Fawcett-Majors retired; dogs at least used to be able to identify with her teeth.

It is a well-documented fact that there have been no authenticated cases of dog bites among marathon runners (individuals who have completed a race 42.195 kilometers in length) since the publication of *On the Run from Dogs and People*. There have been instances, however, where marathoners reported dog bite incidents. A three-day seminar related to "Canines and the Long Distance Runner," was held in conjunction with the Mayor Daley Marathon in September, 1977. Dog wardens appeared in Chicago from as far away as Australia bringing case histories of runners attacked by dogs. But inevitably these cases failed to meet the criteria established by the American Domesticated Joggers Association that (1) the attack has been made on an individual who had completed a full-length (42.195 kilometer) marathon in the past year, and (2) the bite be authenticated by a veterinarian. Invariably after a marathon dog bite was reported, the bitten individual turned out to be someone who had not completed a recent 42.195 kilometer race. In one case, an individual was running in his first marathon when attacked by a dog at the 20-mile mark. He never got to the finish line. He also failed to see the dog who attacked him, or realized what caused his sudden pain. While being driven to the hospital, he told the ambulance attendant: "I heard about hitting the wall at 20 miles, but I didn't realize it was that sharp."

In one other case history presented at the seminar by an Australian dog warden who travelled all the way to Chicago to offer proof of the attack, the wounded individual turned out to be a legitimate marathoner, but close analysis of the pictures of the reported dog bite by officers of the American Domesticated Joggers Association proved that the wounds had been inflicted not by a dog, but by a kangaroo. Until authenticated cases of dog bites inflicted on 42.195 kilometer runners are presented, the American Domesticated Joggers Association takes the position that anyone who finishes a full-distance marathon is granted immunity from dog bites for at least one year.

Dealing with Dogs

Reports of immunity do the beginning runner little good. The beginner must also face the *fear* of dogs, which in some respect may inflict even deeper psychological wounds. Running is not fun if you are worrying all the time about being attacked. Most veteran runners eventually develop various means and strategies for dealing with dogs. Here are ten tips based on my own experience.

1. *Avoid dogs.* If you see a possibly dangerous large dog ahead of you, detour to avoid that dog. The two breeds of dog that worry me the most are Doberman pinschers and German shepherds. They are big and can be mean enough to bite, so I give them wide berth. If I spot one in front of me, and don't know the habits of that particular dog, I may change course mid-workout to avoid a possible confrontation. Probably even more dangerous are packs of dogs; dogs basically are cowards but they gain bravery in numbers. Also, if a pack decides to attack, they can come from several directions. This is the way wild dogs and hyenas successfully hunt much larger animals in Africa. There is an area about three miles from my house where I frequently see pack dogs, and while I still run through there, I do it probably less frequently than if the dogs were not present.

2. *Respect dogs' territory.* Most dogs, specifically those encountered while passing their owners' yards, have a well-defined territory (or turf) they consider theirs to protect. Never enter that territory. Never tread on that turf. Usually a dog's territory includes the borders of his master's property, his "yard," and he may defend it to the death by barking, growling, snapping, spitting, or acting obnoxious. But one thing to remember about territory-defending dogs is that while they won't easily permit you to cross their border, they usually will not come out across it either. So you can run past them without fear. I usually cross to the other side of the road just in case the dog's concept of border is the middle of the road.

3. *Beware dogs accompanying children.* A dog's mission in some instances may be not merely to protect his master's property, but his master's children. This is a noble calling, but it poses a possible threat to the unaware runner who might otherwise run innocently by, or toward, a child. This could be interpreted by the dog as a threat. One of the few instances I was bit

was when a young girl walking a German shepherd on a leash was unable to control it. (That young girl is now a young woman, and friends tell me she still feels embarrassed about the incident, meaning my wounds healed sooner than hers.) So two simple sub-rules: (a) Don't get between the dog and the child it is trying to protect, and (b) consider more seriously my advice about avoiding the dog entirely by means of a detour.

4. *Meet threat with threat.* If a dog barks at you, bark back at him. Shout, scream, insult, question the legitimacy of his birth. One reason why I have been successful avoiding dog bites lately, is that I do not fear dogs, or at least do not show fear. Dealing with dogs successfully involves psychological warfare. Remember, dogs are basically babies. If they sense you are frightened, it gives them more courage and increases the likelihood they will attack. If they realize not only that you do not fear them but may hurt them, they will rapidly back off.

5. *Never turn your back on the dog.* Dogs are more likely to attack from the rear than the front. They don't want to attack from an angle where they can be struck. After using the advice in the previous paragraph causing a dog to back off, don't assume he will stay backed off. If you start to run, he may interpret your move as fear and strike. Keep looking over your shoulder. If the dog comes at you again, turn. Face the dog. Shout! Make a move as though to hit the dog. When the dog backs off once more, continue your run, but be ready to face him down again if he comes back at you. Reach down and pick up a stone to throw at the dog, or a stick with which to hit him. Even the bravest dogs back down when threatened in this manner. If you can't find a weapon, reach down and pretend you are reaching for one.

6. *Carry a weapon.* Ken Young of Tucson, Arizona often runs with a weapon so fierce that the Geneva Convention should consider banning it. It consists of two pipes connected by a chain, which could be used to snap a dog's nose off. Any dog that attacks Ken is in deep trouble.

Thaddeus Kostrubala, M.D. has a container full of bamboo sticks beside his house in San Diego, which he uses while running on the mesa up above. He claims the mesa sometimes is inhabited by stray dogs and coyotes. I think the bamboo sticks are more valuable for the mystical properties he attributes to them; however, you can't run near Kostrubala's house without a bamboo stick. I stayed there once and went up to run on the mesa, but had to return rapidly and get a bamboo stick because I suddenly felt defenseless. Some runners carry Mace. I rarely carry anything, because I don't want to run encumbered. On certain occasions, however, if I spot a dog ahead that looks like trouble I may pick up a stick (or rock) from the side of a road and carry it with me until I'm past him.

7. *Make friends with the dog.* If a dog approaches, stop. Face the dog. Stand still. Slowly raise your hand and let the dog sniff it. Whimper nice words. "Nice doggy," is appropriate. Eventually the dog will become bored and move away. The main problem with this tactic is that it disrupts the flow of your workout. Years ago, I used this tactic more frequently, but lately I decided that it was more effective and quicker to shout at the dog. There is also less danger that the dog will pick you as a friend, run with you for the next 10 miles, and spend the rest of the day in your back yard. That has happened to me.

8. *Run in company.* A dog that might come after a single runner will be less likely to approach two or more runners. If you are particularly adept, you may even be able to position your running partner between you and the dog, so if anyone gets bit it will not be you. This is an easy way to lose running partners, however.

9. *Educate dog owners.* Although most dog owners are considerate of others' rights, some are not. If they were considerate, they wouldn't let their dogs run loose and you wouldn't find shit on the blades of your lawnmower. Educate dog owners as you run by. If they fail to hold their dog as you run by, ask them to do so. If they do so without your asking, thank them for so doing. They will be more likely to do the same for the next runner who comes by. Don't believe people who tell you, "He won't bite," or, "He's only being friendly." Particularly obnoxious are those dog owners who tell you: "If you stop running, he won't bother you."

10. *Use all of the above tactics.* What works in one situation, with one particular dog, may not necessarily work with another. Be flexible in how you deal with dogs. They are more of a nuisance than a threat, so as long as you do not allow the fear of being bit to infect your running pleasure, you can run despite the dogs around you. Stay away from yaks though.

Close Encounters

On a recent winter morning I went for an early workout along Lake Shore Drive. During a run of six miles (between 5:30 and 6:30 a.m.) along this relatively low-traffic street, I encountered 19 automobiles. The drivers of three of those automobiles needed to move over to avoid hitting me, since I was trapped on one side by a snow bank. On one other occasion I needed to take evasive action to move around a car backing out of a driveway, suffering from the exhaust fumes as I went by.

These 19 meetings were what I call close encounters of the second kind: what happens when a driver in an automobile passes a runner within six feet or so, a distance which could be bridged by a brief flick of that driver's steering wheel. Close encounters of the first kind are what happens when a runner sees a car, but is not physically imperiled—as running parallel to a highway but not next to it. Close encounters of the third kind are what happened to Steve Heidenreich.

Several years ago Steve Heidenreich was finishing his athletic eligibility at Indiana University. A 3:38 1500-meter runner and Olympic candidate, he worked out twice daily. Steve ran once on the track in the afternoon, then after eating and studying went out for a second run on nearby country roads, usually for about five miles.

Few cars used these roads so they seemed relatively safe. Nevertheless, he always stayed near the left shoulder of the road, as runners should always do when running in automobile territory. When you run facing traffic you can step off onto the shoulder if a car approaches you from the front. At the same time you will be on the other side of the road from cars approaching from behind. This is particularly important if you run at night, as Steve did. He had been running at night for nine years and never had any problems.

Then one day Steve woke up in the hospital not knowing how he got there. His parents told him he had been hit, but he was so groggy he couldn't focus on what they were saying. In fact, he couldn't even understand what they were doing in Bloomington, since they should have been home in South Dakota.

"Hit?" Steve wondered. He didn't realize he had been hit by a car and thought at first maybe somebody had a contract out on him. "Track can't be that serious," he groaned.

Only later did Steve Heidenreich learn that he had been in a coma for over a week. He had been struck from behind by a car on his regular evening workout. The date was March 16, 1976. The following day a local high school student from Bloomington, one of the stars of the basketball team, appeared at the police station and admitted that he hit "an animal" about the same time Steve was out running. The police filed charges against the student for hit-and-run. Steve filed a civil suit against him while still in the hospital, but several years later the case still had not come to trial.

Eventually, Steve Heidenreich may be awarded damages. Insurance companies paid his hospital bills. But because of the accident he missed a good chance to make the Olympic team. He may never be able to regain his previous condition and qualify for the team in 1980. Steve also must spend the rest of his life with a steel plate in his head, needed to repair his shattered skull.

Approximately two years after the incident that almost killed Steve Heidenreich, a friend of mine from Indianapolis named Steve White was running along a back road near his home after work and got clipped from behind by a car reportedly going 55 mph. Steve was lucky. He came out of the encounter with only a broken pelvis and a badly twisted ankle. He could have been killed. Other runners have been killed by cars, and as more and more people take to the roads it is inevitable that others will be killed or seriously injured.

We are all playing with numbers. On a typical morning run, I encounter approximately three cars per mile. Project that number over an entire week during which time I may cover 100 miles while preparing for an important marathon, and that means 300 cars came close enough to hit me, probably a very conservative figure. If you cover 50 miles a week, you will be threatened by nearly 10,000 cars in a year, but depending on where you run that number might be 100,000.

How many Americans out of 100,000 are crazy? How many don't know how to drive? How many drive while drunk? Once within the last few months a woman swerved her small car at me even after I jumped off the pavement to avoid her. I think she was simply a lousy driver temporarily blinded by the sun, but does it matter who is at fault when a runner gets hit? Tim Topa, who managed the Athlete's Corner at our local shopping mall, came to talk to my YMCA running class one noon about shoes and told me that cars often seem to aim at him while he runs on back country roads near his home. Is he paranoid or merely perceptive? While writing this book I got a call from Hank Austin of Muskegon, Michigan, who told me how a driver purposely tried to run him off the road. The driver picked on the wrong man. Austin is a member of the Muskegon County Sheriff's Department and arrested the motorist for assault with a deadly weapon and attempted murder. "I wasn't trying to kill him," pleaded the motorist at a preliminary hearing. "I only wanted to scare him."

Consider finally the comments of Thaddeus Kostrubala, M.D. at the 1976 conference on marathon running in New York: "Why do they identify us as a threat? Why do they try to run us down? Why have they run some down? In an informal discussion with Tom Bassler about deaths of runners, he said, 'Yes, there are deaths of runners, and it's proven—that in cases of runners hit by automobiles, it did not appear to be an accidental death.'

"So what are we dealing with here? What kind of forces are we messing with? At times when I get into the meditative state, I sometimes have the feeling that a basic hostility exists between the world and the machine and the world of man; and that by running with very little equipment, running along finding my body and soul, somehow these machines don't like me, and there is a fusion of mutual hostility at that point."

Dealing with Drivers

Because few communities have adequate jogging paths available year-round and screened from traffic, runners must run on the road coexisting with automobiles which outweigh them by more than 20-1. The only way to survive is to run defensively. Some tips for staying alive:

1. *Run on the left side of the road, facing traffic.* This way you can see the lane of traffic nearest to you and step off onto the shoulder when a car approaches. You may still get hit from behind by a car passing another car, but your odds are better this way. Besides, the law requires pedestrians to walk in this manner and it applies to runners as well.

2. *Cross to the right side when approaching a blind spot*

where oncoming traffic cannot see you. (Look behind you before you do so.) Usually this occurs on short, steep hills, but it also can occur on blind turns where a wall, trees or other obstructions may block a motorist's view. Even if there is enough room for the car to pass safely, your sudden appearance may panic a driver and cause him to swerve into another car. You don't want to be responsible for someone else's accident.

3. *Avoid high-speed, high-traffic highways.* Pick your running courses carefully to avoid driver conflict. If possible, run on tracks or in parks that are traffic-free. But if none are available, remember that you may have an easier time surviving an encounter on a 25-mph street than on a 55-mph road.

4. *Try not to run in the dark.* Schedule your workouts for daylight hours, when you can be seen more easily. If this seems impractical considering your work schedule, then buy bright clothes so you can be more easily seen. An essential item of equipment for night running is a reflective vest. Jog-A-Lite (Box 125, Silver Lake, NH 03875) makes a lightweight patrol boy's style belt that is easy to wear and even easier to see. It could save your life.

5. *Assume that every automobile you meet is being driven by a drunk or a maniac.* Many of them are.

Why Doctors Are Dangerous

While working on this book, I received a telephone call from an editor attached to the staff of the National Safety Council. She explained that the Council planned to publish a new publication entitled *The Good Life* and wanted an article for the first issue on physical fitness titled: "Spring Training: It's Not Just for Athletes." The point was that warm weather was coming, and if you want to become active in sports in the summer, you should get in shape in the spring by doing mild exercises such as jogging.

"And we assume," said the editor, "that somewhere in the article you will advise people that before they start to exercise, they should get a medical exam."

"No, I won't," I responded.

The editor seemed astonished: "Why not?"

"Because I don't necessarily consider that good advice."

Let me explain why. While writing a previous book titled *Fitness After Forty*, I devoted a chapter to "The Semi-Obligatory

Physical Examination Disclaimer." Almost any fitness article or book aimed at the popular market includes the suggestion that before jogging (or swimming, or cycling, or playing racquetball, or engaging in any activity—except sex—that will raise your pulse rate), you should see a doctor and obtain his approval. A few nervous race directors even require participants to have physicians sign their entry blanks certifying that they are fit to compete. This is a form of buck-passing. Everybody wants to avoid liability in case a runner suffers a heart attack. Nobody wants to assume responsibility to tell someone, "okay, you can run," so they placate the American Medical Association and say, instead: "See a doctor."

This is what the National Safety Council did. At the end of a paragraph in which I suggested that people looking ahead to a summer of sports should begin a gradual conditioning program designed to have them in shape *before* someone thrusts a ball and mitt into their hands at the office picnic, one of their public health consultants, without consulting *me*, inserted a sentence—"It's a good idea to get a medical examination first."

This means that if someone reads my article, starts to jog without getting an examination, and suffers a heart attack, the National Safety Council can point to that sentence and say: "See, we told you so." The semi-obligatory physical examination disclaimer strikes again!

Why do I consider such advice wrong and why do I consider some doctors dangerous? Why would Dr. Sheehan, in fact, list doctors as the natural enemies of runners? Because doctors often will tell you not to run. Not all doctors warn people about the perils of running, but enough of them do that generally people with the letters M.D. behind their names should be avoided as much as possible.

During the spring of 1978, I ran a 20-kilometer race in Dallas. Director of the race was a minister named Gene Greer, who is about 50 years old. At a pre-race dinner his wife described the results of her last physical examination. Her low blood pressure and her level of condition impressed the physician. "That's because I'm running," explained Gene's wife.

The physician seemed puzzled: "Why would a woman your age want to run?"

See, they just don't understand. Most doctors are used to dealing with sick people rather than healthy ones; when a

runner walks into their office they sometimes cannot comprehend why he is not overweight, out of breath, and suffering
from the symptoms they see in all the rest of their patients.

If a nonrunner walks into a doctor's office suffering from all
of the above and wants relief, the doctor may feel more comfortable prescribing medication than telling that person to run.
In fact, having recently read an article in the daily newspaper
about someone who died while jogging at the YMCA, the doctor
may even caution the patient against jogging—or running more
than a mile, which is what this book is all about.

Here is the point: Each year 1,000,000 Americans die from
cardiovascular disease. Half of all Americans who die for *any*
reason in 1978 will do so of this disease. Almost all of these
heart attack victims are nonrunners. Runners occasionally suffer
heart attacks, but with much less frequency. Runners die for
other reasons, such as being hit by a car or from the bite of a
rabid dog. So if non-runners instead of runners die prematurely
of heart attacks, it is best to become a runner. Become a runner
gradually, and follow a well supervised program, but become a
runner. Avoid doctors who might discourage you from running,
particularly non-running doctors. In other words, seek a second
opinion.

Fortunately, individuals such as George Sheehan, M.D. and
organizations such as the American Medical Joggers Association
have begun to educate the medical profession about the virtues
of fitness through running. An increasingly large number of
physicians do run. Physical examinations have become more
sophisticated, particularly with the widespread utilization of
treadmills for stress tests. These tests are often administered by
exercise physiologists in consultation with a cardiologist, and
they may offer you a good indication of your relative level of fitness.

But stress tests can be expensive, anywhere from $75 to $150,
or more. And not all people who administer stress tests tell the
prospective runner what he needs to know: not merely if he can
run, but at what level he can run. Out of 90 health centers in
the Chicago area that provide stress tests using some form of
treadmill, I know of only three that also obtain a measurement
of maximum oxygen uptake, which would permit an exercise
physiologist to predict at what level the individual tested should
exercise for best fitness results.

Until health centers begin to offer meaningful assessments of a person's health, I will resist the temptation to issue the semi-obligatory physical examination disclaimer that you see a doctor before beginning to run. Anyone who follows the schedules appearing at the ends of chapters two and four, and the advice contained in those chapters, will suffer little harm, because they provide easy entry to the running sport. If jogging is too uncomfortable, if you remain out of breath for long periods after you exercise, if your pulse rate fails to return to near normal after several minutes' rest, if you encounter symptoms such as pains in your chest or left arm, *then* you should consult a doctor. Even this may not mean you should not run or exercise (since heart attack victims now run marathons), but only that you should proceed at a much more gradual pace than even I suggest.

Probably the best time for a beginning runner to see a doctor is not before he starts, but three months after he starts. Since you have not already killed yourself, the doctor will be less inclined to tell you not to run. And if the doctor should ask you a question similar to the one asked Gene Greer's wife: "Why would someone your age want to run?" simply ask him: "Why would somebody with your education ask?"

13

The Running Lifestyle

Your diet and living habits
are part of it too

One of the participants in my YMCA running class, Glorianne Mather, told me of a visit she had recently from a neighbor. The neighbor began to talk about this "skinny man" she always saw running up and down the street. The man (who happened to be me) seemed to spend all his time running. "What is he trying to do," asked the neighbor, "kill himself?"

Then Glorianne declared: "And all the time this woman's sitting there puffing on a cigarette!"

Glorianne refrained from going into her anti-cigarette lecture, which might have included information that cigarette smoking each year causes 320,000 premature deaths in the United States, and $20 billion in medical expenses, lost working time, and fire damage.

I didn't start running because I thought it would improve my health. I started running because I wanted to win a letter in high school. I continued running because I discovered I was good at it and I enjoyed doing it. Thirty years later people say that running might allow me to live longer and, as Dr. Thomas J. Bassler of the American Medical Joggers Association suggests, offer me some immunity from heart attacks, but that's not my motivation for continuing.

Nor does running motivate most of the 30,000 or more Americans the National Running Data Center identified as having completed marathons in 1977. We run because running is fun. If the Surgeon General should issue a report tomorrow that marathoning is injurious to our health, most of us would shrug and continue, just as millions of cigarette smokers continue despite similar warnings.

Mallory's Secret

Most cigarette smokers like Glorianne Mather's neighbor don't understand us. They don't understand why we are running. They fail to comprehend why we get tired and sweaty, and run in some of the abominable weather that we do. This is less true today than it was five years ago, because with more and more people running there are less and less other people to ask why.

But people such as Glorianne's neighbor still ask why; as runners, we must learn to cope with these people, just as we had to learn to cope with dogs, drivers, and doctors.

There is a pat answer to the question of why we run, particularly to why we run marathons. The answer is the same as the one the famous British mountain climber George Mallory would have given if he had been honest when asked: "Why do you climb mountains?" Mallory's answer was: "Because it's there." Mallory should simply have admitted the truth: "Because it's fun."

If Mallory had offered that response nobody today would remember him because people would not be able to quote his enigmatic answer. Mallory did not provide a popular answer because he was smart enough to realize that the general public would not agree that struggling up a 28,000-foot mountain in freezing weather and possibly killing yourself might be fun. And most of the general public is not ready to accept that running 26 miles 385 yards might also be fun.

Don't tell them.

Don't let them know our secret. Don't admit that you enjoy running. Learn to cope with these people in another way, as Mallory did. There exists a well-proven way for pacifying the nonrunning public. You can now tell people like Glorianne Mather's neighbor that you run because you know it will improve your health and therefore you are going to live longer. They may turn away shaking their heads, still puffing their cigarettes, unwilling to accommodate themselves to such a life style, but you will at least have provided them with an answer they can understand.

There is no question that the health-improving rewards of running and other endurance sports have motivated many people to begin running. A recent Gallup Poll informs us that 11% of all adult Americans (18 million people) jog at least occasionally. One running shoe manufacturer claims that 35 million Americans over 12 ran at least one mile last year. Dr. Paul Milvy, a researcher at Mount Sinai School of Medicine in New York, cites a survey taken at a recent marathon on the East Coast. Marathoners were asked why they ran the race. The reason offered by people running their first race at that distance was, "to improve my health."

That is why people start, but Milvy showed that people continue as marathoners for other reasons. The same survey indicated that those running their *third, fourth,* or *fifth* marathons did so "because it was fun."

They should not have admitted this, but maybe did so because they recognized Milvy as a fellow runner. Probably as a controlled follow-up to that study, Milvy should send someone who was 50 pounds overweight and smoking a cigar to another marathon asking that same question. The response might be different.

It might be difficult to convince Glorianne Mather's cigarette-smoking neighbor that running up and down the street in front of her house might be fun, but most marathoners would not even attempt to offer that reason to a nonbeliever. They can use as an excuse: "It's going to make me live longer."

Numerous studies have demonstrated the relationship between sports, exercise, and longevity. One survey of men at Harvard who lettered in crew proved that they lived seven years longer than their classmates. Graduates of Princeton and Yale who exercised demonstrated similar longevity compared to their classmates who did not. But how do you rule out the problems of pre-selection? Maybe the people attracted to sports such as crew have better health to begin with. Maybe good health causes people to exercise rather than good health being caused by exercising.

Which comes first: the lean meat of the chicken or the cholesterol-heavy egg?

Researcher Paul Milvy admits a prejudice toward running. He began jogging seven years ago and has completed 16 full-distance marathons. He suspects that there may be a constella-

tion of reasons why some people outlive others and suggests that
continuing to exercise may be the most important one of them,
but concedes that meaningful data are difficult to find. He also
projects the heretical idea that running a full-distance marathon
may not be the most important factor in improving the health
of runners, as Dr. Bassler suggests. Dr. Bassler believes that
people who run marathons may be immune from heart attacks.
Milvy insists the marathon life style is more important.

"The overwhelming majority of marathoners do not smoke,
drink sparingly, and minimize their consumption of meat," he
claims. "Perhaps the style of living required for long distance
running may reduce coronary risk factors rather than the act of
running itself."

The Marathon Lifestyle

What is the marathon lifestyle?

"It is living like a marathon runner," says Dr. Bassler. The
marathon lifestyle consists of modifying "standard" American
behavior in five important areas:

1. *Smoking*. Marathon runners do not smoke cigarettes. In
fact, few runners at any distance are smokers. If they smoke
cigarettes before they begin running, they frequently kick the
habit because they begin to enjoy running and realize that
smoking is antagonistic to their success because it affects their
performance. While tennis players occasionally light up after a
match, and have even accepted cigarette sponsorship for one of
their major professional tournaments, most runners recoil in
horror if someone lights a cigarette. In this case, peer pressure
operates in favor of good health.

Some people use running as a means to give up smoking.

If marathon runners are healthier than nonrunners, it may
partly be because of their aversion to cigarette smoke. Population studies made in Chicago, Albany, and Framingham, Massachusetts found that cigarette smokers were twice as likely to
have a heart attack than nonsmokers. Individuals who don't
smoke improve their chances of survival whether or not they run
marathons.

2. *Obesity*. Very few plump, jolly, overweight people are at
the starting lines of long distance races. Marathon runners are
lean, hungry-looking individuals. Again, some preselection is involved because people who were 5'10" tall and weighed 140

pounds (my size) went out for track more often than for basketball or football. But the sport of running has recently begun to
attract even former basketball and football players as well as
people who want to lose excess fat.

At National Running Week in California in 1977, one individual approached Joe Henderson with a photo of himself a year
and a half earlier. Since starting to run, he had shed 100
pounds and so had at least statistically increased his life expectancy.

A study by the Society of Actuaries showed that 30 pounds
overweight shortens a person's life expectancy by four years.
Running is one efficient way to lose weight because you burn
100 calories for every mile you run. You can diet and lose
weight without exercise. Those who keep their weight low by
any means have greater health.

3. *Food.* The average American diet consists of too much
protein; too much fat; and (despite what some diet books claim)
not enough carbohydrate. Yet carbohydrate—especially complex carbohydrates such as fruits and vegetables as opposed to
sugar-enriched foods—provides not only a good source of vitamins and minerals, but also the most efficient food for endurance activity.

Studies show that when people begin to exercise, they instinctively modify and improve their diets. Their bodies tell them
what they need so they listen. Runners avoid processed food and
are not likely to eat meat in large quantities. The typical
prerace meal for a marathoner is spaghetti rather than a thick
steak.

Runners generally have low cholesterol levels, which they
often assumed was because they burned cholesterol during exercise; but their diet was the real reason. Because an individual
with a blood cholesterol level of more than 300 milligrams per
100 cubic centimeters of serum is three times more likely to have
atherosclerosis than if his cholesterol level is under 200, this provides additional protection.

If you eat like a marathoner you can improve your blood
chemistry. Dr. Bassler suggests this is also true with individuals
who eat at the same table. "The next best thing to being a
marathoner is having one in your family," he says.

4. *Carousing.* Marathon runners, who are performance-
oriented, may not necessarily get more sleep than other individ-

uals (and may actually need less), but they follow more regular habits. The need to find time to run ten miles daily during training requires that they organize their time better. If they drink alcohol, usually it is not to excess and their typical alcoholic refreshment (because of a need for liquid replacement) more often will be beer or wine rather than hard liquor. Casey Stengel used to say that it was not women that caused his ballplayers trouble, but everything that those ballplayers went through in the act of chasing them.

Someone who rarely drinks to excess also lessens his chances of getting killed in an automobile accident. Half of all fatal automobile accidents, according to the National Safety Council, involve someone who is drunk. Marathoners also are the least likely people to die of a drug overdose. Running becomes their "addiction," as Dr. William Glaser describes "positive addiction." It improves their health rather than tearing it down.

5. *Exercise.* People who exercise regularly live longer than nonexercisers, as many studies show. One of the best publicized studies, involving 17,000 Harvard graduates, showed that those who engaged in regular strenuous exercise were 64 percent less likely to suffer heart attacks than those who did not.

The question of preselection might again be raised, but even Paul Milvy concedes that running, and particularly marathoning, does lower mortality whether or not it can be proved statistically. "Running forces a life style on you when you become concerned about your health," he explains. "That concern may be a big factor. The whole constellation of factors is what lowers mortality. The scientific proof is not absolutely in, but the evidence certainly points in that direction."

Should you begin to train for races of 26 miles 385 yards? I enjoy running them; but I dislike suggesting that others follow my lead. I disagree with one famous cardiologist who told me that running three miles a day, three days a week, was sufficient to provide good health, and that running a marathon was "an unnecessary display of talent."

Even if, like that scientist, you see no point in displaying your talent in marathon events, at least consider adopting the marathon lifestyle. Do so, and you may affect your own mortality. You may live longer.

You may even live better.

Part 4
Doing It

14

Looking Good

How to run efficiently
with style

A t a spaghetti dinner for runners and officials the night before
the Heart-a-thon, a 13.1 mile race through downtown
Cleveland in September, 1977, Jess Bell gave a brief speech. Jess
Bell is president of Bonne Bell, the cosmetics firm that sponsors
a series of 10,000-meter races for women. In the last few miles
of a race, Jess said, at a point when he is struggling to finish,
and feeling perfectly rotten, other runners invariably pass and
say: "Looking good, Jess." Spectators also use the same expression to offer encouragement: "Looking good!"

The race field next morning included Frank Shorter, the
Olympic marathon champion, who recently had suffered a bad
hamstring pull. Nevertheless, he started strong and held on
during the first few miles to a fast pace set by Bill Rodgers, Bill
Haviland, Randy Thomas, Rick Rojas, Dan Cloeter, and several
others. I stayed in contact myself for maybe a mile and a half
before letting the younger runners, including Shorter, pull away
from me.

Five or ten minutes later, I realized that Frank Shorter,
bothered by his injury, also had let the front-runners go. By the
four-mile mark, I realized that I was about to overtake and pass
the Olympic champion. I remembered Jess Bell's remarks from
the spaghetti dinner and could not resist myself. As I pulled
even with Shorter, I turned to him and said: "Looking good,
Frank."

Frank's response was brief and to the point: "Oh shit!"

We exchanged a few other more polite words, but I was moving faster than Shorter at this stage. I soon left him behind. Soon after passing five miles I began to suffer from my too eager pace. I became aware, hearing footsteps behind, that I was being overtaken by another runner. It occurred to me that it must be Shorter, spurred on by my scurrilous remark. I tried to increase my tempo slightly, but in a race of 13.1 miles you cannot afford to waste energy in duels with individual runners. I resigned myself to having Frank Shorter pass me, obtaining the revenge he deserved.

At the point when I was almost caught, I glanced over my shoulder and, to my relief, realized that it was not Frank Shorter, but some other runner whom I failed to recognize. I relaxed. When the other runner pulled even, however, he looked at me and said: "Frank Shorter told me to tell you, you're looking good!"

How to Run Efficiently

Looking good is a goal toward which we all persevere, whether we are of Frank Shorter caliber or beginners first starting to jog in the YMCA. This chapter will tell you how to run efficiently. Some of you may consider it strange that I should wait until chapter 14 before considering the subject of running form, but that simply reflects my own sense of priorities in the sport of long distance running. It is less important at first *how* you run than it is *that* you run. After you feel comfortable covering a mile or two a day in workouts, then consider style.

While teaching my running class at the Michigan City YMCA, I tampered very little with my students' form. I offered a few tips during early sessions about different aspects of style, but let most of my beginners run and look the way they felt like running and looking. On only one occasion did I notice one of my female participants jogging along carrying her arms too high. Her hands swung up instead of out, a common beginner's flaw. (As to arm motion, I always advise runners to carry their hands in a position where they are "scratching their belly.")

I pulled alongside the female jogger and began to go into my standard scratching-the-belly lecture, telling her she should lower her arms. She told me she was running that way because her bra was too loose.

If it is a loose bra that causes you to run awkwardly, I cannot help you, but there are certain tips on form that may enable you to look better while you run, and looking better should help you to run faster or farther—which probably is the goal of many who read this book.

Not all good runners looked good when they ran, however. The classic example was Emil Zatopek, the Czechoslovakian who won gold medals in the Olympics in the 5,000 meters, 10,000 meters (twice), and marathon in the late 40s and early 50s. When Zatopek ran, his shoulders seemed tight, his head bobbed, and his face was contorted with apparent agony. I watched Zatopek run a 5,000-meter race once in Nuremberg, Germany, and it was astounding how he could look so bad yet win so easily.

Jim Ryun also had troubles with his form, particularly at the end of hard races. Coming down the final straightaway in a mile run, his head flopped from side to side so much, it looked as though it might come off. Yet this was during a period when Jim set world records in the half-mile and the mile.

But one quality that Zatopek and Ryun possessed—and what any successful runner must possess—was efficient leg action. From the waist down their form was flawless. So in any consideration of form, we must begin at the foot of the matter.

Feet First

One of the most critical areas of running form is the point at which the foot hits the ground. The action of the foot striking the ground then pushing off propels the runner forward. Unless you are running down a very, very steep slope, you don't accelerate while you are in midair. Therefore what you do while in contact with the ground can be critical to your ability to run.

Most good runners probably don't know how their foot contacts the ground. They don't know, because they don't think about it. They don't think about it, because running probably comes natural to them. As long as running is such a natural activity, they probably are better off not worrying about foot plant because anything they do differently will probably have a negative effect on their ability to run fast. "You never tamper with success," advises podiatrist Richard Schuster. The best advice you can give to a good runner is to keep running that way and stay out of human performance laboratories where physiologists try to tell you what to do. The smart physiologists *learn* from good runners, rather than try to teach them.

There is no secret to letting your foot hit the ground, but beginning runners think there is. Essie Epstein, a woman in my running class, approached me one day. "How should my foot land?" she asked. Apparently, Essie had been out jogging over the weekend with her son Buckeye, who played football and was one of the top high school wrestlers in the area. "Mom, you're landing flat-footed," he told her. "You should be running on your toes."

I advised Essie to go home and tell her son that Frank Shorter runs flat-footed. Never accept advice on how to run from football players. Accept advice on how to throw spiral passes or how to tackle 200-pound fullbacks from football players, but not advice on how to run for distances longer than 20 yards.

At the same time I received a letter from a runner on the East Coast whose heels hurt, not when he ran but when he bumped them or lay down with his heels on the floor. The answer to his problem was at the end of his letter: "I've read that one should place his heel down first when jogging instead of toes first, so I do."

Don't land on your toes; ballet dancers land on their toes! Don't land on your heels; race walkers land on their heels! Land on your feet; runners land on their feet!

Let me tell you about the way I plant my foot—or at least the way I think I plant my foot. I have not been photographed in slow motion in a human performance laboratory lately, so I cannot be 100% certain, but I did give the subject of footplant serious attention while writing this book, and I think I know how I run. You can determine how you run by going about it the same way.

What I did was concentrate on what my body was doing while running. While moving along at a comfortable pace, I tried to focus my attention on what was happening down there below my brain. As part of my method, I asked myself questions: What part of my foot is contacting the ground first? Is it the ball of my foot? Is it the heel? Is it the toe? Am I landing flat-footed? Am I missing the ground completely and landing on my face?

I decided that I am first contacting on the ball of my foot, or forefoot, then a fraction of a second later coming down on my heel. This fraction is so miniscule that it is nearly a flat-footed plant and slow-motion cameras might even interpret it as such, but I am convinced that the weight of the landing bears down first on the forefoot and only secondarily onto the heel.

At this stage, the foot is planted firmly on the ground with the weight of the body balanced above it. As the body continues forward, its weight shifts across the foot from heel to forefoot to toe until a final pushoff into mid-air before the next foot lands. The order of contact thus is: ball-heel-toe. I am convinced that this is the most efficient way to run.

The Gospel According to Sam Bell

Not everybody agrees with me, but Sam Bell does. Sam Bell is the head track coach at Indiana University. At a clinic we participated in before the Pizza Hut Marathon in Bloomington one November, Sam presented a lecture on running form that made so much sense to me that I reprinted it in *Stride On!*, a small, regional publication I edit for runners in the Midwest.

Sam Bell said this: "There are a lot of misconceptions about what you should or shouldn't do when you plant a foot. One of these misconceptions is that the heel lands first. This happens only with very inefficient runners. Usually you either land on the ball of the foot, or you land on the whole foot. If you watch a runner like Shorter or Rodgers in slow motion, you find that the foot plants on the outside of the ball, then the heel drops, and finally the foot rolls inside. It happens all the time.

"When a runner lands on his heel there is a slap every time his foot comes down. There are about 45 foot strides in the 100 yard dash, and there are a few 100-yard stretches in 26 miles 385 yards, so multiply 45 by that number and you get an astronomical number of foot strikes. Therefore, it's very important that your foot strikes the ground properly. You should be aware of it in your training, your jogging, or whatever you're doing, because unless you have some anatomical problem, improper foot strike can be corrected. With an anatomical problem you may never overcome it completely, but by becoming aware you can overcome part of it."

Don't go out tomorrow and force yourself to start landing on the ball of your foot because Sam Bell or I told you to do it. You'll probably step in a rabbit hole and blame us for your broken leg. What you should do is go out and at least *think* about how your foot is landing. Find out what you do, then decide if you can change or need to change. But don't drastically alter your running form so that you begin doing something that is unnatural to you. If it feels right to you, it may be right, and attempts to change may cause problems.

The best way to apply this method and learn about your running form is about two-thirds of the way through a workout. If you plan to run for an hour, shift your attention to your foot plant at about 40 minutes into your run. This is the time when runners often experience the so-called "runner's high," an increased sense of consciousness, that certain state of euphoria that comes when all body systems are working in synchronization. If such is the case, this might be a good time to ask yourself: Why? If you are running efficiently, maybe it is because you are planting your foot properly. If at this stage in your workout, you make subtle changes in the way your foot touches down, does it give you a greater degree of efficiency? If so, you may be able to utilize this insight gained in your running form to allow you to run smoother from the beginning, or to maintain smoothness at the end of a workout, or race, when fatigue has caused your form to disintegrate badly.

Beginning runners, of course, need to monitor their bodies at earlier stages. Someone who has not yet covered two miles in a workout will be unable to wait for the 40-minute high to analyze performance, because that person will have staggered into the shower before 40 minutes. Pick instead a point where you are about two-thirds into the run, then monitor your movements.

Higdon's First Law, when it comes to form, is: *You learn to run by running.* Often the body is smarter than the brain, and it will instruct the brain what instructions to send down. As you run more and more—particularly long distances—your body will find an efficient form, which will include better foot plant.

I am convinced that when this happens, you will discover that you are landing ball-heel-toe rather than heel first. I feel that a runner who does this will transfer less shock to the leg, which could be an important factor in avoiding injuries. It stands to reason that if a person lands on his heel first, the total shock of that impact will be transmitted up the leg. But if that person cushions that landing by coming down on the ball first, *then* leveraging down onto the heel, the shock will be dissipated, spread over a wider area. The pivoting foot acts in the same way that a shock absorber does in an automobile. This is why it is important to lean forward and land on your forefoot while running downhill, which is a subject we'll discuss in a later chapter.

Subotnick Speaks

You are entitled, of course, to a second opinion. I obtained one myself while writing this book when I wrote Dr. Steven Subotnick, author of *The Running Foot Doctor*, and a close personal friend. Steve is a podiatrist and has analyzed running form through use of slow motion films. In a recent letter to me, he made the following comments:

1. *Fast runners.* People with track backgrounds, or those who have done intervals or speed work, have a tendency, even when running distances, to land on the ball of their foot, sink back onto the heel, then come off the ball of their foot again. It is very difficult to break any of these former athletes from their older sprinting or speed styles when they become distance runners. I am not so sure that this is the best form, however. Contacting on the ball of the foot, rocking back on the heel, then coming off the ball of the foot again, seems to be the best style for people running fast, anywhere from 6:00 per mile or faster. If you can maintain a 5:30 pace for a marathon, then you can very well contact the ground this way.

2. *Beginning runners.* In regards to beginning runners, they have a tendency to overstride and land far back on the heel, then their foot slaps down. This, in fact, is not good. What they should do is let the foot land on the surface on the outside of the heel about one-half inch to three-quarters inch forward from the most rearward projection of the heel.

The reason to land on the heel is that if you do, the heel will pronate a certain amount causing the subtalar joint to pronate, and this is important since subtalar joint pronation causes dissipation of stress. Then the whole foot comes on the ground and the mid tarsal joint goes through its motions. Following this, the foot becomes a rather rigid lever, and you do not want to have too much pronation and you actually come off a rigid lever foot at the metatarsophalangeal joints, or the ball of the foot.

The problem for normal runners, or long distance runners who are running 6:30 per mile or slower, is that they really should be hitting heel or foot, then bounce off the ball of their foot. In other words, it should be heel-foot-ball. You do not want them to land on the ball of their foot, then sink back, because any imbalance of the ball of the foot will be magnified; the arch will collapse; they will land on the heel the wrong way and spring off a foot that is pronated and does not become a rigid lever.

What happens in good runners like you who have had speed training and track training is that their body and style appears to adapt around any deficiencies they have, and they learn how to run properly landing on the ball of their foot, bouncing back, then coming off by either rotating their feet and/or rotating their feet out.

All in all, I think a jogger should be taught to gently land on the outside of his heel and try to get the heel and foot to the ground under the body, not in front of the body or the ground will push the body back. Not spring off the toes, yet let the foot gently roll over the ball of the foot where the metatarsal-phalangeal joints are. The jogger should realize that there is a lot of stress going through the heel and also stress going through the ball of the foot when running properly.

That may be more than you ever wanted to know about foot plant, yet in one sense both Steve and I cannot answer what may be an unanswerable question: Are good runners good because of their foot plant or do they plant their foot in that manner because they are good runners? Runners who go 5:30 or faster land the way I say; runners who go slower land the way Steve says. Can slow runners (as Sam Bell seems to suggest) improve their speed by changing their foot plant or are they doomed to running slower than 5:30 miles because they must contact heel first? Can you convert a slow runner into a fast runner simply by having him move his plant further forward onto his foot? Probably not, but if Sam, Steve, and I agree on anything it is probably that runners who land too far back on their heels do so because of overstriding. They mistakenly believe they can increase their speed by lengthening their stride, which is a mistake, as we will see in the next section.

Before leaving the subject of heels, however, let us consider at least briefly some comments made by Jim Fixx in his best-selling book, *The Complete Book of Running*. In a training run with Bill Rodgers, Jim deprecated his own running ability and talked about the slap-slap-slap of his feet hitting the pavement as he came down on his heels compared to Bill Rodgers's more fluent motion: "His feet strike the ground softly, at the heel, then roll forward until only a spot of toe links his body to the earth." I thought Jim Fixx wrong in analyzing his own foot placement, as

well as that of Bill Rodgers, and by chance I had the opportunity to make my own analysis of the Fixxian footplant.

This occurred at around the 18-mile mark of the 1978 Boston
Marathon. I had run with Jim Fixx once the previous November
after we appeared together on a local TV program. He had
come to Chicago to promote his book, which I had not read at
that time although I did soon after. At Boston he passed me just
before the Newton hills, and although he spoke to me in passing
and I responded with a few words, I had not recognized him because, bothered by an injury, my mind wasn't focusing very well
at that point. Only when someone called him by name did I
suddenly realize: "My gosh, that was Jim Fixx." I feared he
might have thought I snubbed him out of jealousy that the
Book-of-the-Month Club chose his book instead of mine, so I
pulled up behind him to offer some friendly words of encouragement.

Then, remembering what he wrote about his heels coming
down first, I looked at his foot plant. Jim was coming down with
what looked like a standard flat-footed landing, probably not
that much different from the way Bill Rodgers, who had started
the same race, was landing—or *had* landed. Bill Rodgers at that
moment was standing in front of the Prudential Building with a
laurel wreath on his head.

So I moved even with Jim and told him: "Dammit, Fixx, I
don't care what you wrote in your book: you don't land on your
heels!" Now he knows I'm jealous.

Before we leave the subject of Jim Fixx, let me relate some
other advice on running form offered in an otherwise fine
book. He suggested that runners should "lean slightly forward"
when they run, for which statement he was castigated unmerci-
fully by Olympic marathoner Kenny Moore, writing a book
review in *Sports Illustrated*. Kenny commented that biomechanical studies by Bill Bowerman at the University of Oregon con-
firmed that the most efficient running posture was straight up,
not leaning forward. Kenny will be pleased to hear that when
Jim Fixx runs marathons he runs with his torso straight up and
down just like all Great Runners. So believe what Jim Fixx does,
not what he says. Whatever the reason why he finished eight
miles behind Bill Rodgers that day, it was not because of his
form.

"Fixxation" on Stride

Jim Fixx also suggested that he felt he took three strides for every two by Bill Rodgers, that Bill floated through the air between strides, but this probably was Jim's imagination. Although you might think that the more distance you cover with each stride the faster you can go, this is not true. The most efficient stride in long-distance running is a very short one. In fact, one reason why some beginning runners do land (incorrectly) on the back of their heels is because they overstride, extending their legs too far forward in an attempt to cover more ground.

Back in the dim cloudy past of my running career, back when you could make five-cent phone calls, I ran a three-mile cross-country race in Appleton, Wisconsin. My school, Carleton College, had a dual meet with Lawrence College of that town. We ran on a golf course, and spectators could look across several fairways to see us running mid-race. After I finished third or fourth in the race, one of the spectators commented on what a beautiful, *long*, flowing stride I had. It was 1950, back when running shoes were black leather, the real Dark Ages. I began to pride myself on my long stride.

Four or five years later, having graduated from college, I visited Finland with an AAU track team. In five races in Finland I won three times and placed third twice. After one of the races, a well-known Finnish coach commented on what a beautiful, *short*, efficient stride I had.

My improved racing ability may not have been entirely due to shortening my stride, but there was certainly some relationship. On the Finnish trip with me was Jim Beatty from the University of North Carolina, at that time about a 4:09 miler. Jimmy was a short, stumpy little guy, but he seemed to go down the straightaway in about three strides. He covered a lot of distance with each step, but against top competition he lost more than he won.

Jim Beatty retired for about a year after graduation, then returned to track under the tutelage of former Hungarian coach Mihaly Igloi. The next time I saw him was in 1959, running the mile in a televised indoor track meet, and the first thing I noticed was that he seemed to have cut his stride in half. He also had chopped approximately 10 seconds off his mile time. He was winning a lot more than he lost. During a period between 1959 and 1963, Jim Beatty ranked as one of the top runners in the world at distances between 1500 and 5000 meters, although injuries limited his Olympic success.

I know how I shortened my stride, thereby improving my mechanical efficiency, and I suspect the same happened to Jim Beatty. During the five years between that meet in Appleton and those races in Finland, my weekly mileage in training had increased from probably less than 25 to more than 100. My quality improved too—to where I could do a dozen or more 440s in near 60 seconds. So it became a matter of survival. When you train that much and that hard, you learn to run efficiently out of necessity.

Physiologist Peter Cavanagh, who heads the Biomechanics Laboratory at Penn State University, reported on some interesting studies he made related to stride length at National Running Week in 1977. By analyzing the strides of first-class athletes, he determined that every runner has a certain stride length at which he uses minimal oxygen. Because our ability to run fast is limited by the amount of oxygen we can burn, it becomes critical to determine that stride length.

Cavanagh made the determination by having ten subjects exercise on a treadmill moving at a set speed. They ran in rhythm to a metronome. When Cavanagh increased the beat of the metronome, they had to increase the number of footsteps they took—meaning they shortened their strides. They took short staccato steps. When the beat of the metronome decreased, they had to lengthen their stride. They began to bound. During this time Cavanagh used a breath-collection device to monitor the rate at which they were consuming oxygen. This enabled him to determine at which point the runners burned the least oxygen, therefore were moving with an optimum stride length. He could then compare this to previous measurements of their normal stride.

Peter discovered that eight out of the ten subjects overstrided, but by such *small* margins that the subjects were going about their running very efficiently. This suggested two conclusions to him:

1. Runners can adapt their stride by training. If they keep running, their body movements eventually come along. This is the lesson learned by Jim Beatty and myself.

2. During the course of training, runners can achieve what he called "a remarkable level of self-optimization." We become very good by practice.

Of course, Peter Cavanagh was measuring well-trained runners, far removed in form and ability from those individuals I worked with at the Michigan City YMCA. Beginning runners would be less likely to achieve the process of self-optimization. After all, it took Jim Beatty and myself many years before we finally achieved short, efficient strides. Maybe, and maybe not.

The stride lengths of my beginning joggers probably were efficient at their own level of ability. Many of them seemed to cover inches with each stride instead of feet or yards, but this seemed an efficient length for their particular level of ability. They had not yet learned to balance their bodies over their feet. So it became a necessity that they take short, mincing steps to maintain their balance. Beginning runners become inefficient in their stride only if they feel they have to adapt their running style to some picture-book concept of reality. This might be called the Fixxation Syndrome. Jim Fixx thought maybe he should have a stride like Bill Rodgers, whereas his stride was perfectly adapted for the particular blend of abilities that went into Jim Fixx.

If you want to determine your optimum stride length, one way would be to visit a human performance laboratory and have someone match your oxygen consumption to the beat of a metronome. But there is another way and it relates to the way I taught you to monitor your foot plant. When you find yourself at the 40-minute point in that hour run, when vibrations are the smoothest, your kharma has come together, and your feet seem to float over the surface as though your body were weightless, ask yourself: what is my stride length? You probably have found your optimum stride length at that point.

After finishing this chapter, I mailed a copy to Kenny Moore for his comments. His response concerning stride length is worth repeating. Kenny wrote: "I have been in several running clinics where people running right beside me have complimented me on my long, flowing stride, and looking over I have always seen that their strides were far longer than mine. Sometimes it took a request that they force themselves to run in step with me to convince them. There is something about economical rhythm that fools people into thinking long stride."

So the answer to the question of what is the best stride length relates to Higdon's Second Law, when it comes to form: *Anything that makes you feel good probably is right.*

Running Tall

Sam Bell talks about hanging from a sky hook. "We like our athletes to have their center of mass to be carried as high as possible," Sam says, "because the lower you carry yourself the more slumped you get, and the less room you have for your lungs. You've got to run tall and give your lungs as much room to expand as you can."

Running tall, whether hanging from a sky hook or not, is very important. As mentioned before, it is a mistake to lean forward when you run. Most runners do run erect if left alone, simply because: *The body inevitably assumes the position most comfortable for the activity in which it engages.* So goes Higdon's Third Law related to form. If people lean forward when running, it is probably because they remember having seen photographs of sprinters displaying great forward lean. They think: Sprinters are fast. I want to be fast. Therefore I must lean.

Not so! If sprinters appear to lean, it may be because photographers, when taking pictures of sprinters, position themselves near the starting line at which point sprinters coming out of the blocks have not yet come erect. This results in dramatic photographs. But sprinters do not attain full speed until they stand tall, just like distance runners, after covering 10 or more yards. The only time they lean after that is if they lunge at the tape while crossing the finish line—another moment photographers love to capture. The lunge into the tape is a movement that the average jogger probably never needs to master. To make certain that I am correct in offering this advice, I pulled several recent copies of *Track & Field News* out from beneath the coffee table and examined the photographs of all the athletes—male and female, sprinters and distance runners. All run in an erect position.

These were world-class performers, of course, and the temptation is to say this might not work for beginning runners. But what works for Lasse Viren also works for other runners. One day during a lecture on form before my class at the Michigan City YMCA, I happened to spot another individual who jogged at the Y at noons. He was not enrolled in my class. He was merely a middle-aged man dressed in common grey sweats and an ordinary pair of running shoes jogging around the gym at a steady if unspectacular pace. "Look at him," I told my class. "There's a man with perfect form." Yet I doubt if the man had much instruction in how to run; he was just doing what came natural and felt comfortable. And while none of my students could be mistaken for Olympic prospects, they all began to display good form after a few weeks running—and with a minimum of effort on my part trying to tell them what to do.

However, I may have taught by example. Whether subconsciously or consciously, they probably imitated the way they saw me run. I have often wondered if I developed my particular style of running—straight up with short steps—in this same manner.

See How They Run

In 1952, while still at Carleton College, I ran unplaced in the American Olympic trials for 10,000 meters, won by Curt Stone, a runner with the New York Athletic Club. I did not get much of a look at Curt's form except from the rear, when he lapped me. Later, I sat in the stands and watched the trial race for the American team at 5000 meters, in which Curt ran again. I recall being impressed with the smooth, economical way in which he ran. Of all the runners on the track, the top American distance runners of that era, he demonstrated the best form. He also won the 5000, setting an American record. Form is not enough, of course. You have to train hard and have a certain innate ability. Curt did the former and possessed the latter.

Curt Stone retired soon after the Olympics, but my career as a runner had just begun. Many, many years afterwards, a veteran track coach approached me and commented: "You know who you run like?"

I was curious to know. "Who?"

"Curt Stone."

Several other people at various times have told me the same. I do not recall consciously modelling my form after the runner I saw that day running the 5000 at the Olympic trials, but maybe that was the subconscious result. Or was it possible that his running form impressed me, because I instinctively realized that I already looked like him when I ran? Maybe I merely decided I could look like him.

Whichever way I developed my form, you can improve yours in this manner: *Look at other runners and see how they run.* That is Higdon's Fourth Law related to form. Notice their posture, their arm carry, the tilt of their heads, their stride, and the way their feet hit the ground. You need not copy everything you see, but merely knowing how other good runners run may help make you a better runner.

Arm Swing

Now that we have got you looking good from toe up through the chest, what are we going to do about your arms? The main function of arms in a distance runner is to serve as counterweights in pendulum motion, so to speak, to compensate for the motion of the legs and keep the body properly balanced. As the left leg goes forward, the left arm comes back. It is such a basic movement that it does not have to be taught.

Arm *carry* is another matter, and it is one of the few areas of running form that can be very noticeable if done poorly and can be improved with a minimum of effort and attention. If you will bear with me one moment, we are going to return to kindergarten basics. *Regard thyself in the mirror*, which is Higdon's Fifth Law related to form.

Stand facing a mirror, your arms dangling down to your sides, your hands clenched in fists. Your elbows should be almost brushing the tops of your hips, your pants, your belt, or whatever you have on down there. Now, keeping your elbows in that same position, raise your forearms so that they are parallel to the floor. This forms a 90-degree angle at the elbow joint. Your fists will be forward, pointing at the mirror at this point.

Now, letting your elbows swing freely, rotate your forearms (still in their parallel to the floor position) so that your fists touch your belly. Your knuckles should be maybe two or three inches apart. This is the basic position you want your arms to be in while running.

But we are going to have to do something about those hands, still clenched in fists. Relax them. Allow your hands to loosen so that they now are cupped rather than fists. The tip of your thumb should almost be resting on the edge of your index finger. This is the way most experienced runners hold their hands when they run.

You are not going to run very far or fast with your arms in a static position locked to your belly, so start to swing them. Let them swing from your shoulders rather than from your elbows. They should swing forward rather than from side to side. As they swing forward, your hands should transcribe what might be an imaginary triangle with the peak forward motion of your hands at the peak of that triangle. As they swing backward, your hands should come to a point about even with your hips: left hand stopping at the left base point on the triangle, right hand at the right base point. Swing your hands in this manner while standing in front of the mirror to see what good form looks like on you, then compare that to the form you see displayed by other runners. Not all runners display perfect, or even good, running form, but the better ones do.

In describing arm form I like to suggest that runners scratch their bellies as they run, alongside the navel. If you can brush your belly, you are carrying your arms at approximately the right height and swinging them in the proper manner. And if you are able to scratch, that means your hands are cupped and relaxed as well. Another way to test your arm carry is that if you bring them in close to your body, you should just about brush your hip bones with the insides of your forearms.

Having practiced in this manner before a mirror, take what you have learned out to your favorite jogging course and practice in motion. Don't force this so-called "ideal" form if it feels unnatural, because we all have different bodies that perform in different ways, but by experimenting with arm carry you can find a way to swing your arms that is comfortable for you.

There are two gross errors to avoid in the area of arm carry. One is excessive side swing. While running on Lake Shore Drive recently, I saw a woman runner whom I knew approaching from the opposite direction. Before we met, she gave a wave and turned off on a side street to where she lived. When I passed that side street, I glanced up after her retreating figure—being appreciative of such things—and noticed that she was swinging her arms from side to side. In fact, her arm swing was so pronounced that her right hand would carry out past the left side of her body and the left hand across the right side of the body.

Because of wider pelvises (necessary for comfortable childbirth), women run differently than men, so I thought maybe excessive side swing was a peculiar feminine form characteristic. This may partially be true, but several weeks later I saw a high school boy running along the road with an even more pronounced swing. Side swing is inefficient since it dissipates energy sideways, working against the forward thrust of your legs. To determine whether or not you have excessive side swing, pay attention to the manner in which your elbows swing. They should not be swinging in a plane that is too far out of line from the direction in which you are running.

The second gross error is asymmetrical arm carry. This fault often is more pronounced in young, team runners who do a lot of fast interval training on tracks. Tracks have turns. In going around turns with power, runners often compensate for the centrifugal force pulling them to the outside by leaning, shifting the angle of their trunk, ducking the inside shoulder, and pumping more forcibly with the outside arm. Even distance runners running at a relatively moderate pace make subtle alterations in the way they carry their arms while running in circles.

This is fine, except that many runners not only run turns this way, but they soon get in the habit of running down the straightaway with the left arm in tight and the right arm pumping back and forth. Sometimes they even run this way on roads where any turns are several miles apart. This is an inefficient way of running and should be avoided.

My oldest son Kevin had such a flaw in his form. During the track season in high school, he not only did most of his training on the track, but also raced in track meets two or three times a week, sometimes several events a meet. At times his right (outer) arm swing was so pronounced that it seemed as though he were slapping his hip when he ran. I noticed that this form fault usually became more pronounced at the end of a race, when he was under maximum stress.

When Kevin graduated from high school, he enrolled at Southwestern Michigan College, which has as its head coach Ron Gunn, one of the most knowledgeable students of distance running in the nation. Soon Kevin had improved his arm carry, developing a more natural symmetrical form. Kevin's teammates kidded him about his arm slap and that might have contributed to his improvement, and I'm sure his coach worked with him on form as well, but probably a more important reason was that Southwestern never goes near a track during the cross country season and does fast track running not more than once a week even during the spring. So Kevin's natural tendency to run smooth reasserted itself. But runners who train or race frequently on tracks probably should be careful to avoid running down the straightaways the same way they run around turns.

Head

If you run down the road with your body, the head will come along. Only a few comments need to be made about the way you carry your head.

Hold your head high. Mark that down as Higdon's Sixth Law related to form. Those are the words from a popular song, but they also serve as good advice for runners. You don't want to run along with your chin slumped on your chest, because that will cause your shoulders to slump, tipping your center of gravity too far forward for efficient running. At the same time, you don't want your head thrust so far backward that it will restrict your breathing by putting pressure on your throat. When I first learned to run as a youngster, I remember reading books by famous coaches saying that I should focus my eyes on a moving point 10 yards down the track in front of me, and that would keep my head in line. That is reasonable good advice, although the focus point of 10 yards may be somewhat arbitrary. Just look on down the road in front of you and you probably will be all right. If you find yourself staring too high over the horizon that may mean your head is back too far, a common problem when runners fatigue and start leaning backwards. Or if you are looking at your shoes, you probably have your head too low. Either that or you have a very expensive pair of shoes.

Sam Bell had some interesting comments about the face when he spoke at the Pizza Hut Marathon clinic. "One important index for a coach is facial muscles," he indicated. "Usually they are an indication of what is happening to the whole body as far as relaxation is concerned.

"Facial action does have a bearing sometimes on how you'll hurt. Even when you're hurting, if you can keep relaxed in the facial area it will keep you relaxed in the shoulders, the back, and eventually down through the glutes, the hamstrings, the calves, everything else that's involved. You need to be aware of relaxation, because every time you tense a muscle, it creates strain and leads to tension in other places and this creates fatigue."

Fighting Fatigue

Fatigue is an important factor in maintaining good form. *It is not enough merely to possess good form, you must possess it continuously while running.* You have encountered Higdon's

Seventh Law related to form, and it may be the most important one of them all.

Even runners with normally good form may experience problems, however, at the end of a hard run or long race where they have pushed themselves to exhaustion. When subjected to extreme stress, the body often rebels. Muscles tighten. Legs cramp. A general sense of exhaustion begins to overwhelm the runner. Soon the runner begins to focus on pain rather than the actual act of running, and at this point his form may deteriorate. His arms will raise, his chin will tilt, and soon the runner may actually be leaning slightly backwards as though his legs want to keep running but the body does not want to follow them. Instead of the flat foot placement talked about earlier, the foot now lands back on the heels causing the body to jar, resulting in more pain, and inevitable the next day: some very stiff muscles.

One way to avoid such problems is not to push yourself to the point of ultimate fatigue, but this is easier said than done, particularly for racers. In racing, runners must push themselves to the limits of their endurance otherwise they never fulfill their potential. And in attempting to stretch to the edge of their ability to achieve better and better performances, they ultimately make mistakes of pace judgment and wind up finishing poorly, looking like the runner described in the previous paragraph.

Top runners, however, often succeed because they learn to ignore, or at least not be overwhelmed, by the fatigue signals being relayed from their muscles. They control fatigue. They focus on proper body movements and successfully battle the body in its attempts to lose form. They succeed through concentration.

The April, 1978 issue of *Psychology Today* contained an article by sports psychologist William P. Morgan of the University of Arizona entitled "The Mind of the Marathoner," in which he talked about how some runners diverted themselves from the running movement by pretending they were doing something else. They perform mathematical computations in their head or hum music in their mind. But this was not true with world-class runners, who often focused their minds entirely on the running activity. Morgan wrote:

"The best marathoners, according to recent studies, attempt to *associate* with the pain and discomfort. The elite, or world-class, runners constantly monitor bodily signals of respiration, temperature, heaviness in the calves and thighs, abdominal sensations, and the like. Instead of diverting the mind with mantras or mathematics, they keep reminding themselves to 'stay loose,' to 'relax and not tie up.' This may be the reason that laboratory studies show they use significantly less oxygen at the same running speed than other, nonelite runners."

Morgan discovered what I suspect almost all fast distance runners know instinctively: that you can run at top performance only if you concentrate intensely on every step that you take. During interviews sports reporters frequently ask the question: "What do you think of while running a marathon?" The answer I give them is: "I think about running." I don't fantasize myself winning Olympic gold medals, but rather I concentrate intently on running as smoothly as I can. I concentrate on the step I am taking. When finished with that step, I concentrate on the next one. Then the one after that. If we accept Sam Bell's figure of 45 steps per 100 yard dash, that comes out to approximately 18,720 strides in a marathon race. The day when I can concentrate fully on each one of those 18,720 strides I know I'll be able to run a fast race.

Of course, outside thoughts do intrude. You have to break pace slightly to obtain water. You may need to glance at your watch at a check point, then compute your pace. You may notice scenery, other runners around you, the crowd.

Little conversation goes on at the front of the pack when runners are serious about performing at peak efficiency. Partly this is because they don't want to divert the oxygen necessary to talk, but even more: they don't want to divert their minds. Sometimes I have run shoulder-to-shoulder for 10 miles or more with very close personal friends and we barely acknowledge each other's presence. We save our conversation for after the race.

In contrast, runners at the rear of the pack often are less performance oriented and more inclined to accept a race as an enjoyable jaunt rather than as intense competition. I started the 1978 Boston Marathon in the last row (it took me 6:00 to get to the starting line after the gun went off), and back there people were laughing, joking, talking to each other. They waved at the crowd and seemed to be more aware of those around them than of their own body movements.

Of course, sooner or later it gets down to the nitty gritty and by the last six miles those same carefree individuals were locked within themselves, fighting their own personal battles, conscious of every step they took. I am not necessarily championing one method of running over another. I simply report the way it is.

Some years ago I wrote a book called "Finding the Groove," which was a series of interviews with auto racing drivers such as Mario Andretti, Bobby Unser, and Richard Petty on how they drove. One thing that piqued my curiosity was: what peculiar skill or talent permits a man to drive a race car faster, or better, than another man. It was obvious that some cars were faster than others, but it also was obvious that some drivers were better, and therefore faster. Yet there was no particular physical attribute that related to driving skill. Or at least it has not yet been studied adequately. Physiologists at human performance laboratories have not focused much attention on race drivers.

I learned while writing "Finding the Groove" that coordination was important, but not completely so. Strength was important, but not vital. Good eyesight was important, but some excellent drivers wore glasses. In terms of physical fitness among athletes, I suspect auto racing drivers rank extremely low on the scale, below even baseball players. Finally, after talking to dozens of drivers, I deduced that the one attribute that the good ones had in common was an ability to concentrate. They could drive their race cars down the straightaway at the Indianapolis Motor Speedway at speeds in excess of 200 mph and when they reached the corner turn the wheel at precisely the right moment, four turns per lap, lap after lap, 800 times in a 500-mile race. The secondary drivers failed to go as fast because they could not concentrate as fully, or as precisely, and got sloppy in their driving, particularly late in the race.

And the same is true of long distance runners, which brings us to Higdon's Eighth (and Final) Law: *You have to concentrate to look good.*

15

Textures in Training

There are many ways to increase your speed and distance

In the first chapter of this book we talked about looking through the fence at the fast young runners on the track. You may decide to join them after you have been running for three months or more. After some beginning runners learn they can run far, they may want to see if they can run fast. They become performance-oriented. They shift their goals away from mere physical fitness and turn toward the twin gods of speed and achievement. Or maybe twin devils, since a desire to go faster and faster becomes an obsession with some. This usually occurs after a runner enters his first race.

More and more Americans—by the tens of thousands—are beginning to enter long-distance races. At first, it is merely enough to finish. Then runners realize that perhaps with more *specific* training, they may finish higher in the field. They want now to *race* not just run.

This proclivity in mankind should neither be discouraged nor encouraged. If an individual makes a decision to improve his or her running ability beyond the point of physical fitness I do not try to discourage them, particularly because I have been per-formance-oriented almost my entire running career. Although I still enter races for sheer fun, and occasionally run slower than I could and accept subpar performances (for example, I started in the *last* row in the 1978 Boston Marathon just to be part of the crowd*), most of my running is predicated on a desire to be best in the world at what I do.

---

*The crowd was so big that I crossed the starting line six minutes after the starting gun sounded.

Before embarking on a racing career you should be aware of the sticker on the package that warns that if racing is not injurious to your health, it will do little to improve that health, may even harm it. You reach a point of diminishing returns in terms of physical fitness. Dr. Cooper, the *Aerobics* author, identifies this as around 30 points a week to get you in shape or keep you in shape; but 60 points will not put you into *twice as good* shape.

Speaking more specifically of running (Dr. Cooper awards points for other activities), you can get yourself in shape for most running events — even a marathon — by putting in five training hours a week: about 30 miles of running. You can do this by running an hour every other day, with shorter runs on the off days. If you enjoy running at this level, there is no need to change your schedule by increasing mileage. However, you might want to consider a change in quality rather than quantity. Or you could change what I would call the "texture" of your workouts by adapting some of the training methods used by the top racers. There are two reasons to join the runners inside the fence:

• *To test yourself.* You want to improve your times. Running becomes a means to an end.

• *For variety.* You want to improve your running experiences. Utilizing different training methods while running becomes an end in itself.

Because few things in this world are totally black or white, your actual reasons may fall somewhere between these extremes. Maybe other runners you know are into different training methods and you simply want to join them. Rationalize no further. You can train any way you want by using methods that appeal to you. For those interested in expanding their training horizons, here are some of the most popular different styles of training to run long distances. For those who run the same distance at the same speed over the same course day after day, you may proceed to the next chapter. (Do not collect $200 for passing "Go.") For reasons of organization, let us consider training techniques in two categories: first, training with a watch; second, training without one.

Training with a Watch

1. *Time Trials.* You engage in a time trial every time you

clock yourself over a specific distance. The beginning jogger who measures a mile with his automobile odometer, then times how fast he can run that distance, is in a time trial. He may not be engaging in a wisest first-day workout, but he is following a practice common to many coaching regimens.

I dislike time trials. I consider them a waste of time. They are psychologically dangerous for a competitive athlete if that person later fails to produce in competition what was timed in practice. I had a good friend who ran a 9:20 practice two-mile, yet never got beneath 9:30 in competition. Perhaps this bothered me more than it did him but I never want to be in the position of having to *waste* a good performance.

I run time trials occasionally, but they are often at odd distances (three-quarters of a mile, a mile-and-a-half) that I never run in competition. And invariably, with competing runners behind me, I go past those intermediate distances (en route to a mile or two mile) faster than I did in practice. My motivation is much higher when forced to produce and win.

I sometimes run long workouts as time trials, particularly over cross-country courses where I never race. I time myself, then compare my time with past workouts to get an idea of my level of condition. I also use certain races as a form of time trial. Many of the all-comer track meets I run in, particularly during summer months, are time trials for me. They are competitive situations technically, but mentally I treat them as merely another form of workout. This also is true when I race on the road.

As I write this paragraph on Monday morning, I am planning to run in a ten-mile race next Sunday. I will go into the race, planning to run at a steady subcompetitive pace merely to test my level of conditioning at this point in the season, looking forward to much more important races several months in the future. I sometimes fool myself and run fast times in such "timed workouts," but most of my best performances come when I want to run flat out and after I have pointed for that specific race. I point for some races months in advance. We will discuss that subject in a later chapter: "Going All the Way."

2. *Repeats.* When you do two or more of a specific distance during the same workout, allowing yourself full recovery between each, it is called doing "repeats." An example would be to run a quarter-mile, walk or jog until you feel recovered, then run another quarter. You simply repeat what you do. You

usually make no effort to measure the length of your recovery when running repeats, but simply go when you're ready—or go when the coach says you are ready. At least that is how I define a repeat; others may differ.

These repeats do not have to be done at full sprint speed necessarily, but often this is the case. I frequently include repeats in my summer training regimen, because warm weather is no deterrent to this form of training as it is to other techniques that involve continuous motion and continuous heat build-up. You can stop between repeats and have a drink of water, even lie in the shade if you want. One frequent repeat workout I did when I trained for track meets at the University of Chicago in the late 1950s was to do three separate miles in an hour (*3 x mile* in my training diary), giving me 25 minutes rest between each allout effort. I usually ran these miles in the neighborhood of 4:30: within 10-15 seconds of what I could run one in a race at that time in my career.

I run repeats more frequently at shorter distances: 220-yards, 330-yards, or 440-yards—sometimes one of each in a single workout. I usually walk about a quarter-mile between each repeat, with a five-minute rest in between. I rarely run more than three and try to run each of these faster than 60 seconds. I don't always succeed. This is partly because I might schedule a day of fast repeats after a long workout the day before and partly because I can't run fast on tired legs, but the object of my workouts is to try to run records in races, not during practice.

During the spring of 1971, when I was about to turn 40 and start running master's races for the first time, I included one 3 x 440 workout at full speed in my program each week. Each 440 yard repeat was a struggle because I had run very few fast track races during the previous several years. I was barely able to break 70 seconds at first. I reached a point by June when I could run a flatout quarter in 64 seconds. My last of three repeats was usually the fastest. I competed later that month in the National AAU Masters track-and-field championships in San Diego and had to go to the last few yards before edging ahead of Peter Mundle in the 10,000-meter run.

My final quarter in that race was 63.8, faster than I had been able to run a single quarter in practice! Without the repeats all spring, I doubt if I could have mounted such a sprint. Yet by the end of the summer, I was running repeats at that distance as fast as 56 and 57 seconds, meaning that an ability to go faster in previous workouts was related to my being unaccustomed to the rhythm of high-speed running rather than a lack of basic speed or conditioning. If you expect to run at a specific pace or speed in a race, you must practice at that speed.

You also may want to practice at a speed considerably faster than what you will run in a race. One reason is that running fast helps stretch muscles. Joe Henderson says that if you don't like to do stretching exercises, you should at least do speedwork. Another reason entirely unrelated to your eventual race performance is simply that running fast feels good. Speed has a sensual quality to it: the wind in your hair, your arms churning, your spikes biting into the track. It's fun!

I wouldn't recommend this type of running for a beginning jogger who takes up the sport after 20 years of sedentary living, but try some fast repeats after you have been running for a while and know you no longer are threatened by either a pulled muscle or a heart attack each time you get your pulse up near 75% of maximum.

How many repeats should you do? I set three—sometimes four—as the maximum for this type of workout. Once you move past three or four, you convert the workout into an endurance workout rather than a speed workout. You also may cross the thin line that separates repeat work from interval training, the next type of training to be discussed.

3. *Interval training.* One difference between running repeats and running intervals is that with the latter you usually run more of them; but a more important difference is that you measure the time and/or distance between the fast runs—in short, the interval. I often hear runners talk about "running my intervals" as though that were the fast part of the workout, but actually it is what goes between, as the word interval would indicate.

Gerschler and Reindell, two West German physiologists, popularized interval training during the early 1950s when I was introduced to this method while in the Army in Germany. I trained in Stuttgart with Stefan Lupfert, who was the German indoor national champion at 3000 meters, and Dean Thackeray, a fellow soldier who made the American Olympic team as a marathoner in 1956. A typical workout for Lupfert might be a dozen 400-meter runs (12 x 400) at a 65- or 70-second pace.

This normally would not test a runner of his caliber, except that he would jog 400 meters in roughly two minutes between each run. Thus he would not fully recover before running another fast 400.

One advantage of interval training is that it permits you to practice at race pace but at a level of reduced stress. In fact, you control that level precisely. A 9:00 two-miler could not cover two miles in practice every day at 9:00, but he could run 440s in 67 seconds to simulate the stress. Runners who utilize interval training usually become very good judges of pace.

Interval training also allows you to plan your workouts with greater accuracy. You cannot compare one day's workout with another—or week to week, or month to month—unless you know exactly what each workout consists of, including the amount of rest between hard runs. Well-organized coaches eagerly embraced interval training, because it allowed them greater control over what their runners were doing in practice each day. They could see the results on the stop watch. It also gave them something to record on their workout sheets—probably why this form of training appealed to the often "methodical" Germans.

I experimented with every variation and pattern of interval training during ten years of intensive competition: I varied distances of my fast runs from 110 yards to one mile; I varied the intervals at similar distances and also varied the speed of the jog. I would occasionally mix distances such as: a fast 660, followed by a 220 jog, a fast 220, then a 220 jog. Sometimes I went for volume, once doing 50 x 440 in 75 seconds with a 30-second jog between. Sometimes I opted for speed, doing 220-yard sprints faster than 30 seconds each.

But often I became injured because when I pressed myself near the maximum in running—at any speed or any distance—I risked muscle damage. The most successful runners are those who walk the tightrope between too little training, and too much. You cannot attain maximum results unless you stay on the line, but the danger is that any excess will cause disaster. I suffered my share of disaster, but I also competed extremely well while on that tightrope.

Interval training theoretically should permit you to avoid injuries because you can organize your workouts better. But interval training often results in injuries for several reasons:

- It often is done at high speed; you risk muscle damage any time you run near your maximum.
- It is usually done on tracks where the stresses of going around turns may contribute to problems.
- It involves continuous stopping and starting, so the need to accelerate and decelerate may cause trouble.
- It is frequently used to excess by coaches who want to manipulate every step of their athletes' training.

The obvious remedies would be: (a) run at less than maximum, (b) run on surfaces other than tracks, (c) avoid abrupt transitions into or out of fast runs, and (d) use intervals as merely one course in your training menu, not the entire meal.

How often you should include some form of interval training in your workouts depends on your inclinations and ambitions. Frank Shorter believes that most world-class distance runners employ some form of interval-like running at least three times a week. But Frank defines "interval-like" workouts quite broadly, and includes various forms of fartlek (see following section) as well as races under this category. What Shorter means is that top runners like himself do fast workouts at race pace at least three times a week, but that there are other ways to achieve these workouts beside running in circles around a track while someone stands nearby with stopwatch in hand.

If you are a beginning runner and started to run following the advice that you jog until tired then walked until you felt rested, you employed a variation of interval training. Hopefully you did not get too involved with time and distance, but were training at that embryonic stage just like the top Olympic champions. Once the embryonic jogger achieves the conditioning to run continuously for one or more miles, however, he often forgets how he achieved that level. Interval-training is left behind.

Perhaps this is wise, because hard interval-training does contribute to injury. Interval-training in moderation, however, can contribute to improved performance and add variation to your training. By running and resting you can approach speeds you normally could not achieve during long continuous runs. Racing the stopwatch in practice *sometimes* can be fun.

My feeling is that every runner—even fitness joggers—can

benefit from one interval workout a week or a few times a
month. If you are performance-oriented you should definitely
consider adding one or two interval sessions, or some other form
of fast training without a watch, to your weekly regimen.

Training without a Watch

1. *LSD.* Author Joe Henderson coined the phrase LSD, "Long
Slow Distance." Henderson published a book in 1969 *Long Slow
Distance—The Humane Way to Train.* It came as a reaction to
the mechanistic interval-training theories that came into vogue
in the United States during the early 1960s after the successes of
Jim Beatty, Jim Grelle, and Bob Schul, pupils of the ex-Hungar-
ian coach Mihaly Igloi.

Henderson's star example was Amby Burfoot, winner of the
Boston Marathon in 1968. Amby trained almost exclusively on
relatively slow, long workouts on the road, but was able to run
26 miles 385 yards at near 5:00 per mile pace while winning at
Boston. Several other runners, Henderson included, achieved
success by avoiding tracks and speedwork and running at gentle,
easy speeds.

Like many reactions, the LSD movement probably went too
far in one direction, and runners began to assume that they
could achieve success with *only slow* running, or *too slow* run-
tance, which is as inefficient as too fast. Soon Amby Burfoot's
performances deteriorated due to the continuous LSD training
routine. He realized that some of his success was caused by intensive speedwork while on a college track team immediately
before the slow road work. Many other LSD disciples did not
realize that Joe Henderson could race successfully after that LSD
training partly because of excellent natural speed. He ran a
4:18 mile in college and has run 440 in 52 seconds. Another factor was that 5-10 percent of his weekly mileage came during
races, which gave him the speed work he didn't get on the track.
Joe considers this to be very important.

At one of the sessions of National Running Week in 1975, Joe
Henderson and I engaged in what we now laughingly refer to as
"The Great Debate." He supposedly was going to champion
LSD running, while I would argue that runners needed speed-
work to achieve fast performances. What happened was that
The Great Debate turned into The Great Agreement, because
we both believe that LSD and a certain amount of speedwork

result in the best performance.

If you plan to compete in long distance races, you certainly need to include some LSD running in your training. LSD is not a new concept. We were doing a variation of it when I was in school in the early 1950s, except we called it "overdistance." Our concept of overdistance then, however, was not like our theory today. If we were going to race a mile on Saturday, we ran an easy mile-and-a-half on Monday. If our Saturday race was two miles, our Monday distance was three. Distance runners now race at distances from six to ten miles, so their long workouts often are anywhere from 10 to 20 miles. This also prepares them for the occasional marathons they race.

There are three criteria which allow you to determine if a workout can be classified as LSD. First, it must be long in the sense that you run farther than your average racing distance (unless that distance is the marathon). Second, it must indeed be *slow*, probably at least a minute per mile slower than your normal racing pace. Third, it must be (to borrow from another Henderson book, *Run Gently, Run Long*) *gentle*. You should finish with some reserve after your LSD workouts, not fully fatigued after having staggered the last few miles. If you pushed that near your limit in a long workout, you probably fit the next classification.

2. *FCR*. Credit Ron Gunn, the track coach at Southwestern Michigan College, for this expression describing an LSD workout at or near top speed. FCR means Fast Continuous Run.

Drawing a line between LSD and FCR is impossible because of the great variations in ability of those who run. It is principally in the mind of the runner: if he thinks he is going fast or slow that day he is probably going fast or slow. I will sometimes start on what had been planned as an LSD workout, then convert to FCR at midrun simply because I am feeling good. (And the opposite sometimes happens: an FCR deteriorating to LSD.)

The shift from LSD to FCR often happens spontaneously. I may realize halfway through a run that I have dropped my pace to near 6:00 per mile instead of a planned 7:00 or 8:00 effort. This is the way I like to train because it means that my body has dictated that I will run at a certain effort that day. Many years of experience are necessary, however, before some runners learn to accurately read their bodies.

Similar to LSD, there are three criteria that classify a workout as FCR. First, it must be *fast*, probably within a minute of the pace at which you might cover that same distance in a race. Second, it must be *continuous* in that you not only run fast but hold that pace steadily during the entire length of a fairly long workout. Third, you must push to near the limit of your energy on that particular day, and finish feeling as though you have been through a *tough*, not gentle, workout.

I will frequently enter minor road races, intending to use them as a form of FCR training. I do run not to win, or even record a low time, but mostly to have a hard, fast workout under controlled conditions. One other factor in FCR running is that, though not necessarily done under the stopwatch, it should be done so you have a general idea of the pace at which you run. Experience normally takes care of this.

3. *Fartlek*. This Swedish word translates roughly into English as "speedplay." Fartlek might be described as an unstructured form of interval training. It first became popular after the success of Swedish milers Gunnar Haag and Arne Anderson in the early 1940s. They trained in the forest by doing sprints at varying distances.

Fartlek can be done on the road or in any area where you can find a wide open running area, but it can be most successfully accomplished on golf courses because of their combinations of smooth surfaces (good for sprinting) and varying terrain. Fartlek usually consists of fast runs of indeterminate distances mixed with easy-recovery jogs. The mixture depends on the runner's inclination and discretion. I usually run fartlek with a gentle run until warm, then select some landmark such as a tree and sprint to it, jog until recovered, then select another landmark as the finishing point for my next fast run. Jog, sprint, jog, stride, run, walk, jog, sprint. Fartlek is best accomplished when you mix in different distances, paces, and recoveries. One fast run might be a flatout 80 yard sprint, the next one 600 yards at a moderate striding pace. Sometimes I jog between fast spurts and other times I might walk. The interval changes constantly, as do the fast segments.

One of my favorite workout areas is in the Moon Valley wilderness a mile from my home, a hilly area criss-crossed with trails. The up-and-down nature of the terrain is such that it almost forces me into a fartlek-style workout: driving to go up one steep hill, floating across the top of it, then sprinting down the other side, finally slowing once more along a flat. One sand dune in this course is so steep it would severely test the cardio-vascular reserve of even the best conditioned Olympics athlete.

One advantage of fartlek is that it can be a gentle or extreme-ly tough workout, depending on your inclination. That is one of fartlek's disadvantages, too. The runner needs to be well disci-plined to train this way; no coach with a stopwatch will be standing beside the track telling him how and when to run.

4. *Speedwork:* This is a variation on interval training, because speedwork usually consists of a series of sprints at full speed, anywhere from 40-220 yards, then jogging or walking to recover. I include this form of training under "Training Without a Watch" rather than the previous section, because I do not time runners at distances under 220 yards. I have seen coaches stand at the 60-yard dash line and time their distance runners who are sprinting continuously out of blocks in a work-out. While such training may work for sprinters (and I'm not certain of that), I suspect it does little good for distance runners, and may even damage them by causing excessive fatigue and muscle injury.

If you work out at a track, it might be better to do your "wind sprints" on the soft grass of a football field rather than on the harder track. This may be poor advice, however, if the grass is too tall or the surface is uneven because of football cleats. I prefer doing speedwork on a golf course, usually selecting some fairway (par five holes are the best) for my workout. Rather than sprint a specified distance, I select two landmarks and sprint from one to the other, then either turn and jog back or jog up a bit further and sprint back in the other direction. At top condition, I do these in "sets" of ten: 10 x 110 with a 110 jog between. After doing ten, I walk for a few minutes then do a second set of ten. Sometimes after a sprint workout between two landmarks, I go back and pace the distance covered and find it was 150 or 220 yards. If you learn nothing else, learn this: it matters less what you do than how you do it.

In the past I have done as many as five sets of 10 x 110, but I rarely do more than two sets now. To do more converts a speed workout into an endurance workout. You may be better off building endurance by other methods—such as LSD.

Most of these training techniques are applicable to your regi-men only if you plan to race. The person who runs to improve

his physical fitness or simply to make life more enjoyable probably will not want to start running fast, interval-style workouts
on the track under the eyes of a coach with a stopwatch. If you
like to race, however, you may be able to improve yourself by
adding texture to your training.

16

Putting It Together

Finding your natural level
and training there

During 1977 and 1978, caused partly by the success of Jim Fixx's best-seller, *The Complete Book of Running*, jogging and running became very popular. One young student at the elementary school where my wife teaches showed up tardy one morning. He brought, as is customary for admittance to class, an excuse stating the reason for his tardiness. The excuse said, "I was out jogging."

So was everybody else judging from the evidence from the Gallup Poll and other indexes of public opinion. Among runners and joggers, there are five levels of dedication. Let us consider them, one by one:

1. The Fitness Jogger. Fitness joggers, who follow schedules similar to the one printed in the early chapters of this book, begin by working out three or four times a week. They progress until they can cover two or three miles a workout, which converts to ten miles a week. Maybe they get in 10-15 miles.

Ten miles of running at approximately 10:00 per mile scores 30 Aerobics points according to Dr. Kenneth H. Cooper's charts. If your main purpose in running is to obtain a reasonable level of fitness, and possibly prevent some future heart attack, that is all you need do.

2. The Recreational Runner. When fitness joggers have been at the sport two or three months and want to do more, they start adding an occasional slightly longer run. Or they begin to work out daily as they find that running becomes easier. They may push their weekly mileage into the 20-30 range.

At this level people begin to move beyond fitness and accept running for other benefits, mostly enjoyment. They have reached, or at least approached, a happy medium. They are earning more than their share of Aerobics points, yet have not yet pushed into the danger area where runners start becoming injured. Dr. Richard Schuster suggests that most runners who incur injuries cover more than 30 miles a week. So runners who keep their mileage in the 20-30 range probably can avoid paying medical bills at either end of the spectrum: either to cardiologists or podiatrists.

3. The Runner. Nevertheless, many push on to a new level of running simply because 20-30 miles a week is not enough to satisfy their urge to run — or they want to compete. The third level of running is your one-hour-a-day runner, the individual who sets aside at least that much time each day to train. If that person skips a day, or goes less than an hour once or twice during the week, he usually balances the ledger with a longer run on the weekend.

Seven hours of running a week comprises less than 5% of someone's time, but with that small a commitment that person can run 40-60 weekly miles — or enough to permit almost anybody to compete in races near the limits of their ability, and even finish marathons with reasonable comfort. Most of the runners who participate in weekend running events (regardless of where they finish) probably fall into this third-level category.

4. The Racer. Individuals who have the time available, and have greater competitive ambitions (they want to finish near the front of those weekend runs, rather than merely participate), begin to increase the length of some workouts, or run twice daily. They reach the fourth level of running. They cover 70-80 miles a week, which permits them to maximize their ability. This brings them into the area of maximum running, the level occupied by the racers. At the same time, an individual can be classified as a "racer" without necessarily competing in races, or even running fast. Racing may partly be a state of mind.

Although it is impossible to pick a single mileage figure with any precision, 80 miles a week of running seems to be the point of no more returns. Or at least *few* more returns. For 99% of all runners, pushing beyond this weekly mileage will not permit them to run any faster, and it actually may cause them to run slower because of the increased likelihood of injuries. When you run farther than 80 miles a week, unless gifted with an extremely well-balanced body, it is not a question of *whether* you will get injured, but *when* you will get injured. (We will discuss injuries, and how to avoid them, in a later chapter.)

5. The Elite Runner and/or Mileage Freak. Risk of injury notwithstanding, runners and racers do go beyond the 80-mile limit and up to what might be described as the fifth and final level of running. This is the area of the elite runners and the mileage freaks. Some individuals, either because of Olympic ambitions,. or maybe because they simply love to run, increase their workouts both in number and length and crash the 100 mile barrier.

The most visible elite runners are those who receive the low-digit numbers which permit them to start in the front line of major races. You usually can spot an elite runner even without the identifying number, partly by the way that person looks, dresses, or carries himself (or herself). Some people look like they are going to run fast, and usually they do.

Not everybody who trains more than 100 miles a week has Olympic ambitions, thus the sub-category of mileage freaks. For some, it is enough merely to wring every last bit of potential out of their body in order to be able to race at 100% efficiency. A 40-year-old athlete who runs 3:29:59 and therefore qualifies to run in the Boston Marathon achieves a victory possibly as satisfying as that achieved by Bill Rodgers, who won at Boston in 1975 and 1978. Not everybody would classify that person as an elite runner, although I might.

But then there also is the area of the mileage freaks, people who pile up miles in their training diaries, often merely for the sake of those diaries. John Joyce of the Leaning Tower YMCA told me of one individual working part-time on his staff, who used to run 30 miles a day, usually through the forest preserves, often in two or three daily workouts. (With that much running, you almost would need to work part-time.) Yet that individual never competed, except for one marathon that Joyce convinced him to run to see what he could do, more from Joyce's curiosity than that of the runner. The runner finished in 2:52, "without the slightest strain," said Joyce, who suspected he could have pushed to go faster than 2:30 if he wanted to. The runner never ran another race, because competition did not interest him.

Only running interested him. Recently married, that individual lately has decided to cut back on his running and now covers only 18 miles a day.

Reaching a Level

Although some individuals start at the first level of fitness jogger and remain there all their life—if they do not abandon running for some other activity, or lack of activity—many beginning runners progress to at least one level higher than where they start. Fitness joggers become recreational runners. Runners become racers. Most people, however, do not jump much beyond a second level. People who start as fitness joggers probably never quite reach the category of racer. Those in the elite category probably begin their careers as runners rather than fitness joggers.

Once an individual reaches a certain level in running, however, that person may not necessarily remain there. In fact, more than likely that individual will move back and forth between that level and the one immediately below or immediately above, depending on variations in motivation or available time. A runner becomes a recreational runner for several months because he temporarily loses interest in racing, or becomes a racer for an equal period because of increased incentive for some particular event, or series of races.

Moves upward or downward of more than one level within a single year probably are rare, except during periods of injury. Occasionally I have made such moves. I have functioned both at the recreational level and the elite level at different parts of my career. Most of the time I fluctuate between runner and racer, although with the current popularity of running and the pressure to perform well at major races I find myself being drawn upward into the elite level more frequently lately.

The level at which you decide to participate in running partly dictates what type of training (as covered in the previous chapter) you will do. I know many runners who do nothing but LSD training day after day. Or sometimes it may be SSD, for Short Slow Distance. They establish a set course and run the same distance at the same speed at the same hour each day. If they enjoy running in this manner, there is no reason for them to change. However, I happen to believe that variety is the spice of life. By changing the pattern of your workouts, you often not only can make workouts more enjoyable, but you can train yourself to run faster—which for many runners is the name of the game.

Tear and Repair

Merely understanding different training techniques is not enough; you must know how to put them together. Specifically, if you want to improve as a runner, you have to know how to blend hard days with easy days. Bill Bowerman, former track coach at the University of Oregon, was one of the first coaches to talk about the hard-day/easy-day approach to training—although if you examine some of the schedules published by other coaches in past eras you realize that they often followed a similar pattern, whether they or others recognized it or not.

The hard-easy approach recognizes that ordinarily it takes the human body more than 24 hours to recuperate from a difficult workout. That being the case, you do not want to run difficult workouts more than two days in succession, otherwise you run the risk either of injury or excessive fatigue. The East Germans even monitor fatigue levels of their athletes by actually measuring blood pH after each workout.

Ron Gunn, track coach at Southwestern Michigan College of Dowagiac, Michigan, operates on a pattern similar to that of Bowerman, alternating hard workouts with easy workouts, although labeling them differently. He speaks of days in which his runners either tear or repair. A "tear" day is one on which they have an extremely demanding workout, or maybe a race. Sometimes he schedules two tear days in succession, but more often a tear day is followed by a "repair" day, one on which they run at a relatively easy pace. Of course, what a well-conditioned college runner might consider a repair workout might put a beginning jogger into the hospital. In running, times and distances often are relative, but principles remain the same.

Usually runners arrive at Southwestern Michigan College each fall already in excellent condition from a summer of running anywhere from 50-100 miles a week. Each morning they rise early and run four or six miles on their own and at whatever pace suits them. The main workout of the day is scheduled for late afternoon following classes.

The Ron Gunn pattern for a typical week is tear-tear-repair-tear-repair-tear-repair. For example:

Monday: Tear. A fast, continuous run (FCR) usually around

eight to ten miles on the roads and at a pace faster than 6:00 per mile. To avoid boredom and having his runners compare their times from one week to the next, Gunn usually runs workouts over a variety of courses in the countryside around campus. Usually these courses are named after All-Americans who graduated from SMC, such as the Roscoe Run, or the Ofsansky Loop. His runners rarely run the same course more than once or twice a season.

Tuesday: A second tear day. Perhaps some long repeats of 880 yards to 1¼ miles (not always measured) on a nearby golf course, a long hill, the roads, or even the track. During the fall, Gunn's teams never go near the track and even during track season work out on it only once a week.

Wednesday: Repair, what Gunn calls his "go fishin' day." This might involve an easy LSD workout on the road or maybe slow running through the trails of the forest behind campus.

Thursday: Tear. A hard workout of short intervals or sprints of no particular distance or direction around the golf course. One runner sometimes will lead along a winding route, then when he turns back, everybody sprints to the start following the exact path they came out. This teaches the runners to pay attention to the course on which they are running, an important factor in cross-country success. (See the chapter on cross-country.)

Friday: Another repair day. The team members run easy the day before a race, covering only a few miles in practice. Distance and speed is partly dictated by how important the next day's race is.

Saturday: The final tear day of the week revolves around a track or cross-country meet.

Sunday: Repair, involving either total rest or a relaxed run, depending on how each runner on the team feels. For some this might be an easy 15-mile run.

Gunn predicates his entire schedule on a tear-repair basis with a major race on one weekend followed by an easy open event the next, which his top runners may decide to pass. He also sometimes schedules junior varsity meets mid-week to permit everybody on his squad, regardless of ability, an opportunity to compete. As the season progresses, the major races get tougher and tougher. Utilizing this program Ron Gunn developed Southwestern Michigan College into one of the top two-year running schools in the United States, and earned it the nickname of "the Oregon of the Midwest." In ten years his teams won three National Junior College Athletic Association titles (including one tie) and finished high most other years. In the 1977 NJCAA cross-country championships in Tucson, Arizona, SMC had five runners in the top 25 positions (thus earning All-American status) even though finishing second to Allegheny College, whose top five runners included two Kenyans and one Englishman.

Training Patterns for Beginners

The beginning runner may look at the workouts Ron Gunn prescribes for his athletes and decide: That's fine for a college All American, but I'm 45 years old and never ran a step until two months ago. True, but while the dosage may be different, the pattern can be the same. One other individual that Ron Gunn coaches is an insurance broker named Bill Livingston, who lives in Dowagiac. He started to jog just before turning 40 and within four years qualified for the Boston Marathon by running a time under 3:30 for the 26 mile 385 yard event.

In having my running class report to the Michigan City YMCA three days a week on Monday, Wednesday, and Friday, I followed a tear-repair program. The pattern was tear-repair-tear-repair-tear-repair-repair. Tear for my YMCA joggers was a mile or two of easy jogging and walking on Mondays, Wednesdays, and Fridays. On repair days they did nothing.

Invariably, some of them discovered that they enjoyed running so much that they began running on their own on the off days. Chet Dubie soon was covering ten miles in a workout, entirely indoors at the YMCA. Diane Alexander began to run four and five miles in her neighborhood. Paul Marshall worked his way up to six miles and began to look forward to a local 15 kilometer race in the summer. One day, however, Paul told me: "If I try to run six miles two days in a row, I have much more difficulty the second day." Working at a much lower level of fitness, Paul had simply discovered the principles that people like Bowerman and Gunn used to develop national championship teams.

I simply advised Paul: "Take it easy the second day. Then you can run hard again the day after that."

This is good advice for all runners. As you begin to improve in conditioning, consider how you might begin to vary your workouts so as to not merely become a better runner, but to enjoy your running more. Using the training techniques discussed in the previous chapter, here is how you might pattern your workouts in one typical week. Rather than identify specific workouts on particular days, I merely have numbered them. But you could begin your week on Sunday with number 1.

1. *Long, Slow Distance.* Take an easy run on the roads over a relatively long distance. How long depends on your particular level of conditioning. A beginning jogger might go three or four miles. For racers, a good rule of thumb is anywhere from 25 to 50% further than the distance at which you normally compete. If your favorite racing distance is 10 miles, you may want to cover 12-15 miles. (This rule does not apply to marathons, however, which will be discussed in a separate chapter.)

2. *Easy run.* Take a relaxed workout at a relatively short distance at whatever pace feels comfortable to you. Seek out a different course: perhaps a golf course or the woods. Enjoy the scenery. If you run with someone, have a good conversation. Spend a little extra time taking a shower. Sing.

3. *Interval training, or repeats.* If you have been jogging or running more than three months, work with a stopwatch so that you get some measure of your ability. You do not need to run 440s in 60 seconds to be able to benefit from this type workout. Despite being a highly competitive runner, I sometimes run interval 440s as slow as 90 seconds. Beginning runners may want to go even slower than that and walk instead of jog in between.

4. *Easy run.* A run similar to the one taken two days earlier in which you relax after the previous hard day's workout and rest so that you can work hard again the next day.

5. *Untimed fast running at different distances.* Take a fartlek workout, preferably on some area with a soft surface such as a golf course. But you can run fartlek on the roads if you have to. A hard cross country workout over varying terrain that forces you into changes of pace may serve the same result.

6. *Rest.* Nothing says that you have to run seven days a week, although many runners do, either because they think it makes them better runners, or because they enjoy it. Take a day off, without guilt. Go for a bike ride or a long walk instead. Or stay home and read a magazine—not *Runner's World*, but *Time*, or *Esquire*, or anything to get your mind as well as body away from

running for a while.

7. *Hard run*. For most people this means competition, although you may not be ready for that yet. If you don't compete, try taking an FCR workout, which might mean going anywhere from 50 to 75% of the maximum distance to which you've proven yourself capable of covering—but at a slightly faster pace. If you don't go the entire distance at that fast pace, maybe at least finish the last third of the run moving fast. If you are a raw beginner, having started to jog after many years of sedentary life, you may want to be cautious about subjecting yourself to extreme stress, however.

Two-Week Training Pattern

One of the flaws of the above schedule, of course, is: what do you do the second week? Well, the obvious solution is that you can repeat what you did the first week, which is what most training guides that you see in books and magazine articles assume. Whenever a running magazine profiles some elite runner, whom we all are supposed to emulate, they show only one week's training. No matter that he may have done something entirely different the other 51 weeks of the year. In my yearly schedule, the patterns of my training weeks are like snowflakes: no one is ever quite the same.

There is no reason why training schedules cannot be developed on a pattern that encompasses two, three, or even more weeks. Garry Bjorklund follows a three-week pattern in his training, covering as much as 160 miles in one, 100 in another, 60 in the third. That is not the only reason why he is one of the top marathon runners in the world (he ran 4:06 for the mile in high school, so obviously he has some talent), but he may be several years ahead of most of us in training theory.

Don't let what Garry does scare you, however. Following is a pattern of training for a two-week period of time that almost anybody can follow.

1. *Long, Slow Distance*. An easy LSD run on the roads over a relatively long distance. If you are used to running ten miles in competition, you might want to cover as many as 15 miles in such a workout.

2. *Interval workout*. Assuming you didn't overextend yourself yesterday, you now want to stretch your muscles by doing some-

thing at a faster pace. Take a workout on the track. A typical one might be 10 x 440 yards at the pace of the shortest competitive track distance you usually run. (If you are a 10:00 two-miler, this would mean 75 seconds.) Walk or jog 440 yards between, depending on your level of conditioning.

3. *Easy workout*. Run a relatively short distance at around the same pace you ran the LSD workout two days ago. Do it in a different area, possibly a cross country course.

4. *Fast Continuous Run*. If ten miles is your race distance, a hard five or six miles will suffice. Do it on the roads if that is the most convenient surface. I would avoid running this type of workout on a track, however. I have no particular reason for this statement other than I don't like counting laps.

5. *Easy workout*. Relax. Another day of repair.

6. *Fartlek*. Best done on a golf course or on cross-country trails, a fartlek workout can be as hard as you want to make it. Sometimes I run fartlek as merely gentle changes of pace and sometimes I include full-speed sprints over extremely difficult terrain, including uphill.

7. *Easy workout*. There is no law that says, if you are interested in becoming a tougher-than-nails runner that you cannot jog. I do a lot of easy jogging. Sometimes I stop in the middle of an easy relaxed run and talk to people, or walk, or watch the sunset. Running is supposed to be fun, isn't it?

8. *Long Slow Distance*. Repeat the approximate distance you ran one week ago, but maybe choose a different course. Some runners have regular groups with whom they run LSD each Sunday, and this is fine. If you are on a progressive program, you may want to run slightly farther than you did last week—but don't make the mistake of assuming that you have to add one mile each week in order to improve. Sooner or later that kind of progression will catch up with you and convert what should be an easy long workout into a long, difficult one.

9. *Repeats*. Pick some short distance and run it several times full out, with ample time between. My favorite workout of this nature is 3 x 440, but I sometimes run shorter distances. I also sometimes run longer ones.

10. *Easy workout*. Back to the golf course or cross country paths for another day of repair. You may need it if you're not used to speed workouts like the one yesterday. I live on the lake and run frequently on the beach, sometimes barefoot, during the summer.

11. *Interval workout.* If you ran 440s last week, maybe this week you should run a different distance and at a different speed. Go 10 x 220, but at a faster pace. Or do 5 x 880 at a slower pace. If I am on a progressive schedule I may try to run the same basic workout, but at a higher degree of difficulty. If I ran 10 x 440 in 75 seconds last week, I may do the same number in 74 and try to improve a second a week. Or I could run more of them. But as with progressing your LSD workout, sooner or later you reach a point of diminishing returns.

12. *Easy workout.* No rule book says that the only easy workout is one that is slow and continuous. Sometimes I run at the track and do 110 yard runs at a relaxed pace on the infield grass, walking in between.

13. *Rest.* Take a day off now and then when you do nothing. Rest your mind as well as your legs.

14. *Race.* Or a fast continuous run (FCR). We will discuss the subject of racing in more detail later in the book.

17

Perhaps You Need a Coach

How and where to find
someone to help

Knowing the names and meanings of various training techniques will allow you to join in the conversation at the next Runner's Brunch you attend, but it will not necessarily make you a better runner. More critical is how you (or your coach) *adapt* these accepted training techniques to you, the runner. How you blend these ways of running into your own training will determine your success as a competitor.

I said success as a *competitor*, not as a *runner*. Most runners define their own success by establishing goals and movitation, hopefully in relation to their ability; they can succeed merely by running in any manner, using any form at any speed over any distance.

Underachievement may be a greater virtue than overachievement, particularly if the underachiever is able to display a balanced personality: able to enjoy the theatre, books, family, in addition to regular daily runs or races on weekends. George Sheehan, M.D., once said that people should not run merely to improve their health or to live longer. "You could get hit by a truck and never live out all those extra years running supposedly is generating for you," says Dr. Sheehan. "You would have wasted all that time when you could have been playing a harp or cello." Running at least is supposed to make you feel better, but there is no guarantee there either. It depends on your approach to running. People who run 150 miles a week in twice-a-day workouts may win all the trophies, but may not be the world's best adjusted individuals.

Having said all that, I realize you still want me to tell you how to win that trophy. I'm not sure I can do it. Perhaps you need a coach. People frequently come to me and ask if I can help them improve their running, although more often their questions are stated in terms of time: "How can I break three hours for the marathon?"

Dr. Steve Subotnick asked me that question recently, although he should have known better. My response was, "Find a downhill course and use a skateboard," but he refused to accept that. Steve has run 3:14 and would like to go faster. He probably could if he moved his weekly mileage up from 55, used some of the training methods discussed in this book, and stopped being a human being. But he also might run slower. He was already limping from an injury, partly because he raced in marathons almost every other week the previous winter and nobody was around telling him to stop; at least, nobody he would listen to. There is a saying about lawyers that he who serves as his own attorney has a fool for a client. This is true of runners too.

Running under a Coach

Do you need a coach? Some runners may be unable to avoid one. Those who want to compete on their high school or college track team may find that accepting a coach is part of the price they must pay for competing at that level. I have seen exceptional runners destroyed, or at least wasted, because of poor coaching. On the other hand, I also have seen talent wasted because a runner failed to obtain good coaching. One of the advantages of running for a team, particularly for younger athletes, is that you can let a more knowledgeable individual worry about your daily workouts and help you progress. One disadvantage, particularly for more mature athletes, is that no one system of training works best for everybody. A coach who must work with 50 runners of varying abilities and motivations may not be able to give certain runners the attention they need.

I frequently encounter runners who are dissatisfied with their coach. They subscribe to *Runner's World* and *Track & Field News*, and have read all the books by Henderson, Sheehan, Ullyot, and Higdon, thus know everything there is to know about running—or at least more than their coach. Their coach has them doing nothing but intervals on the track, and they know that they would be better off going for long cross-country runs in the park. Or their coach has them doing too much slow running, and they think they should be doing speedwork. In the specific sense they may be right, but from a general viewpoint they are wrong. A little knowledge is a dangerous thing. Remember the principle laid down in the previous chapter: *It matters less what you do than how you do it.* If you accept that as your philosophy, you can survive under even the worst coach.

Accepting team discipline is one of the prices you pay for being part of a team. If you refuse to accept it, you can quit and do your running elsewhere. This was not true when I was growing up, because scholastic and collegiate competition was practically the entire ball game, or entire track meet. Today, ample competition outside the school system exists for runners in all events and at all levels in at least most areas whether you belong to a team or not. And you may not necessarily want to compete; you can just run.

Finding a Coach

The problem for most runners, however, is not escaping from under the thumb of an autocratic coach, but finding one, autocratic or not. There are very few paid running coaches in the United States other than within school systems. Some track clubs have people who coach runners in their spare time for no pay, but these individuals are rare. If you find one, send his children presents every Christmas and his wife flowers every Mother's Day.

One problem is that everybody wants to run today, but nobody wants to stand on the sideline with a stopwatch. Perhaps we could come up with some form of tithing system for runners: in a ten-year period, if you run for nine years then you take a one-year sabbatical to coach others. This would provide more runners with adequate coaching, but until everybody gets "religion," and starts to tithe, we will have to survive with the makeshift system we have.

Here are the most obvious places to find a coach:

• **Schools.** If you attend high school or college, simply go out for the team. This obviously will not work if you have graduated and work for a living, so go to the nearest local track, introduce yourself to the coach, and ask if you can use his facilities. Most coaches willingly accommodate outsiders if they follow the rules and don't get in the way. Perhaps you will be able to ingratiate yourself with the coach by offering help as an official, knowledgeable ones being in extremely short supply. Maybe he will help you with your training. Many of today's coaches also run, so you may even find a training partner.

• **YMCAs.** Many YMCAs have active jogging programs, and many runners begin in such facilities. Unfortunately, many of these jogging (also labeled fitness or exercise) programs are taught by people without a broad background in long distance running. They are well-meaning swimmers, gymnasts, or cyclists who happened to be teaching people how to run because their work schedule reads "teach running." Eventually these people learn from doing, so the level of instruction continues to improve as running becomes more popular. At the present time what you learn at the Y may benefit your heart, not your competitive speed. Many YMCAs serve as centers for running activities at all levels of accomplishment, however, and you may be able to get help and advice from other people in their programs.

• **Athletic Clubs.** The rich man's YMCA. Some decades ago, exclusive downtown athletic clubs in major cities offered practically the only means of competition and coaching beyond college. It was a status symbol for rich businessmen, even if their only physical activity at an athletic club was using its dining room and bar, to brush shoulders with athletes. Many such clubs fielded track teams. These expensive athletic clubs fell out of favor soon after World War II because many of them discriminated against minorities. A few, such as the New York Athletic Club, remain active in the competitive athletics, but most do not. With the increase of jogging, however, perhaps more of these clubs may be motivated into providing coaching for their members. A trend that may become more common in coming years is the athletic club centered on fitness rather than golf and tennis. The most successful example is Dr. Kenneth Cooper's Aerobics Center in Dallas.

• **Running Clubs.** Such clubs often have members but no facilities. A few, such as the University of Chicago Track Club, may be organized around college and its coach but open to runners outside the school. More often, clubs are organized by a group of runners for social as well as competitive purposes. You can usually locate these clubs by going to any large race in your area and looking at chests. This may not be good advice if you are male and the chest happens to belong to a female runner who is standing next to her husband, but you mainly want to read the words on the shirts covering those chests. Many runners wear t-shirts advertising the last race in which they competed, but a group of others proudly will be wearing shirts advertising organizations such as the West Valley Track Club, the Baltimore Olympic Club, or the Evanston Running Club. Talk to them and ask them about the club and what it has to offer. Some coaching may be available. You may want to join.

• **Other runners.** If you cannot find a coach through a club, talk to other runners that you meet, regardless of their t-shirts. Perhaps you will find one kindly enough to help you with your training. If that person is not willing to follow you around with a stopwatch, you may at least obtain advice on some general aspects of training. Maybe that other runner also is looking for advice, and if so perhaps the two of you can form a club and hire a coach. A long journey begins with a single step.

• **Clinics.** One popular recent phenomenon has been the establishment of clinics where runners can go and listen to running lectures and ask questions about problems they have with their training. I lecture at dozens of such clinics each year, as do most of the other better known runners. Many of these clinics occur the day before important races, and in a sense are one-shot (or at least once a year) affairs. But many large cities also have independent clinics where runners can listen and then run, or often just run.

The Run Chicago Clinic, organized by Noel D. Nequin, M.D., meets the first Sunday of every month in Lincoln Park and usually features (a) a speaker, (b) stretching exercises, and (c) runs of varying distances and speeds. I organized a similar running clinic in the Indiana dunes in the spring of 1978. The San Diego Marathon Clinic sometimes attracts as many as 500 runners to its weekly Sunday morning affairs. Runners run in groups according to ability. The organizers of the Honolulu Marathon sponsor similar clinics, one reason Hawaii ranks as the number-one running state (in terms of percentage of participation) in the United States.

• **Camps.** Dozens of running camps have started in recent years. They are week-long affairs where runners usually spend each day listening, running, and talking. I have lectured at camps from North Carolina to Pennsylvania to Utah and thought their programs excellent. I recently established a camp in Dowagiac, Michigan. You can obtain excellent advice from some of the top runners and running coaches in America in this manner.

Such camps fulfill your needs for only a week or so, then the runner must go home and be coachless until the following summer. Although there are numerous ways in which runners can obtain coaching help, there are not enough coaches in places where the majority of people running today are going to be able to take advantage of them. What this may mean is that the runner interested in improvement must learn how to coach himself.

Runner, Coach Thyself!

If you want to achieve success as a runner, you need a plan. You probably need to know not merely what your workouts are going to be next week and the week after, but you probably should have an idea of where you want to be in terms of conditioning, and what you will be doing, six months from today. You may even want to plan years ahead, particularly if running is to become a lifetime activity for you. I have not given much thought to the quantity and quality of my workouts in the year 2000, but in planning my training I often think at least several years in advance.

This occurs often because I focus on specific races or events, as do many runners. Because of its tradition and glamour, the Boston Marathon has served as a focal point for many runners, some of whom started running because of a desire to run Boston some day. The Olympic Games have served as a similar focal point for many young runners, while runners over 40 point for the World Veterans Track and Field Championships, held every other year.

But planning ahead need not be restricted to the competitive elite. An individual may started a jogging program determined to lose so many pounds and reach a particular weight by a predetermined day. Or that person may want to run a certain distance without stopping, or achieve a level of fitness measured by a stress test in a human performance laboratory. Maybe the goal simply is to "feel good," obviously much more difficult to measure.

When I look forward to a specific race — and right now I am pointing (in April) for a major effort in July and another one in September — I give considerable thought to planning. I decide what type of training I need to prepare myself for that event. If a marathon, I may need long distance runs at specific mileages. If it is a track event, I may need more interval training at specific speeds. It is usually a combination of both.

I may spend several weeks thinking about a specific race and establishing a plan. Then I may spend more time revising that plan. I usually do this in solitary workouts, so it isn't as though I were taking large gaps out of my work day. In a sense this frees time to occupy my mind while running. But on certain occasions, I may come home after a run, and plot workout progressions on paper, including times and distances for specific weeks. If I know I want to be running 10 x 440 in 65 seconds the week before I compete in the world championships, I may begin that pattern of workout running 440's in 75 seconds ten weeks ahead of time and work my way down a second a week. I know that schedule will achieve my goal, not only in that final workout, but also the specific race.

Keeping a Journal

A beginning runner has no yesterday when it comes to running. That yesterday may have consisted of smoking, drinking, watching TV, and all those other things some nonrunners do. But the beginning runner can have a running "yesterday" several years from now by recording what happens today.

What this means is that every runner should keep a diary, or journal, of their running experiences. You are going to make mistakes; unless you learn from those mistakes you will make them again. Not only that, you will achieve success. To duplicate that success, you need to know why.

If you injured your knees, was it because of excessive mileage, or was it because you tripped over a log in the woods? If you improved your time at some distance, was it because of extra mileage the previous three months or because you had a cold and did little training the week before the race? Or was the reason, both? If you can't remember details about your training and activities you may never know the answers to these questions.

Most runners who record workouts simply jot down each day's mileage. They total this mileage each week, each month, and each year. I recently received a clipping from a newspaper in Chillicothe, Ohio from my friend Ralph Pidcock. The photo with the story showed him crossing a bridge, completing his 25,000th mile: enough to carry him once around the world. Unless you actually run around the world, of course, you will never know you have run enough to circle it unless you count miles. But there are other things you may want to include in a training diary:

• **Sleep.** If you feel tired while running, maybe it is from reasons other than the difficulty of your workouts. Maybe you are not getting enough sleep. Record when you go to bed and when you rise, plus any naps you take.

• **Body weight.** I have discovered that my best performances usually come when I weigh less than 137 pounds. But I often become injured when down as low as 131. I remember this because I record my weight at least on a semi-regular basis. Weigh yourself at the same time of day and on the same scale or you won't make accurate comparisons. You also may want to weigh yourself before and after workouts to get an indication of how much liquid you lose through perspiration. Some losses in body weight are seasonal; I weigh less in the summer than in the winter because I always weigh myself after workouts and sweat more in warm weather.

• **Time of day.** How much time do you take during your workouts, which may lead you to the question: How much time do you waste?

• **Surface.** What were you running on and what was the condition of the surface? Was it a fast surface or a slow one? Because many injuries are related to workout conditions, you need to know on what you train.

• **Weather.** The temperature, humidity, or wind velocity can have a major effect on your ability to run successfully.

• **Workout.** What did you do, and at what effort? If you run your best times after a month of interval training, you must know it. But don't be fooled; that six months of LSD you put in before going onto the track may have been an even greater factor in your success.

• **Assessment.** What was the quality of your workout? How tired did you feel after it? If you have an injury, does it feel better or worse as a result of that day's run? Numerous factors affect ability to perform. The more information you provide, the better you will be able to assess what happened.

I have recorded workouts on calendars, in note books, and on specially prepared workout sheets. I am now using a series of loose-leaf pages I designed myself called "The Runner's Diary." Similar workout books can be purchased, usually through ads in running publications, particularly *Runner's World*.

One of the major advantages of having a coach is that you are accountable to someone. You are not running in a vacuum but are performing daily workouts under an individual's supervision. A coach always motivates me in workouts to have someone running with me and pushing the pace or have a third person observing. Even if not standing beside the track with a stopwatch, a coach is someone to report to: "I just ran ten 440's, coach."

The diary you keep of your workouts thus can become your coach. If you decide to skip a day, training becomes a matter of "nonrecord" because you write nothing in your diary that day. The missing mileage will show up in your total at the end of the week, unless you make it up. The diary becomes one way of motivating yourself to achieve success at your chosen goal.

Of course, a diary can become a trap too. I know runners who either have injured themselves, or have not recovered from injuries because of being chained to their diaries. They were going to get those 100 miles in every week whether it did them any good or not. Common sense should always prevail—although that is easier said than done.

One last word before we leave the subject of being coached: either by someone else or yourself. It is helpful to establish goals in your running, but establish realistic goals. Not everyone can win a gold medal in the Olympics. Everyone cannot expect to do two miles nonstop. Assess your abilities and lack of abilities, and establish some realistic goal that you may be able to attain in a few months. If you attain it early, set a new goal. If you fail, either lower your sights or plan on spending more time achieving that goal.

The eventual goal of running should be enjoyment, so don't let artificial ends get in your way.

Part 5
Competition

18

All About Racing

The ins and outs of getting there and what to do when you arrive

Recently I attended a podiatrist's meeting and heard Dr. Steve Subotnick make the statement: "You have two choices in life: either to smoke, eat bad food, and die—or run a marathon." Steve spoke partly in jest, although when you hear some people talk in evangelistic terms about the benefits of jogging, running, and long-distance racing it almost seems that simple.

I resist the role of proselytizer. I see people all the time who are overweight, smoke cigarettes, drink too much, and in poor physical shape. A sound physical fitness program might offer them a better life, but if they dislike exercise, the 15 or 20 minutes they spend doing it might be the worst minutes of their day. Just because I enjoy running does not mean everybody else will.

The temptation also is great to convert joggers into runners and ultimately to racers. Many long-distance races are like the Blueberry Stomp in Plymouth, Indiana, each Labor Day. This 15-kilometer race starts immediately before a major parade; 25,000 people often line the race route which in the first and last mile coincides with the parade route. There are bands and clowns and horses and floats and a lot of runners bring their wives and children and picnic afterward. The Governor presents the winners with trophies and everybody gets gaudy t-shirts even for finishing. The Blueberry Stomp is merely typical of many such races all over America. Runners go, enjoy, and their instinct is to convert everybody to racing: "Hey, you ought to try it. It's fun."

221

Racing is fun because of what goes on around the races, but I try to resist trying to oversell this form of running as something for everybody. Yet before the recent Bonne Bell 10,000-Meter Run for women in Chicago, I would pass female joggers on Lake Shore Drive and ask: "Are you planning to run Bonne Bell?" I also encouraged several of the students in my running class at the Michigan City YMCA to participate. But it was their choice, not mine; I was merely making them aware of an opportunity to achieve another dimension in their running.

Almost every beginning runner who remains active more than three months sooner or later must face the question: "Should I race?"

Should You Race?

The most honest answer I can give to that question is that you will probably never know unless you try it at least once. One reason people in the past avoided races is that they did not want to feel embarrassed. They did not want people to laugh at them because they finished last. They feared looking foolish: an understandable reason.

I am not going to con you. If you start to race, a time will come when someone will laugh at you for the simple reason that some people are clods. I recently ran a ten-mile race in Berrien Springs, Michigan. At the gun, Bill Rodgers and a group of other fast runners bolted off the line while I lagged behind. I was running more or less alone yet still averaging a 5:20 pace around four miles when I passed some people standing on the lawn of their house. One of the men chortled: "Boy, he ain't never gonna catch them other runners. Hahahahaha."

Yet I finished 14th out of nearly 300 runners, so you can imagine what he thought when the wave of runners in the middle of the pack passed his front lawn. If he stayed out there that long. He probably went inside for a beer. So if they laugh at me, sooner or later they are going to laugh at you. Bill Rodgers gets laughed at on occasion as well, and he was the top-ranked marathoner in the world in 1977. But I never laugh at a fellow runner for finishing last, and neither does Bill. Despite differences in our ability we share a common activity. Anyone who runs becomes the recipient of tremendous waves of support from everyone else in the running community. If you don't believe me, attend any road race as a spectator and see how those in the rear of the field are received as they finish. They may be ignored on occasion, but so are the front runners. Nobody ever jeers.

Even the behavior of the clods is less offensive now, because running is considered "in" by most of the general public. My biggest hassle while training now is not fighting off dogs or enduring the taunts of teenage comedians, but rather suffering a sore arm from waving back at people who wave at me. So I developed tactics to cope with this problem. One time I wave with the right hand, the next with the left. The next person gets a nod of the head, another a smile, sometimes a spoken greeting. That gets me through races, and workouts as well.

Being Loved

One way to be loved is to finish last. Hunter Goin finishes last quite often. Hunter belongs to my club, the Indiana Striders, and his name often occupies the bottom line in race results. I sponsored a 10,000-meter race called the Frostbite Frolic in Long Beach in January that attracted maybe three dozen runners. Hunter crossed the finish line last. But Hunter is capable of finishing last in much larger fields than that. He doesn't intend finishing last, but it usually happens. One thing is certain in most Indiana races: you rarely have to worry about being the last-finisher, because Hunter will be still out there on the course. Unless you drop out; then Hunter is going to beat you because Hunter Goin never fails to finish.

Hunter Goin also is a movie star, because they made a film of the 1977 Mayor Daley Marathon and at one stage the camera focused on Hunter running in a group of other runners. He didn't finish last in that race, because with the increasing popularity of long distance running a lot of other Hunter Goins have begun to surface. One thing to remember: no matter how slow you think you are, sooner or later somebody will come along who is even slower if you keep at it long enough.

Hunter does not seem discouraged by his numerous last-place finishes. In fact, each year the Hoosier Road Runners Club awards a trophy to the individual who competes in the most point-races each year, and Hunter Goin often wins it. Nobody feels sorry for Hunter, nor does Hunter feel sorry for himself. I cannot recall anybody ever saying to me: "Gee, if Hunter only would add some interval work to his training, maybe he would improve to next-to-last." How fast he runs seems unimportant to him or to his friends, who accept him for what he is. What is important is that Hunter Goin seems to enjoy what he is doing, and we enjoy having him around doing it.

The Hunter Goins also communicate very easily with the Bill Rodgers' and the Frank Shorters. Runners at all levels of ability possess a shared interest. The fact that one finishes first in a race and another finishes last seems not to matter when they get together afterward. If fear of appearing foolish keeps you from competing, fear not. Everyone loves a slow runner. You can be right back there with Hunter Goin if you keep at it long enough.

Getting to the Race

You probably won't have difficulty finding a race to run; more often the race will find you. Long-distance running has become so popular in the United States that most major cities have at least one mass race that attracts several thousand entries and considerable publicity. Most such cities also have dozens of smaller races or low-pressure fun runs that attract varying numbers of runners. Watch your local newspaper and you usually will see news items about upcoming events. Even if you do not feel ready to race, you can attend one and obtain entry blanks and information about others later in the season.

Other good sources of information about running events are your local YMCA or track coaches at high schools and colleges. You may find a local running club whose members can help ease your way into racing. The most active organization of long distance runners is the Road Runners Club of America, 1111 Army-Navy Drive, Arlington, Virginia 22202. Write that organization and ask for the name and address of the branch nearest you. Always enclose a *large* stamped return envelope; you are more likely to obtain a fast reply. (Jeff Darmon, RRCA president, commented to me while requesting the word large be added to the previous sentence in reference to envelopes: "I am always amazed that the amount of information requested is usually inversely proportional to the size of the envelope sent." *Runner's World* (Box 366, Mountain View, California 94042) also includes monthly information on races in many areas; one problem being that so many races exist that listing them in any single publication no longer is possible. Many regional, state, or club publications and newsletters contain running information.

If all the above fails, simply stop the next runner that you en-counter while jogging down the road and ask. Well, maybe you shouldn't *stop* the runner, but at least run alongside for a short distance while you ask your questions. Pick someone who looks like a racer. One problem in stopping runners is that so many new people lately have joined the sport that they may be stop-ping *you* to ask questions. Tell them to buy this book.

You can get plugged into the system sooner or later. Once that is accomplished you will have no difficulty locating more races than you can possibly run.

Going to the Race

No policy exists to tell you how you can enter races, because races occur at all levels of organization. At some loosely organ-ized fun runs, for example, a single official carrying a stopwatch may appear 15 minutes before the scheduled start and begin handing out numbers and safety pins. At many low-key events runners do not even enter; simply show up and run. Someone reads off times as the runners cross the line, but nobody bothers to record them. *Runner's World* magazine sponsors numerous fun-runs, awarding certificates for achievement depending on a runner's time, often on the honor system.

You must enter major races sometimes as much as a month in advance, although one week is more common. Some races accept post entries (people who enter on race day), but penalize these latecomers by charging a higher fee. A few events limit entries, permitting a set number to start, or require that runners meet a specified time standard. The Boston Marathon requires entrants to have run a previous marathon faster than three hours (3:30 for women and men over 40). Certain events such as high school or collegiate races may be limited to eligible run-ners. There are races for women, men over 40, and children in various age categories.

The simplest rule before going to any race is to obtain an entry blank and follow the instructions that you find on it. Don't trust the times and dates you see listed on race schedules which are often prepared months in advance. Make sure there actually is a race before you travel very far to get to it.

You may need an AAU card to enter some races. The Ama-teur Athletic Union once controlled all track-and-field as well as long distance races in the United States. That is no longer true.

Even when the entry blank asks for an AAU number, you may not be required to provide one. Race organizers formerly requested that competitors obtain a physician's signature before competing, but this gesture has almost disappeared.

The AAU has been waging a battle with organizations such as the USTFF, the NCAA, the RRCA, and others over who should have jurisdiction over amateur sports, but as a new racer you do not want to get involved in the politics of running. The AAU is an effective organization in a few states, but in other states seems to subvert the sport. More often the AAU is merely neutral, doing neither much good nor much bad. If required to register in the AAU the first time you enter a race, slide along, pay your money ($3.50 per card in most associations) then make up your mind, based on your experience, if it is worth renewing it a year later.

The Hoosier Road Runners Club in Indiana, because of interference from the Indiana AAU, resigned en masse. Because our club organized most of the AAU races, the Indiana AAU long-distance running program virtually ceased to exist. The races continued although under different names. I have not held an AAU card for three years, yet have run as a member of the Hoosier RRC in local, national, and international races with very few problems. AAU officials tried to block my entry into races three times: but on two of these occasions I ran anyway. I see signs that the AAU is improving in certain areas but deteriorating in others.

At the Race

You will sometimes receive instructions by mail on how to pick up your number; you will sometimes receive the number itself. But most likely you will need to report to a specific place before the race.

Do not panic. The scene may seem hectic, but look around for signs. Do what the signs tell you to do or where to go. Stand in the line that looks appropriate, making certain if you are a woman that it is not the line to the men's toilet, vice versa if you are a man. Somebody will sooner or later hand you a package with a number or simply a number itself. If you have to pay at that point, come equipped with exact change. Smile a lot. Be polite. Sign anything they hand you. Get out of the way fast so the other thousand runners behind you in line can get served.

Now go stand in line for the toilet, making sure it's the right line.

Most numbers should be pinned to the front of your shirt with safety pins. Sometimes race sponsors offer only two pins in the envelope, often small ones. I usually bring extra pins for all four corners of the number, to prevent it from flapping in the breeze. That tip probably is as important as teaching you how to run fartlek.

You may be able to find a place to change clothes, although at the smaller ones, you may change in your car. Runners frequently just come ready to run, already dressed in their racing uniform (if they have one) and warmup suit. Even if you plan to go out somewhere to eat after the race, you may want to come dressed to run, particularly since warmup suits now have become both attractive and fashionable. Following the Bonne Bell 10,000-Meter Race for women in Chicago, my family and I stopped off for brunch at a fashionable restaurant. Other people in the restaurant, having just come from church, wore suits and dresses but we neither looked out of place nor felt that way.

If you do plan to shower and change after a race, however, be sure to bring a towel as well as a combination lock for protection.

Before any race you can see runners sitting around going through the rites of their avocation: taping toes, rubbing petroleum over their bodies, dusting their shoes with talcum powder. I use few such aids. I simply put on my shoes and shorts and run. If you remain in running long, experience sooner or later will teach you what preparations you need if you need them.

Experience also will teach you to provide for your eliminatory needs, because large numbers at any race usually means long lines to the toilets. I try to visit the toilet before I arrive at the race, either at my home or hotel, or by stopping for gasoline (and a rest room) just before arriving. At Boston, however, I often just use the woods nearby. Another way to avoid lines is to wait until the last two minutes before the race, when all the other competitors are standing on the starting line. But this takes nerves of steel, and stomach muscles of the same material.

Going to the Line

Runners begin drifting toward the starting line from 30 to 5 minutes before the scheduled gun. Simply follow the mob.

Races today have a much better record for getting off on time than previously. They often began 15 or 30 minutes late depending on when and if officials appeared. Today, large races require so much coordination between officials and traffic police, that they often start with such split-second accuracy you often can set your watch by them. The starter will not wait for you, so be ready to run.

Start far in the back if you are a newcomer to racing so you won't interfere with faster runners. Notice I said "faster," not "fastest." Race sponsors increasingly provide the fastest runners with low numbers and a reserved position on the front row so that they can run unimpeded. Sorting out the ones behind them is done more haphazardly. Sponsors may place signs identifying areas for runners capable of running a 6:00, 7:00, 8:00 or even slower mile. Sometimes such signs are not easily spotted in a mass of humanity and even when seen may not be understood by someone who never has raced. Start in the last row if in doubt.

It is possible for someone unqualified to push their way to near the front row and stand near a Don Kardong or a Garry Bjorklund when the gun sounds. Some people do it because of exhibitionism, others because of ignorance. These people do not penalize the fast runners who will be off at the gun and away from them anyway, but the average runners in the middle will have to go around them eventually and may be blocked in their efforts to run a respectable race.

If the weather is warm (and few novices run their first event in snowstorms), you may be able to leave your warmup suit in your locker or car. But you may need to stand near that line five or ten minutes before the gun sounds, and if the weather is cold you may want to keep your sweat suit on to avoid freezing prematurely. (Once the race begins, you need less clothes to keep warm.) If someone has accompanied you to the race, they may hold your warmups when you strip at the last minute. One advantage of belonging to a running club or any such group of runners, is that somebody is usually along willing to grab sweats. If not, and the race finishes at the same point it starts, you may be able to simply leave your gear under a convenient tree. In 1978 before the Boston Marathon, which is a point-to-point race, I wore a raggedy pair of sweats I planned to throw away anyway and simply left them at the curb after I stripped. But I cannot do this often, otherwise I will run out of raggedy sweats.

Warming Up

I always warm up before any race to make certain I am loose and ready to run. I have seen physiological "studies" that seemingly prove that runners do not benefit from a warmup and other "studies" that prove the opposite. I don't care what the physiologists say; I know what my body tells me. I need to warm up if I expect to obtain maximum performance at any race.

The first time I appeared at the Boston Marathon in 1959, I was surprised by how few runners warmed up properly. I went out in the field behind the gymnasium in Hopkinton to do a mile or so of jogging and about the only ones out there were the two Finnish runners, me, and a handful of others. The Finns usually finished in the top few positions so this should have told everybody something.

Now at Boston, it seems like more runners warm up, although the percentages may not have changed. There are simply more runners. Many marathoners apparently feel that if asked to run 26 miles 385 yards, they should not also be expected to increase that daily amount to 27 or 28 by a preliminary warmup.

I warm up for a road race similar to the way I had been taught to warm up for a track race. I usually begin by jogging a mile or two at an easy pace, then stop and do some stretching exercises for five minutes or so: nothing in the way of severe calisthenics, just some gentle tugging and massaging of muscles that will be carrying me through the race that day. I may then stride about 100 yards three or four times. How fast I do these strides depends in part on how fast I will be racing that day. If the race is a mile, meaning a first-lap pace of near 60 seconds for 440 yards, I will need to stride (or sprint) faster than for a marathon where an opening 440 in 80 or 90 seconds may keep me on pace. (Even that may be too slow in a crowded field where I must start fast to avoid being trampled.)

I rest between the jogging, stretching, and striding. Lie down. Relax. When I go to the line, I may do some easy jogging, stretching, and striding. Lie down. Relax. When I go to the line, I may do some more easy jogging, stretching, and shaking, partly to stay loose but partly from nervousness. Experience will tell you the best warmup for your particular needs.

Part of the reason for my warmup is to loosen not only my body but also my bowels. I don't want to have to stop mid-race and search for a toilet. And it also gives me something to allay nervousness in the hour before the gun.

I find myself more and more frequently utilizing a pre-warmup the same day. If I awaken around 6:00 AM for a race scheduled to start anywhere from 8:00 to noon, I may go out for an easy shakedown of one or two miles, then return to bed.

Those runners who do not warmup at Boston may not need as much warmup because of their differing philosophical approach to the race. If you are not performance-oriented and don't plan on finishing in the medals, you probably do not need to cut that extra 30 or 60 seconds off your time by being instantly ready. A relaxed runner simply can start slow and warmup during the first few miles before getting into the flow of the race. This may save that person some energy that later can be expended toward the end of the race. Possibly. But slow runners may expend more energy running stiff than they would in a warmup.

During the Race

Follow the leader. Unless you are blessed with unusual speed or talent, or the race is a small one where the field quickly separates, you need not worry about which way to go. There will be dozens, maybe hundreds, thousands, of other runners ahead of you leading the way. If one gets lost, everybody gets lost.

Nevertheless, it helps to have some knowledge of the course you will be running. Drive over it the night before if you have time. If that is not possible, examine a map of the course to get a general idea of what turns you will take and what landmarks you will pass. There may be mileage markers so you can tell how far you have gone, but sometimes you may miss them. It helps if you remember that you pass a big lake at the half-way point.

Although you should run workouts on the side of the road facing traffic, you may be asked by police to run a race with traffic at your back. Or in some races where automobile traffic has been eliminated, such as the New York City Marathon, you may run right down the middle of the street. Run defensively, just as you would in practice, and don't run blindly through intersections — even with traffic policemen standing nearby — assuming that cars will stop just because you wear a number on your chest.

Officials read times to runners at different intervals at most races, usually at the first mile, then in increments of two, three, or five miles; or sometimes in kilometers. Find out in advance where they will be giving you times and anticipate them if you care about your pace. If you are running far back in the field, however, you may discover that the officials have left before you arrive at the markers; another reason to wear a watch and time yourself.

In hot weather it may be important that you take liquids along the course, so do not fail to do so. The elite runners some-times are so impervious to dehydration that they whisk right past the water points, not wishing to slow their stride and lose a single second. Or they may have friends hand them plastic squeeze bottles filled with some specially prepared liquid. I have trained myself not merely to run, but to drink on the run.

You should not bypass any water stations, particularly if the day is hot. Most runners grab cups of water or other liquids from the hands of those manning the water points, but invari-ably they spill some in this way, and they may spill more trying to gulp it down. If you are not attempting to break a world record, stop to walk as you pass a water point and carefully drain each drop from the cup. Take another cup if you want. Unless you consciously force yourself, you may not get enough liquids in you on even moderately cool days. You can pick up the pace again after drinking, and you will have lost less time than you think. On hot days accept all other aid offered in the way of sponges or sprinkling from hoses.

Don't be afraid to stop and walk, for refreshment or simply from fatigue. If the hill ahead of you seems too high to run, walk up it. "Honor" be damned. If running down the other side jars your muscles too much, walk down. If you know you are going to walk at some point during a race, it is best to walk before forced by fatigue to do so. If you stop with some reserve, it will be easier to start running again.

Anticipating possible collapse in certain races, I sometimes practice what I might call a disaster drill to become familiar with the rhythm of stopping and starting again. One secret I have used in marathons, and which may make finishing easier for you, is that I never stop to walk without first deciding how soon I will start running again. I pick out a tree, or a lamp post, or a parked car 50,100, or 200 yards ahead at which point I return to a running pace. That may carry me only a few steps further, but when I walk a second time, I pick out still another point. Using this method I sooner or later get to the finish line.

If forced to sit or lie down, however, I find it very, very difficult to resume the chase.

Finishing

Sooner or later you will cross a finish line if you persevere. As you come across the line listen to hear if someone is reading your time, or look to see if there is a clock displaying that time. Unless you wear a watch, it may be your only way to obtain your time for many hours, days, and weeks after the race, if ever. Though some race organizers now computerize results, the glut of runners causes even the computers sometimes to fail.

Different races handle their finishers in different ways, but you will usually be funneled into a chute. Trust the officials around you. Obey them. Do not stop on the finish line once you cross it, but walk to avoid getting in the way of those finishing behind you. Somebody at the end of the chute will either record your number or tear off some preattached card enabling them to identify your finishing position. Sometimes they hand you a slip or stick telling you where you finish. Sometimes they will ignore you. This is all right too. If you don't obtain your time or place in this manner, don't bother the officials at the line. They probably will not be able to help you, and you may only make their job much harder. I told you to wear a watch.

Cool down slowly after your race. You may want to change into a dry shirt. Don your warmup suit if the weather is too cool. Use liquid refreshments if available. Relax and get to know the other runners. You all will have great war stories about your battles out there on that day.

Competing in a long-distance race usually is much less complex than indicated in this chapter. Thousands of runners have been going to races for years without much advance instruction. They simply go and do what other people do, and learn by seeing how other runners act. There is nothing complex about racing. You will be able to obtain information about future competitions after the race—*if* you want to attend them!

This last is very important. You do not need to race to be a runner. To some, racing is an end in itself, and they point all their training for competing on weekends. Others, however, are turned off by the whole scene. They do not want to either win, lose, or compete in a herd of hundreds or thousands of others. That is fine. Every individual should find their own niche.

You will never know if you enjoy long-distance races unless you try—at least once.

A GUIDE FOR BEGINNING RACERS

PHASE ONE

The training principles for long-distance races differ little from the guide for beginning runners in chapter four. The main change is: Instead of testing yourself every second week by testing how far you can run, you test yourself by entering a race. Another difference is that you may want to increase your mileage if you decide to race. You also may want to substitute interval-training, repeats, or fartlek for previous fast/slow workouts depending on the experience you have gained. Phase One of this Guide for Beginning Racers starts where the final phase of the Guide for Beginning Runners stopped. Because most races are on a weekend, modify your training by shifting the hardest day of the week to one of those days and begin from there.

PHASE TWO

Plan to run five to six days a week, taking a day or two off depending on your fatigue.

Sunday: Four to six miles at a comfortable pace.
Monday: Interval training: 5 x 440, walk or jog 440 between.
Tuesday: Easy jogging or rest.
Wednesday: Four to six miles at a comfortable pace.
Thursday: Fartlek 30 minutes, or some fast repeats such as 3 x 220.
Friday: Rest before competition.
Saturday: Race one to three miles. Enter for fun, not competition. Select some low-pressure event, perhaps a fitness mile or fun run, for your first effort against other runners. Try to ignore their presence, however, during the race. Do not attempt to sprint at the end, but finish comfortably.

Move to Phase Three after you have tried this level of racing several times, or if you feel that you want a greater challenge.

PHASE THREE

Plan to run six days a week. You must be regular and consistent with your training if you want to become a racer.

Sunday: Six to eight miles at a comfortable pace.
Monday: Interval training: 6-8 x 440, walk or jog 440 between.
Tuesday: Easy jogging.
Wednesday: Fartlek 30-45 minutes, or some fast repeats such as 3 x 330.
Thursday: Four to six miles at a comfortable pace.
Friday: Rest for tomorrow's race.

Saturday: Race three to six miles. Pick some event that attracts a small field of local runners. Begin at a slow and comfortable pace and do not push yourself too soon. If you feel good in the last third of the race, maintain the steady rhythm with which you began, or try to increase your pace. Do not necessarily race every weekend, but once you feel comfortable at this level of competition, move to phase four.

PHASE FOUR

Plan to run six to seven days a week, taking a day off before the race only if you feel you need some extra rest.

Sunday: Ten to twelve miles at a comfortable pace.
Monday: Interval training: 10 x 440, walk or jog 440 between. Once you feel comfortable with this number, run your 440s progressively faster in succeeding weeks, but do not progress more than one second a week.
Tuesday: Easy jogging.
Wednesday: Fartlek 45-60 minutes, or some fast repeats such as 3 x 440.
Thursday: Six to eight miles at a comfortable pace.
Friday: Easy jogging or complete rest.
Saturday: Race six to ten miles. Go to one of the better weekend runs that attract a large field. Estimate the time it will take you to go the distance and try to maintain that pace.

After you become comfortable competing at this level, move on to Phase Five.

PHASE FIVE

Run every day unless you feel you need an occasional day off.

Sunday: Fourteen to 16 miles. You may have found some runners who take long workouts each weekend. Go with them if you don't feel trapped by their pace.
Monday: Interval training: 10 x 440 (or begin to substitute other distances such as 220s, 660s, 880s, miles). Jog between.
Tuesday: Easy jogging.
Wednesday: Fartlek 60 minutes, or some fast repeats. You also may want to try some flatout sprints such as 10 x 100, jogging between.
Thursday: Eight to ten miles at a comfortable pace.
Friday: Easy jogging.
Saturday: Race 5 to 15 miles. You should begin to know some of the other runners in the field who are near you in ability. You may not necessarily want to race to beat them, but you can run competitively with them. Begin to experiment with your own pace. Go out at a faster pace than usual to see if you can survive. Are you able to push yourself during the middle of the race when others around you start to fade? Can you dig into your reserves and still muster a bit of a kick at the end?

If so you have become a racer. Continue to explore the edges of your ability, realizing at the same time it is less important that you achieve a victory over others than over yourself.

You are ready to take the final step to phase six.

PHASE SIX

Stop thinking of yourself as a runner and consider yourself a racer. By joining a running club and subscribing to newsletters, become aware of the various levels of races in other parts of the country. Begin to plan your races months in advance. If there is one race or time of year when you want to be at your best, plan your training to reach a peak of conditioning at the proper time. Do not lose your humility and think that simply because you race you are better than you were at your previous levels. You are simply a different individual. Be free with advice to other runners coming up. You may want to give some serious consideration to running your first marathon at this point. Examine the Guide for Beginning Marathoners at the end of the next chapter.

19

Stalking the Wild Marathon

Facts and training secrets for conquering the beast

The first marathon, run during the initial modern Olympic Games in 1896, covered a mere 25 miles. It commemorated the feat of the legendary Pheidippides who, following the Battle of Marathon, supposedly ran into Athens with news of the Greek victory over the Persians, said "Rejoice, we conquer," then died. I say "supposedly," because historians suspect that the legend owes more to fiction than to fact.

At the 1908 Olympics in London, officials shifted the marathon starting line to Buckingham Palace so the queen could watch the beginning of the race. By chance, Buckingham Palace was exactly 26 miles 385 yards from the finish line in the Olympic stadium. That mileage thus became the official distance still being run.

Next time you pass 25 miles, your feet sore, your legs aching, your breath coming in gasps, with the finish line still more than a mile away, think "God save the Queen!" Or words to that effect.

We will never know if the marathon would possess the mystique it has today if the distance had remained 25 miles—or at some other distance such as 40 kilometers. There is certainly a lack of appeal to the name: the Boston 40-Kilometer Run. Marathon has a much better ring to it.

The word "marathon" is much abused. In my community each year they hold bridge marathons for card-players. The recent promotion of a Chicago radio station titled "Marathon

1978" was actually a fund-raising drive for the Chicago sym-
phony Orchestra. An oil company uses the name. Newspapers
frequently talk about labor leaders or heads of state engaging in
"marathon negotiations." Certain members of the general public
seem to equate "marathon" with any long-distance race,
regardless of length. So do many new runners.

A woman called recently and said: "I'm interested in entering
your marathon." She was referring to a 15-kilometer run. I still
have a trophy from the "Freeport Harbor Marathon." It was
three miles — six laps around the town square. Yet to any long
distance runner the word marathon means precisely 26 miles
385 yards — and the course better be certified as accurate or the
race director will receive complaints.

Would the marathon have the same mystique under any other
name? Probably. The mystique of this unique event grew because of the people drawn to it; particularly because of the
hordes of relatively untalented runners to whom finishing this
distance becomes a supreme accomplishment no matter how
slow their time. Once you have run 26 miles 385 yards, your life
will never again be the same. No matter what happens to you
from that moment, you can always look back and say: "I once
finished a marathon." You may even want it engraved on your
tombstone — if you ever die. Some people believe marathoners
may possess immortality.

Talk to any first-time marathon finishers a week after their
accomplishment. Their legs will have ceased to hurt by then,
they will be walking naturally, their blisters and sunburn will
have healed, they may even be back out running at their regular
speed again. But the glow will still surround them.
"Did you finish the marathon?" Instant smile.

Deciding to Run the Marathon

I try not to be a proselytizer for running. I am not an evan-
gelist in the sense of a Ken Cooper bringing his message of
aerobic fitness to the millions. I do not say, as Dr. Steve Subotnick says, "Run a marathon or die!" I try not to convert people
to running other than by my daily presence on the road. If
people want to try it, fine; but I don't tell them to try it.

But once a person begins to jog then moves from fitness jogger to recreational runner, I think that person should seriously

consider a marathon. Why? As Senator Robert F. Kennedy said during his final campaign in 1968: "People ask me why? I ask them, why not?"

So I tell other runners to go out and run a marathon—at least one, just so they can say they did it, then go back to a normal two-miles-a-day fitness regimen. My position on whether or not to run marathons has shifted in the past few years, but that is because the focus of the event has shifted from a rather grueling and unsmiling race to a joyful participatory event.

During my first visit to the Boston Marathon in 1959, the field included only a few hundred veterans. I could count the number of American marathons on one hand, and there were not that many more other races over ten miles. So few were the long distance runners that I knew practically everybody in the field at Boston, because I saw them race after race, year after year. The numbers explosion was yet to occur.

Most of these veterans were dedicated, serious men who trained hard and raced hard. Back in this era few people finished much after 3:30. Hardly anybody ran that slow. Even the slowest runners trained to complete the race at a 7:00 or 8:00 pace, and soon quit if they began to fall behind because nobody ran any slower than that. Dr. Kenneth Cooper showed up at the Boston Marathon in 1962 while doing graduate work at Harvard Medical School and finished 101st just under four hours in last place. (To place 101st at Boston in 1978, you had to run 2:26:56.) The only reason Ken received his time was that his wife Millie begged the officials to stay until her husband crossed the line. It was like running in a vacuum, so few people were around him.

Today, the bulk of the field has just begun to cross the finish line between 3:30 and 4:00. Officials at the Mayor Daley Marathon in Chicago continue timing finishers through six hours now. The Honolulu Marathon prides itself on timing everybody, no matter how far back, and boasts their "record" time as over eight hours. While serving as a consultant for the first Chicago Distance Classic in 1977, I wanted to get an idea of when we could expect the maximum number of finishers in that 20-kilometer run. I assumed the rate at which people finished would follow the classic bell curve with a few at the front, a few at the end, with a peak in the middle. Then I analyzed the results of the Revco-Western Reserve Marathon held a few months before and discovered to my surprise that no such curve existed. The few in front and few in back were there, but the middle was a long plateau (instead of a curve) that extended from 3:00 to 4:30. Runners seemed to be spread out evenly, with as many crossing the line near the end of that period as before.

More people run marathons today at a relatively gentle pace: one reason why I tell recreational runners that they should try one — *at least one.*

Another reason is the tremendous sense of accomplishment it will give them. One of the participants in the 1977 Mayor Daley Marathon was the wife of Charles Murphy, a well-known Chicago architect. She finished somewhere over five hours and staggered immediately to bed where she lay unable to move for the next 18 hours, groaning and moaning. Murphy later commented: "I was going to call an ambulance, except all the time she lay there she kept repeating over and over, 'This is the greatest thing that ever happened to me!'"

Murphy also recently had purchased his wife an expensive emerald broach. He later told Lee Flaherty, president of Flair Merchandising and sponsor of the Mayor Daley Marathon: "I paid all that money on the emerald broach and you spent maybe five cents for the certificate she received for finishing the marathon — and if it came to a choice, I know which one she would keep!"

As Don Young, a Chicago public relations executive, commented while standing near the finish line: "Welcome to the world of personal achievement."

How Difficult Is the Marathon?

Flaherty made a 20-minute film during the marathon. He included an interview with an attractive, middle-aged woman who had come all the way from California to participate. Her face glowed with her sense of accomplishment, and after discussing the tribulations of her hours on the road, she said, almost as an aside: "I've only been running for four months."

I have shown that film before numerous groups of runners while lecturing at clinics and, invariably, a groan of scepticism escapes from the crowd at her remark. Most of the audience understands the price you must pay, particularly in hours and miles of training, to be able to run 26 miles 385 yards. I also suspect that the woman meant she had been running only four months to prepare for that particular race, or if she did take her first running step that recently, maybe the previous 30 years had been a career as a mountain climber, roller derby star, or ballerina. I keep asking friends of mine from California if they recognize her, but nobody does. One of these days I'm going to track down that woman and ask her if she really ran the race on only four months training.

Nevertheless, it probably can be done. It depends on the point of view you bring to the race. Four months have passed since the first day I met my class at the Michigan City YMCA, and although the class is no longer in session most of those individuals now are running on their own. Four or five of them could go out next weekend and finish a marathon, although I would not suggest that they do so. They would take longer to recover than Charles Murphy's wife. For their own comfort, if they should decide to make such a commitment, I would hope they plan a more gradual buildup to such an event.

Almost anybody can finish a marathon. Barring any limiting physical defect almost any moderately conditioned individual can cover 26 miles 385 yards at an easy walk. If you walk at a modest three miles an hour, you can make the finish line in nine hours. Marathoners run into problems when they try to reduce this time to eight, seven, six, five, four, three, or nearly two hours. Fast runners have more trouble finishing marathons than slow runners. I made four attempts at the marathon before I crossed the finish line, but that was because I always wanted to *win* the race rather than merely *finish*. If your motivation is to finish the distance, your goal and approach are different.

People have finished marathons who were blind, had one leg, or had no feet. People also race marathons in wheel chairs although that brings their accomplishment closer to a bicycle race. During the marathon connected with the World Masters track-and-field championships in Sweden in 1977, I was passed near the 15-kilometer mark by a blind runner over 40 from Germany named Werner Rathert. He was being guided by a tether to Manfred Steffny, a former German Olympian. I was stunned by the speed at which they were moving since I was en route to a 2:38 that day. I eventually repassed the blind runner, but learned that he has a best-time of 2:36, which probably should not have amazed me since another blind German athlete named F. Assmy won the 100 meters and 200 meters in the 60-64 division. There seem to be no handicaps in running, only variations of ability.

The Ultimate Experience

I do not recommend that anyone run a marathon on only four months of training. I suggest that if you are a total beginner you spend at least a year in preparation, preferably two years. You may be physically ready sooner than you are mentally ready. Why rush to eat the dessert. Explore the many delights of long-distance running before tasting what for many is the ultimate experience. Savor what you have and you will enjoy your accomplishment more. That sounds like an argument for chastity before marriage, but that is how I feel about the marathon.

In a postscript to my book *On the Run from Dogs and People* written in 1971, I suggested a two-year buildup to the marathon — and still consider the advice sound. The first year was to have been spent by a previously sedentary individual shedding excess poundage, abandoning all bad habits in relation to cigarettes, diet, liquor, and sleep; and reaching a point where an occasional hour's run could be enjoyable, not a strain.

The second year would permit a move from jogging to running. Because we have already covered some of the training by people who compete in ordinary long-distance races — up to 20 miles — let us consider some aspects of the marathon that are different.

Marathon Fact 1: It is a very long race in terms of mileage. The marathon is more than twice as long as the average distance run competitively in the United States. The most common length for long-distance races seems to be ten miles. Fifteen- and twenty-kilometer races are often scheduled, as are shorter distances, but though races are held at 25 and 30 kilometers and occasionally 20 miles, races at those distances are relatively rare. So if you plan to run a marathon, it means that you must often double the distance you normally cover in competition.

Marathon Fact 2: It is a very long race in terms of time. Apart from the distance covered, think of the time it takes.

Most runners will spend three or four hours on the course, often in difficult weather, sometimes under a hot sun. Even three or four hours lying on a beach or sitting at your desk performing some task can be taxing. You are going to spend three or four hours on your feet in a marathon concentrating on the same task (moving one foot in front of the other) time after time after time.

Marathon Fact 3: There is a wall. Unless you pace yourself extremely well and have trained with great diligence, you will hit this wall at 20 miles. Without getting too involved in detail, thé body can store enough glycogen to provide energy for two hours of activity; when it is gone the body must begin to convert fats into glucose for fuel. The body does this very, very grudgingly. It is said that the first half of the race is 20 miles; the second half of the race the last six. After that, the final 385 yards are a snap.

Marathon Fact 4: The race is psychologically as well as physically demanding. Apart from any physiological barrier, there is a psychological barrier that occurs in any endurance race when about two-thirds of the distance has been covered. Milers encounter this "down" point in the third quarter but they have only little more than 440 yards to finish. Your last "quarter" in the marathon includes six miles of more running.

Marathon Fact 5: If anything is going to go wrong, it will. Minor irritations become major irritations when extended over several hours. Tiny imperfections in a shoe that will cause only slight discomfort in a ten-mile race will raise massive blisters in 26 miles 385 yards. I wore one competitive vest in many short races without a problem, but the shoulder straps kept slipping off my shoulders when I wore it in a marathon. I had to constantly reposition the shirt on my torso, as though the vest rebelled at being worn for the excess distance. Various other parts of your body and equipment will similarly rebel if subjected to the marathon.

Marathon Fact 6: The event is running's biggest production number. It is the difference between *The King and I,* with its magnificent costumes and startling scenery, and a Harold Pinter play like *The Caretaker* with its half dozen characters on a single set.

Marathons are big. They attract more runners and more spectators and more publicity; particularly the big ones such as

Boston, New York, and the Mayor Daley. There are bands, banners, and often helicopters swooping overhead. There is danger that the runner may become so overwhelmed by the pageantry that before he knows it he has been swept past the first mile en route to 26 faster than he could run that distance in a single race.

How Far Should You Run in Practice?

In the TV movie, "See How She Runs," Joanne Woodward is asked about her ability to compete the Boston Marathon, the goal she has chosen to revitalize her life as a middle-aged house-wife. Her response is: "They say if you can run 13 miles in prac-tice, you can go the whole distance." I'm not sure who "they" were who supposedly offered that advice, but it is not very sound. In her preparations for Boston, the character Woodward played in the movie finally struggled through one 13-mile work-out, hitting the wall at around 11 miles. She staggered to the finish line of the Boston Marathon, bleeding from a fall, prac-tically on her hands and knees in the dark of night long after the last official starters had finished their bowl of stew in the Prudential building garage. If finishing like that is your goal, a single 13-mile workout will probably guarantee it.

To finish the marathon in reasonable comfort and respectable time, however, you probably should do more. Maybe "they" told the character played by Joanne Woodward that if she ran occa-sional 13-mile workouts in practice in reasonable comfort, she could go 26 in a race. But she heard only what she wanted to hear.

Training to run a marathon is not very different from training to run any other long-distance event. The same train-ing patterns work as well for marathons as for ten-mile races. If you are an hour-a-day runner covering 50 miles a week, you need not add many more miles. But you should make some im-portant modifications in your schedule. The seven secrets in finishing your first marathon:

First Secret: Get out for a longer run at least once a week.
It need not be excessively long to begin with. If you have become accustomed to running an hour several times a week, add an extra 10 or 15 minutes on one of those occasions. The best time to do this is on the weekend, when you may have more time. Or if you think of your long run in terms of miles instead

of minutes, and you have been going eight miles, add an extra mile or two.

If this seems like too much of a strain, maybe you are going the extra distance at the same pace as your normal workouts. So slow down. Do the extra time or distance at a gentler pace so as not to convert what had been a normal workout into a difficult one. Be content to go farther, not faster. When you feel comfortable at this extended distance you are ready to consider the next secret.

Second Secret: Begin to run continously farther. Several weeks after having increased your distance from eight to ten miles, add another increment to your run. Move from 10 to 12 miles and see how you feel. Explore the edges of your fatigue and as you become comfortable with one distance move up another. But don't move too fast. If two-mile progressions seem difficult, move up in one-mile stages. When you move to a new level, remain on that plateau for a while and gather yourself before the next jump. Your body should dictate how soon you are ready to move, but I recommend that you stay at one mileage at least a month. Consolidate your gain before moving on. The secret in making the move easier is:

Third Secret: Rob Peter to pay Paul. Just because you increase your mileage in one workout a week, you need not increase your total mileage or your normal time commitments. Cut your workout in half the day before your scheduled long run to allow yourself to train long while well-rested. If you have been covering eight miles on the day before, cut the workout to four miles. Or take a day off. As you increase mileage on your one long day, you also may want to schedule a second half-workout the day after your long run to permit proper recovery. At the same time, you should keep another point in mind.

Fourth Secret: Mileage may be less important than time. Remember that not merely are you going to have to cover 26 miles 385 yards, but you are going to be on that course for a specific time, whether four hours or what. It may be important that you adjust to the demands on your body for such a long time. So go for several runs where you simply spend the time running that period, regardless of how slowly. This also will help you overcome the psychological problem of spending so much time doing one thing.

Fifth Secret: Have a goal. The 13 miles suggested to Joanne

Woodward probably isn't enough. If you are going to finish a marathon, you might as well finish well. A reasonable goal would be anywhere from two-thirds to three-fourths of the distance you plan to race. This would mean 16 to 20 miles on one workout a week. When you reach the point where you have been doing weekly workouts in that 16 to 20 mile range, you should be well prepared to finish a marathon. You may not even need to hit that mileage in practice every week; every other week might be enough.

Sixth Secret: Plan your progression. Have not only an ultimate goal of running a marathon, but plan to run a *specific* marathon. If you know when you want to run your first marathon, you can plan your progression with logical steps that allow you to reach the necessary mileage by a fixed date. If you begin at the eight-mile stage anticipating a race six months hence, you know that merely by adding two miles to your one workout each month will bring you to a weekly workout of 20 miles by race day. Knowing this, you will realize there is no need to panic by doing too much too soon. Six months lead time is probably minimum for someone preparing for their first marathon, but you might want to take even more.

Seventh Secret: Add a second long workout to the middle of your week. This workout should be longer than what used to be your usual regular workout, but not as long as your single long run each week. A good rule of thumb would be to cover three-fourths the distance of this longest run. If you cover 16 miles on Sunday, you might want to do 12 miles on Wednesday. If you reach 20 miles, you may want to have another run at 15 at a faster pace: FCR instead of LSD. Again, rob Peter to pay Paul, blending short days with long days. If you find it difficult to go that far at midweek because of your other schedules, consider doing double workouts on one day—a run in the morning and a run in the evening—to at least get your mileage on one day.

If you utilize these seven secrets, it may not make your first marathon faster but it probably will make it more comfortable. For a more detailed approach, examine the weekly guide lines at the end of this chapter.

Preparing for the Big Day

If you have trained adequately, you should be able to coast

into the race without panic and without worrying that you need to get in that last 20-mile run at good speed the Sunday before to prove to yourself that you can finish. Anything good that happens to you will be a result of the steady six months of work that preceded your first marathon, not what happens the last week. Anything bad that happens to you may be because of that last week.

Relax. Ease off on your training. Allow your muscles some rest and the glycogen level of your body a chance to rise. Most world-class marathon runners spend anywhere from ten to five days tapering their training before very important races, so why do it differently?

You should probably begin easing your training two weeks before the event. The last week should include minimal work. An occasional hard run is acceptable during this period but don't attempt two in a row. Let both quantity and quality in your workouts slide. Take a day or two off. You may want to have complete rest for two days before the marathon, or you might want to rest then go for an easy jog the day before just to be sure you are loose. Most experienced runners develop ways to taper for specific races and if you continue as a marathoner you will too, but in the meantime be content to do less than you do normally.

You may experience some psychological problems, however, while resting because your body will have become addicted to running. You will miss your daily runs, so cutting down too far may be unwise if you become uncomfortable because of lack of activity. You may substitute food for running and gain more weight than you need. So even this tapering should be done in moderation.

A brief word about prerace diet. By the time you are ready to run a marathon, you have probably heard about a special diet called carbohydrate loading, which can cause runners to scale the wall at 20 miles and drastically improve their marathon times. We will discuss this special diet in a later chapter, "Going All the Way," but *don't attempt to carbohydrate load before your first marathon!*

Carbohydrate loading involves a depletion run of perhaps 20 miles seven days before a marathon, followed by three days on a high protein, high fat diet, followed by three more days on a high-carbohydrate diet, then race. The first phase of this diet includes foods that could cause atherosclerosis, so should not be attempted by runners over 40. Runners who have attempted this diet often experience unpleasant side-effects during this phase. You may want to experiment with carbohydrate loading to improve your performance after you have been running marathons for several years, but avoid this diet before your first race or any other big race without prior experimentation.

Although you may want to avoid the full two-phase regimen of carbohydrate loading, you may want to modify your diet slightly several days before the race to include foods high in carbohydrates, because carbohydrates are a better source of fuel for endurance events. The typical prerace meal for marathoners is spaghetti, but also consider a vegetarian meal or fruit plate. I like eating the night before in Chinese or Italian restaurants. But I can't name any good Chinese or many fast Italian marathoners. Eventually it gets down to the steady preparation of miles on the road over a period of many months, not what you eat the night before. With proper preparation you can achieve the ultimate experience: running 26 miles 385 yards.

A GUIDE FOR BEGINNING MARATHONERS

PHASE ONE

If you converted from runner to racer using the schedule at the end of the previous chapter and reach Phase Five you can probably move right into a marathon with few problems. You should be running close to 60 miles a week, including a 14- to 16-mile run on the weekend. Although your weekly long run should probably be somewhat longer, that much mileage is more than ample for marathoning. Simply stay out a bit longer on your Sunday workout, and you will be ready to run.

But many runners decide to become marathoners, skipping the "racer" level. For that reason, the Guide for Beginning Marathoners starts at a level lower than the previous Guide for Beginning Racers.

In Phase One, you should be running 25 to 30 miles a week, hopefully without stress or strain, so that a steady increase of training over the next three to six months will not leave you too exhausted to perform your daily tasks. For your first attempt, select a marathon held over a relatively flat course at a time of the year when you can anticipate reasonably good weather. Hilly courses also are fun, but save them for when you are a veteran. Unless you are already covering more than 25 to 30 weekly miles, begin your marathon preparation at Phase Two.

PHASE TWO

Plan to run five to six days a week, then taking a day or two off to recuperate from hard training.

Sunday: Eight- to ten-mile run. The key to marathon training is a long, but easy training run (LSD for long, slow distance) at least once a week, usually on the weekend when you have extra time. Eventually you want to build your LSD capacity to around 20 miles. Running that far in practice offers no guarantee that you can go the extra six miles 385 yards in a race, but it will make it more likely, and you will finish more comfortably.

Monday: Easy jogging or rest after yesterday's long run.
Tuesday: Interval training. 4-6 x 880 at the pace you hope to run your marathon. Jog or walk 440 between each fast run.
Wednesday: Three to six miles at a relaxed, recuperative pace.
Thursday: Five to seven mile run. This should be at a slightly faster pace than your Sunday workout (FCR for Fast continuous run), but only at about two-thirds the distance. As you progress in distance on Sunday, you should similarly progress on this mid-week workout.
Friday: Easy jogging at whatever pace and over whatever distance feels comfortable.
Saturday: Rest.

This workout pattern should give you 25-35 miles of training, not much different from the mileage level in the final phase of the Guide for the Beginning Runner, but with a slightly different pattern. Remain at this level for one or two months, or until you feel comfortable with your workouts, then move on to Phase Three.

PHASE THREE

Plan to run six days a week, taking one day off for recuperation.

Sunday: Twelve to fourteen mile LSD run.
Monday: Easy jogging or rest.
Tuesday: Interval training. 4-6 x 1320 at marathon pace. Jog or walk 440 between.
Wednesday: Three to six miles at a relaxed pace.
Thursday: Six- to nine-mile FCR run.
Friday: Three to six miles at a relaxed pace.
Saturday: Easy jogging or rest. If you jogged Monday, rest Saturday, or vice versa.

You are now running 30-45 miles a week, a small but significant increase in mileage. Remain at this level at least a month before moving on to Phase Four.

PHASE FOUR

Plan to run six to seven days a week, taking a recuperative day if you need it.

Sunday: Sixteen to eighteen mile LSD run.
Monday: Easy jogging or rest.
Tuesday: Interval training. 4-6 x mile at marathon pace. Jog or walk 440 between.
Wednesday: Three to six miles at a relaxed pace.
Thursday: Nine to 12 miles FCR run.
Friday: Three to six miles at a relaxed pace.
Saturday: Speed work. Run some 100-yard sprints on a soft surface such as a golf course. Don't do too many sprints or at too fast a pace (8-12 x 100 would be right). Try to come away from the workout feeling loose and relaxed rather than fatigued.

Your mileage is now in the 40-55 range. You are beginning to get tough, but don't overdo it. Remain at this level at least a month before moving on to Phase Five.

PHASE FIVE

Plan to run seven days a week, resting a day only if you feel you absolutely need it.

Sunday: 20- to 22-mile LSD run.
Monday: Easy jogging.
Tuesday: Interval training. 6-8 x mile at marathon pace. Jog 440 between.
Wednesday: Three to six miles at a relaxed pace.
Thursday: Twelve to fifteen miles FCR run.
Friday: Three to six miles at a relaxed pace.
Saturday: Speed work, as above.

You may want to run some races of between six and 15 miles at this phase in your training as a tune-up for your marathon. If so, substitute the race for your weekly FCR workout and do speed work on Thursday instead. Depending on what day of the week you race, you may have to juggle the order of your workouts, but try to maintain the pattern of a hard or fast day followed by an easy one. Your mileage is now in the 50-65 range and you are ready to run your marathon. Move to Phase Six.

PHASE SIX

You are well trained because of the hard work you put in getting this far, but you also may be a bit tired, even overtrained. Spend one to two weeks tapering your training before the race. Start to cut your workouts in half, and/or decrease the speed at which you run them. Four to five days before the race do little more than jog or rest completely. Go into the race well rested and ready to perform to the best of your ability.

Then do it.

20

All About Tactics

The art of pacing, passing,
and kicking

The beginning runner, motivated often only by a desire for
fitness, never worries about tactics. For that person it is
merely enough to run, not to race. Even when a beginner becomes
involved in competitive running, it often is more from a spirit of
participation than from a desire to beat an opponent one-to-
one. Tactics is something employed by those fast people up in
the front of the pack, those inhuman specimens who somehow
possess the ability to run at faster than 5:00 pace, mile after
mile after mile. Nevertheless, even though you may never come
into the last lap of an Olympic final with a chance to win a gold
medal, knowledge of tactics may enhance your appreciation of
long-distance running as a sport as well as an activity.

"Tactics" is a military expression sometimes confused with the
term "strategy." Strategy, by definition, is the science of
planning and directing large-scale military operations and
maneuvering your forces into the most advantageous position
before actual engagement with the enemy. Tactics is the science
of arranging and maneuvering military and naval forces *in
active contact with* the enemy.

Translated to running: strategy is training to race. Tactics is
racing itself, particularly how you maneuver in crowded fields of
two or more runners.

Tactics are least important in the shortest and longest events.
In races to 440 yards, runners generally go full speed all the
way, separated by lanes. Little contact and no decisions are

made concerning pace. In the longest races, beyond 10,000 meters, runners compete on wide, straight courses where little contact occurs. Pace becomes an important tactic, but less important than at medium distances.

In the medium distances (road runs less than 10 miles, cross-country events from two to six miles, track races from 800 to 10,000 meters) tactics become critical. Tactics increase in importance when runners move onto tight, narrow, indoor tracks where straightaways are short and hairpin turns make running very difficult.

Of all the runners I have seen race, one stands out as the premiere tactician of all: Herb Elliott. Most track fans remember Herb as a world-record holder and Olympic gold medalist, but I remember Elliott because of his superb use of tactics.

He could lead from the gun; he could burst in the middle; he could kick at the tape. He finished a career unbeaten in the 1500 meters and the mile by effectively employing all those tactics. His most astonishing race probably came in the Rome Olympics of 1960 when he stunned his competitors by starting his sprint with roughly two laps to go. They came back on him near the end, but Herb Elliott still had the victory.

Knowledge of tactics is essential if you intend to race successfully, but too many runners give little thought to this form of the running art.

Using a Kick

There are two styles of running: from the front and from the rear, with numerous variations on both. Those who lead presumably do so because they possess superior endurance and like to break their opponent before sighting the finish line. Those who follow presumably do so because they have superior finishing speed and know they can beat their opponent as long as they can stay with him.

A handful of extremely gifted athletes possess both superior endurance and superior speed. When these occur in one athlete, you have a racer.

Several excellent front-runners come to mind: Filbert Bayi, Ron Clarke, Kip Keino. Keino's 1500-meter victory over Jim Ryun at Mexico City was denounced as a "trick tactic," because teammate Ben Jipcho set a fast pace theoretically allowing

Keino to pull away from Ryun. Nothing was tricky about the tactic. It was simply a matter of strength over speed.

Speed prevails more often. This was particularly true of New Zealand's Peter Snell, Olympic gold medalist at 800 meters in 1960 and 1964, and at 1500 meters in 1964. "Schnell" in German, means *fast,* and Peter was that. His typical tactic was to burst into an apparently frantic sprint at the end of the back straightaway with 200 meters to go. His kick was superb. He did not merely beat opponents, he demolished them. It was almost as though Snell were sitting on the blocks at the 200 meters start, waiting for the others to go 3½ laps so he could race with them.

Kickers succeed for psychological reasons. Not only do they have unbeatably fast kicks, but others *expect* them to have unbeatably fast kicks. Snell toured North America during the spring of 1965 and began the tour his usual invincible self by overwhelming rivals (including a young Jim Ryun) with his finishing burst.

Then, one weekend he traveled to Toronto to race Bill Crothers, the 800-meter Olympic silver medalist. Snell had a touch of flu and was beaten.

This was hardly a disgrace, but word spread quickly among middle distance runners of the world: "Crothers outkicked Snell!" The superb New Zealander's psychological edge vanished overnight and he never won another race on that tour. He soon retired.

One of those who beat Snell that summer was Ryun, who reigned as "boss kicker" for three years until defeat by Keino reduced his psychological edge.

Kickers may not necessarily win more races than front runners, but their victories are more spectacular and so may be remembered longer. As a result, too many runners assume that kicking is the only tactic to guarantee victory. This is sometimes true, but remember that Lasse Viren, a renowned kicker, won the 5000 meters at Montreal by leading the last six laps.

Viren understood a very important tactical rule: *A runner who assumes a back position automatically lets others dictate his race.*

Following The Leader

There are times when a runner who desires victory above all

should be a follower rather than a leader. Four such instances when it is best to follow:

1. *On windy days.* If you run into a wind, you use additional energy to battle it. A tactical runner may choose to tuck in behind an opponent and use him as a windshield, known in NASCAR as "drafting." A runner drafts on a windy day during a track race, by using his opponent to block the wind going down one straight, and block the wind pushing the opponent from behind on the other straight. This tactic works best when the wind blows parallel to the straight, and is of less value in cross-winds that blow across the turns. A runner who uses this tactic must have a strong tolerance for disfavor, since his popularity among other runners (and fans) will eventually wane.

2. *As a psychological weapon.* Some runners have a low tolerance for tension, and wilt under the psychological pressure of another runner dogging their footsteps. Simply by trailing a runner (wind or no wind) you may cause him to worry about your presence and break his concentration. Running is not an automatic function. You cannot run efficiently unless you concentrate on the act; runners lose efficiency if they worry more about those behind them than the track before them. Some runners, *many* runners, give up if passed forceably near the finish line.

3. *If you're faster.* A runner who can run his last quarter in 59 seconds, other things being equal, will defeat a runner capable of running his last quarter in 60 seconds. If you are the latter, you do not want to be behind the former going into the last lap. If you are the former, you need only stick on the latter's shoulder to defeat him. Sooner or later somebody comes along capable of a last lap in 58 seconds, of course.

4. *If the pace is too fast.* Too fast may mean any speed faster than you consider an ideal pace. If you plan to lead the first quarter of a mile race in 62 seconds and someone pulls you through the first lap in 58, you are better staying behind to allow the fast pace to lag before taking command. Sometimes, of course, the pace may not lag and you will find yourself permanently behind. But that's racing.

Leaders Of The Pack

There are occasions when it is unwise to follow another's pace. There are four such instances:

1. *On indoor tracks.* Following may be a poor tactic on the short, 11-lap-to-the-mile board tracks in most major meets. A stretching-out effect occurs on indoor tracks. As the lead runner slows going through the turn, others behind him slow progressively (depending on their position behind him). The sixth runner in a six-man field will find himself slowing while still on the straight or going through the turn. The leader, meanwhile, has speeded up on the next straight. Because indoor straights are short, passing becomes a more difficult task—particularly on the last lap. The same stretching-out occurs in the 3000-meter steeplechase at each barrier where the lagging runners are blocked by runners in the front who lose momentum while in the air.

2. *On rough cross-country courses.* There are two instances when you do not want to follow a runner in cross-country. One is when the footing is hazardous, because running behind someone is a bit like running in the dark. The other is when the course narrows. If you get caught behind a slow runner in the middle of the pack, the rest of the field will draw away from you. In crowded fields, you can get stomped on if you hit a sharp turn.

3. *If you're slower.* This is the flipside of why you can run behind if you have superior finishing speed. If you meet one of those runners, you want to break him before the last straight. If the pace is too slow, you may want to get out in front and keep it honest.

4. *On hot days in road races.* One of the most frustrating experiences for a marathoner is to arrive at a water point during a warm race and be unable to obtain water. This is likely to happen if you are behind a group of runners who take all the available cups before you get there. If the water is being handed out on only one side and your opponent unintentionally blocks you, you also may experience trouble. Speeding up or slowing down to get the water may cost energy, but it may be necessary. The runner who runs alone may suffer loneliness, but he avoids these problems.

Also, you may want to run into the wind on an extremely hot day to allow the wind to cool you.

Heat may be a more critical factor than the wind in limiting your speed.

Another tactical reason for leading the closing stages of a race is that if you are two yards ahead of your opponent with 100 yards to go, he has to run 2% faster down that final straight (covering 102 yards) to beat you.

Rick Wohlhuter understood this when I interviewed him for *Runner's World* just before the 1976 Olympic games. He told me: "One strategy is to say, 'to hell with everybody else,' and just keep them behind. If they work their way to your shoulder coming down that last straight, just hope they will have fought so hard to get there they don't have the speed or strength to go by."

It was almost as though Rick had a premonition of the tactic that Alberto Juantoreno of Cuba would employ against him in the 800-meter finals. Juantoreno blasted into an early lead and although Rick almost reached his shoulder down that last straight, he could not summon enough kick to go by.

Some runners who are pace-setters find it very disturbing when other runners who are kickers trail them for an entire race waiting for the precise moment to storm by. Unless he is very experienced and cool, this exerts excessive psychological pressure on the lead runner. The trail runner knows this and this is one reason he stays behind.

Various methods are used to disengage a trailing runner, probably the simplest one being simply to run off and leave him. This works, obviously, only if you are clearly superior. For runners of near-equal ability, however, the lead runner must employ other tactics.

One method is to vary your pace, alternately slowing down and speeding up. Time your fast spurts (particularly in cross-country runs) after you have passed some natural obstacle or crested a hill so you can catch your opponent off guard and open a slight lead before he recovers.

Since you choose the places for pace changes, you expend less energy than your opponent. You control the tempo. Of course, if your opponent is experienced, he will know enough to hold back and not match your every twitch. A confident kicker may trail almost to the point of losing contact, moving into a striking position only when it comes time to strike.

In road races, while running into the wind you sometimes can limit the benefit to an opponent by weaving, moving from side to side, so he must change position constantly to keep you as a shield.

During a 20-kilometer race in Dallas in April, 1978, I was fighting a losing battle for fifth place maybe 20 yards behind another runner when we came into the wind. Although it cost me some energy, I spurted to within a few feet of his back so he could break the wind for me. He sensed my presence and attempted a psychological ploy to shake me: "You can't draft someone as skinny as me."

He was wrong, of course, because the wind coming off White Rock Lake was severe, and I was able to move with less effort and stay with him. But I lost the advantage as soon as the course shifted so the wind was no longer in our faces. He pulled away from me gradually so I had to go it alone the next time the course shifted.

I learned something that day, however, and the next time someone attempts to draft me I will work on their guilt feelings. Another tactic would be to eat chili and beans as your prerace meal, which would allow you to break the wind in more than one way. This could have disastrous results, however, if you have too much to eat. Then again, some runners draft their opponents so closely they just might follow them into the bushes.

There are other more sensible ways to shake an opponent who either has been trailing or running with you. Sometimes, while battling an opponent in a road race, I spurt when we reach a water point. As he reaches for a cup of water, I start to move. He will lose distance while grabbing the water and while swallowing it. It's difficult to race hard those first few hundred yards after a good drink of water. This is not a wise tactic to employ on very hot days, however.

I once ran a two-mile track race against an opponent who had been told by his coach to follow my pace. Because I was doubling back after the mile, I was not eager to push hard. He was fresh, yet allowed the pace to get slower and slower, particularly after I sensed what was happening and decided to test how slow he was willing to go to remain in second. Finally, after one incredibly slow quarter, I started walking. The other runner, much to his coach's consternation, began walking too. I won eventually with a blistering kick. I think our time was around 11:30. His coach was furious.

The Art Of Passing

There is a time and place to run from behind, and a time and place to run from the front. If you run from behind and want to win, you must pass the runner in front of you sooner or later. You might wait until your last stride of the race, but you must pass or lose.

Passing is a tactical art in itself.

Passing on a road course usually poses no problem, because your straight may be 26 miles 385 yards. You have considerably less distance to get by another runner on a track. Let us consider three possibilities for passing moves:

1. *Coming out of the turn.* This is the most obvious place to begin your pass. You have the maximum distance to run after moving wide and before sliding back into the inside lane.

You need to shift your pace relatively little to pass if your opponent offers no resistance. If he does offer resistance, you have more time to overcome it.

When I intend to pass somebody coming out of a turn (and I am not trying to disguise my move for the element of surprise) I will begin the pass at the apex or mid-point of the turn. As I pass the apex I begin easing my way out toward the second lane so when we reach the straight I am beside the runner, not behind him. This is more efficient than making a sudden move to the side when you hit the straight, because anything done suddenly in a race wastes energy.

Out of the turn is the best passing place, so many runners float through the turns then increase their pace down the straight to keep their opponent from passing. This is a good tactic if you want to maintain your lead.

2. *Going into the turn.* The last ten yards of the straight is where most inexperienced runners trying to hold the lead tend to relax. They figure they have you beaten going into the turn and want to ease off as soon as possible. This is the best time to jump them. Sometimes I make a false move coming down the straight, moving outside the lead runner's shoulder, but not seriously challenging him. Then, I charge past the moment he relaxes at straight's end. I'm in front before he realizes it.

Sometimes I am the one being passed. If a runner challenges me down the straight and fails, I wait until I see him abandon his move and tuck in behind me going around the turn. At that moment I slow down too, forcing him to stay in the outside lane while still in the turn. This psychological ploy defeats many inexperienced runners, who fear that in running wide around the turn they cover too much extra distance which inevitably will cause their defeat.

3. *On the turn*. Several years ago I attended a junior high track meet where two runners had a stirring shoulder-to-shoulder battle the entire race. I overheard the loser's coach tell the runner he added at least 100 yards to his distance by running wide.

Well, if he ran in the third or fourth lane, he might have covered that much more distance. I thought the loser had run a relatively good tactical race considering his inexperience and poor coach. He ran wide on the straight, but moved behind or at least in tight on the turns. But his coach had implanted in this young runner's mind that he *never* should pass on the turns. I pass on a turn if I feel like passing on a turn. You are much better off running a few inches farther and avoiding a break in your tempo than waiting until the straight to go around.

And it is inches rather than feet or yards.

I recall some years ago watching Frank Shorter and Jack Bacheler running a race on television. Jack ran most of the way off Frank's shoulder, and the TV commentator kept talking about all that extra distance he was covering. He ran very little extra distance, and with Jack's long legs compared to Frank's shorter ones, he probably could stride much more comfortably running to the side rather than directly behind.

What that junior high coach and the TV commentator did not understand: when you run wide in a distance race, you rarely run a full lane wide as would a quartermiler running in staggered lanes. You run a fraction of that. When I run second behind another runner I run slightly wide so I can see the track over his shoulder and avoid being boxed. I often like to run half-wide, meaning that my inside (left) leg is behind his outside (right) leg.

It is easier to pass from half behind than from directly behind. Unless he holds you off, you may pass a runner on the turn while still in half-wide position, a bit the way a high jumper clears the bar without ever seeming to be over it completely. You dip your shoulder in front of the passed runner. You have not moved the required one stride ahead before cutting in, but you do not cut in. You have moved from half-wide behind to half-wide ahead, from which you can gradually draw away and take the inside lane, if the lead runner permits you to do so.

If you do not wish to be passed this way, you must be willing to defend your position. You should not permit runners to cut in front of you unless they have the necessary one stride lead. Because most runners who do cut in do so unintentionally, a slight push or soft tap on the arm will usually warn them you intend to hold your ground. If they keep coming, an act of aggression, a sharp blow against the elbow will deter them. If worse come to worst, the beleagured runner can raise his arms and stagger into the infield, hoping to draw the attention of the judges to his plight.

More often there are no judges, or they're not watching, but once in an indoor board race in Philadelphia they were. I had the lead with three turns in a mile race when a runner cut me off and forced me into the infield. That got *him* disqualified. I tried to get back on the track coming out of the turn and he was blocking the inside lane, so I gave him a shove (well, a fairly rough push). That got *me* disqualified. The third runner won the wristwatch.

What irritated me was that, in shoving the other runner I pushed him forward, improving his sprint. I tried to convince the judges that since the other runner was disqualified for cutting me off, he was technically not in the race when I retaliated so I should not have been penalized. They failed to see the logic in my argument.

In long distance races run on a track, fast runners must often face the problem of passing runners as they lap them. Although it is easier to pass a slow-moving runner, the hazards of collision increase because of the great variations in speed.

For this reason I always object when officials order slower runners to move to an outside lane either when being lapped or for the remainder of the race. Officials who make such rules usually never have race themselves.

At a high school indoor two-mile in Bloomington, one year I thought a friend of mine named Marshall Goss was going to have a heart attack or at least suffer a hernia, trying to move runners into the second lane just before they were lapped. Some moved and some didn't, which caused more of a problem than if all had remained near the curb.

I have two reasons for wanting lapped runners to stay inside.

First, I see no reason why slower runners should be penalized for their slowness by being made to run in the second or third lane, and I believe most other faster runners share my feelings. I am usually quite happy to move wide and run the slight extra distance. I don't need an extra advantage.

But second, and most important, if the slow runner is told to stay on the inside, I know where he is going to be and I need not worry about him suddenly moving out into my path.

In the 5000-meter run at the 1975 Masters Championships at White Plains, N.Y., a lapped runner looked over his shoulder and saw me approaching. He remembered the officials had warned everybody to run wide to get out of the way when about to be lapped. But I was closing so fast that I was on his outside by the time he got the message to his tired feet and moved out. He bumped me, but apologized after the race. The officials owed both of us an apology.

During a 3000-meter race sponsored by the Midwest Masters I came into the turn and found my path blocked by four runners jogging abreast and chatting. So I wasted no energies on conversation. I simply cut through the infield. That time, fortunately, the judges were not looking.

Sometimes a fast runner treading his way through lapped runners can use them to his tactical advantage. By artfully dodging inside or out a runner in the lead can break contact with those behind him. When a blizzard caused cancellation of the 1974 North Central Marathon, it forced more than 200 runners to run a 10-mile substitute race on a snowy track. I broke fast from the starting line despite treacherous footing, because I knew we would start lapping trail runners within a mile. Anyone more than 10 yards behind at that point would be hopelessly enmeshed in the crowd.

That is exactly what happened. Only Barney Hance of College of St. Francis and I stayed in contention. Barney would have chewed me up on a dry road course but on that icy track with curb-to-curb runners, neither of us could gain on the other. I had fun playing with him psychologically because when he had the lead and moved wide to pass a group, I often found a gap on the inside and moved ahead of him. The organizers eventually threw sand on the icy curves (improving traction) allowing Barney to demolish me in the last few miles. I was having the time of my life until then playing games with

Barney. Each of us won a watch, although mine stopped recently.

Using And Avoiding Boxes

Tactical knowledge often can tip the scales when two runners of equal ability meet. This is particularly true when it comes to boxes. Experienced runners get boxed less often than novices, or if they do get caught know how to work their way free more easily.

A box occurs when a runner behind the leader suddenly finds another runner on his shoulder, boxing him in and preventing him from passing. If the box occurs on the last lap, it may cause defeat. If it is a moving box, one in which there is not one runner but a stream of runners passing, the one on the inside may go from second to last with little control over his destiny.

If the box occurs in the middle of a race, many runners simply relax and wait for the wide runner to move either forward or back. After all, his junior high school coach once may have warned the outside runner not to run wide. But there are several ways in which a runner can disengage himself from a box:

• **Slow down.** If you slow your pace, the runner boxing you in on the outside will probably move into your former position. But you will have surrendered position. You may have surrendered too much ground on the leader if you do this on the last lap.

• **Ask to get out.** Most boxes occur unintentionally, and if you ask the runner on your shoulder to give you room, he will usually do so. You want tactical advantage over other runners, but you do not want unfair advantage.

• **Shove your way out.** Risky if the judges are watching, this tactic should be employed only if the wide runner is a teammate of the leader and is holding you in deliberately: an illegal tactic that could cause disqualification of both boxing runners. You can push your way out of a box more subtly by exerting gentle pressure while going around the turn and forcing the outside runner wider than he would like to be (opening a gap by the time you hit the straight).

• **Move inside.** This desperation tactic usually will work only on the final straight. Waiting for an inside opening may be your only hope if you find yourself boxed at this point in the race. The lead runner in his closing sprint with another outside runner on his shoulder often moves wide either forcing that runner farther out or, because centrifugal force pushes him toward lane two. This sometimes opens the door for another runner to come through on the inside.

The best defense against boxes is not to get in them; to run off the shoulder of the runner in front of you in the same outside-inside overlap stride mentioned earlier. Thus positioned, you cannot be easily boxed, because by moving slightly wide you can be free of the runner in front of you. You can avoid most boxes by thinking ahead.

The same is true in the rush for position at the start. A runner who starts in the middle often gets caught as others on the outside sprint to reach the pole then slow down once they get there. If I have a choice, I usually start in an outside rather than inside lane—unless it is *the* inside one. When in the middle, I try to edge outward to avoid being hemmed in.

Tactical Sense

Some purists may object to tactical devices to defeat other runners of equal ability. They consider tactics unfair. But to remove tactics from racing would also remove a lot of fun from the sport. I enjoy getting out on a wide-open road course and running solo with only the clock to beat, but on occasion I like to get on a tight track for a tussle with other runners.

These maneuvers, as well as other tactics described in this chapter, do not come easily and cannot be learned by reading a book. Many runners use these maneuvers and tactics without giving much thought to them. The best teacher is experience.

21

Running Off the Road

The beauty of cross-country may be just what you're looking for

Cross-country is a means to an end rather than an end in itself. Many runners use cross-country to prepare for the track-and-field season or for road races rather than as the separate running sport it is.

There are several reasons runners train on cross-country courses rather than on roads or tracks. Variations in terrain and surfaces provide stress that can be an important training adjunct; and workouts over cross-country courses can be less boring than some track laps or long runs on straight, flat, traffic-clogged roads. With certain surface conditions, the chances of injury from hard training can be minimized. All these are valid reasons for using cross-country to prepare for other events or sports. Many skiers, wrestlers, basketball players, and tennis players run cross-country as part of their conditioning.

Another reason is that it is fun to run on twisting woodland trails or over rolling surfaces of well manicured golf courses, particularly during fall: the traditional cross-country season. In the Midwest, the weather is better for running in the fall than at any other time of the year, warm but not hot, moist but not humid, eventually bracing but not cold. Trees turning green to gold to brown provide a backdrop for running I particularly enjoy.

But I also enjoy cross-country as a competitive sport because it is the thinking man's sport. Cross-country is one branch of running where an intelligent approach to competition can affect the result. Most runners *run* in cross-country events, unfortunately, they don't *race* in them. There is a difference.

In the first case, you stand at the line until the gun sounds, then you go as fast as you can until you stop at the finish line. That is what I call *running* a cross-country course. The brain is disengaged and the event becomes simply matters of strength, speed, or endurance.

In the second case, you consider your event, the course, and your rivals long before you stand at the line. You go as fast as you can after the gun sounds, but with a purpose in mind and utilizing techniques specific to *racing* a cross-country course. Strength, speed, and endurance are still important, but the brain is engaged as well.

The difference in a cross-country event several miles long may be only a few seconds, maybe *tenths* of seconds; the difference between victory and defeat for you or your team.

I do not criticize an athlete who takes a casual "runner's" approach to cross-country. I have been preaching that running, first of all should be fun, so if you want to approach cross-country as jogger or fitness runner, do so. But because you try hard does not mean you can no longer have fun. Trying hard — and specifically thinking hard — does pay off in cross-country.

Think Your Way Around The Course

How can thinking affect the result? Consider cross-country as a *technique* event. You will never succeed as a cross-country runner if you don't appreciate that simple fact. It is a technique event because it is run on varied terrain for which differing techniques must be utilized.

This seems like such an obvious statement that many runners give too little attention to techniques that would improve their cross-country abilities. You would not attempt to steeplechase without learning how to hurdle, so why attempt cross-country without learning how to overcome that sport's barriers?

You need know only how to run if you run distance events on the track. If you run cross-country, you must know how to run hills, uphill and downhill. You must learn to adjust your stride for rough ground and varying surfaces. You must know what to do when you get to a sharp turn — especially if you get there at the same time as a half-dozen other runners.

Ask the average runner how he runs around a turn, and the answer you get will be, "Well, you just, sort of—*turn!*" Ask a pole vaulter how he vaults and you would not get such a simple answer. But then vaulters are more conditioned to technique than are most runners.

Let us examine a method for taking turns: you have to set yourself up to turn the way an auto racer gets his machine positioned to take a turn around Watkins Glen. You have to assume the right *attitude*—in the sense that astronauts speak of attitude (or relative position) of their spacecraft, rather than state of mind which is important too.

This means you must begin to go around a turn before you reach it, similar to the way you run a banked turn indoors, although some runners don't know how to do *that* properly. Several strides before you reach the turn, you place your upper body sideways: outside shoulder forward, inside shoulder back, outside arm raised, inside arm down.

Lean toward the inside of the turn and bring your legs into alignment with your shoulders as you reach the turn, allowing yourself to "fall" around the turn, at the same time propelling yourself around it, an action more easily demonstrated than explained. Go out and try some sharp turns on your home cross-country course, then adopt the movements that seem more comfortable to you.

Remember that turns differ. You would not throw yourself into a long sweeping turn as specifically as you might to turn 90 degrees in two strides between trees. Remember also that you must resume your normal upper body movement after you come out of a turn. A common fault of many runners, even on outdoor tracks, is to continue running the straightaway with left arm down and right arm thrashing across their body as if they were still turning. Resuming your "normal" running stride is a matter of concentration, and is easier in the early stages of a race than in the later stage: one reason some runners pull away from others.

You can take turns at maximum speed by setting yourself and avoid sliding off the path, maybe into a tree. Taking a turn aggressively requires energy but so does accelerating after having been forced to slow down. You use valuable energy to catch up after taking a turn too wide and seeing your opponents move away from you.

Another consideration: you gain a half stride or more on your opponents by taking turns properly which may be critical in a tactical race.

I ran a summer four-mile cross-country some years ago against a fast high school runner named Jerry Smith, and Dave Collins of Ball State University. After the race, Collins said that every time we went around a corner I would pick up five yards on Smith.

Both runners eventually beat me, because of superior talent, conditioning, or both; either of which will overcome superior technique. If you are matched against a runner of equal talent and conditioning, however, you can defeat him by applying superior technique.

Collins is a good example of a thinking runner. We had been racing in a summer fun-run, but he had kept his brain engaged while his feet were in motion and had learned something about cross-country technique, or at least reinforced knowledge he already had.

Running In A Crowd

What I have said thus far applies generally to taking turns more or less in a vacuum, alone or with one or two other runners who presumably will not interfere with your well practiced technique. Different problems arise in crowds.

During the 1950s, the annual NCAA cross-country championship was conducted annually at Michigan State on a course that started in an open field with a sprint of about 440 yards before a sweeping 180-degree turn had to be negotiated.

I entered the NCAA championship during my junior year at Carleton College, and began my race at a pace befitting a 10:00 two-miler, which I was at the time. The middle of the pack had become so congested by the time I reached the first turn that there was no alternative other than to slow to a walk. It was like the crowd at the start of the Boston Marathon, and I probably lost 10 or 15 seconds before being able to resume my regular pace. I finished something like 96th in the race.

I returned to the race during my senior year in college with a strategy. I was now a seasoned veteran; no matter that I still was only slightly better than a 10:00 two-miler I sprinted out at the start and reached the turn with the leaders. I was running in fourth place at the half-mile mark. Having overextended myself, I finished something like 96th in the race. But as least I had been thinking.

But this underlines a problem faced by the "average" runner attempting to compete in crowded cross-country races: how do you avoid getting trampled in the pack? The answer sometimes is to go out too fast, realizing that overextending yourself will hurt your performance but knowing that you will lose less than if required to run in the pack.

If everyone goes out fast, of course, the pack will be at the front of the race rather than in the middle, and the runner who has paced himself well can pick his way through the spread-out field in the second half of the race and beat dying runners. This is a technique better suited for placing well rather than winning. It is easier in a six-mile college race than in a 2.5-mile high school race. If the average runner wants to succeed in large meets, the technique of running in a crowd must be learned.

Running in a crowd generally is no problem on a straight. It may be easier to be swept along in a crowd of runners slightly faster than you are. You want to avoid being held back by a crowd of runners slightly slower than you are.

The main problem occurs when the crowd encounters obstacles: a hill to climb, a log to jump, or a turn to negotiate. The pace of the crowd will then change, often subtly; if you are running in the rear you may find yourself unnecessarily slowed. Your only defense is to anticipate such obstacles so you can position yourself near the front, forcing the other runners to follow your pace rather than you following theirs.

The next best technique is to move to the outside if this is possible, particularly approaching a turn. You are better off running wide and covering some extra distance than getting trapped on the inside and having your rhythm broken, or maybe getting tripped.

Another possibility is to slow down and negotiate the obstacle behind the crowd, but you may be giving away ground never to be recovered. A greater risk in an extremely crowded field is that you will have dropped out of the one crowd only to be engulfed by another.

Remember: you will be able to cope with problems only if you anticipate them and plan the proper tactic.

Roughing it

Another problem that the cross-country runner frequently encounters is terrain. There are two major types of terrain. Big variations are known as hills, little variations are known as rough ground.

Let us consider the first variation, hills. You will probably never enjoy true cross-country unless you enjoy the challenge of running hills. Notice that I said the *challenge of hills,* because charging up a steep hill may be enjoyable only in the abstract. It is the reflection afterward, of a challenge met that provides the pleasure of cross-country running. It is why flat, even-surfaced, multilap courses are an anathema to those who love the harrier sport.

Running hills is an art form in itself; each person must seek the technique that best suits his talents but in general the best results can be obtained by following a few guidelines:

1. While running uphill, do not make the mistake of leaning into the hill. Too much forward lean robs you of the leverage you need to get up the hill. It is better to run with a slightly backward incline, maintaining your weight over your "wheels." A more flatfooted stride works best on most hills with medium inclines. On very steep hills, you may be forced by the angle of the slope to get up on your toes and tilt forward.

Hills, like snowflakes, vary greatly. The key to running hills is to run hills. You can't learn a technique unless you practice it, experiment with it, and determine what works best for you.

2. The most important time on any hill occurs immediately after you crest it. You must resume your natural stride as quickly as possible despite the fatigue accumulated in the uphill battle, an essential if you are to avoid losing ground to your opponents and your own timetable. This *running over the top* can be an important tactical weapon in breaking contact with those behind you.

3. The best way to run downhill is to get up on your toes, lean forward and lengthen your stride. Simply let fly. This is not always wise in road races where long hills over a hard surface and the finish line another 25 miles away may require caution. But the hills usually are shorter, as are the races. Surfaces are softer. Discretion may often be thrown to the wind.

Leaning forward while going downhill is a debilitating

exercise that will rob you of the rest you deserve after an uphill struggle, but you will improve your time and finishing position. The secret to obtaining proper forward lean is to tilt forward from the waist. A conscious effort at the top of each downhill charge will do this. It is easier in the first mile than the sixth but the results are worth the extra concentration. As with any cross-country technique, practice is essential.

The second variation in terrain is uneven ground, best negotiated flatfooted. Runners who sprint across uneven ground while up on their toes risk losing their balance. They can get away with it only if they are very familiar with the course. Even then it is a gamble. If you don't understand, take an unsharpened pencil and balance it on its end, then sharpen that same pencil and try to rebalance it. The more surface you can lay down on the ground, the better your balance.

Similarly, the more foot surface you can lay down on the ground while navigating loose ground (sand, mud, etc.), the better traction you will obtain. The technique in traversing loose ground is similar in many respects to running uphill. You want to keep the weight over your "wheels" again. A shortened stride also may be necessary. On the other hand, some loose ground may be avoidable if you adjust your path around it.

The most successful runners are those who are able to suffer sudden changes of pace without losing their running rhythm. Steeplechase runners usually make good cross-country runners, and vice versa. Fartlek running or interval training that forces the runner to shift gears regularly may be a more successful regimen than LSD or FCR.

Many Delicious Flavors

The thinking runner also realizes that every course has its own nuances, its own flavor, that must be approached analytically; it must be conquered by guile as well as by style. The runner who can analyze a cross-country course and determine the best way to run it will achieve success. That success may mean finishing first instead of second, or maybe finishing 178th instead of 179th. It will certainly mean using your potential, and running your race with intelligence as well as with guts. Success, often relative, is still success.

Because my oldest son ran cross-country in high school (and still does in college), I attend numerous cross-country races as a spectator rather than as a participant. The distance in Indiana is 2.5 miles, so usually a visiting team arrives and is escorted around the course by the home team.

The visitors invariably jog the course conversing with each other, paying little attention to the ground they will soon cover at race speed. They sometimes cut corners or avoid loops on the theory that they are saving energy. Their only motive in examining a course before running over it—other than their coach told them to do so—is so they won't get lost. That was probably the coach's reason for sending them out, too.

An important reason for examining a course is to learn the terrain, and navigation probably concerns only the few runners who will lead. Most of the runners will follow sheep-like. If the lead runners get lost, everybody gets lost.

The questions they should ask themselves are:

—If there is an uphill stretch, can it be run without breaking stride?

—If there is uneven or loose ground, can it be avoided by running a slightly different path?

—Are there any obstacles such as fallen logs or streams?

—Is it the type of course that might be negotiated best with flats rather than spikes?

—And if with spikes, what length?

The thinking runner must answer such questions if he wants to succeed on strange courses.

Most runners assume that they can follow home-course runners who already know the fast way around. This may be a false assumption. For one thing, you may be ahead of the home-course runners who may hold back to make you find your way. (A legitimate tactic: why give away your home-course advantage?) But another factor of cross-country running is that most runners, particularly on high school teams, have given so little thought to their sport that they don't know how to run their own course.

A runner being shown a new course should certainly greet all offered advice with skepticism. Our club had a triangular meet with Northwestern and Iowa several years ago, and we were being shown the Northwestern course before the race. We came to a point in the woods where a large tree lay across the path. A side path angled down to the left into a depression, and the Northwestern guide pointed to it: "That's where you can go around the tree."

I noticed that path, and also a third path to the right that seemed shorter and was level. But being a steeplechaser, I decided I could step the tree like a water-jump barrier. I decided to forego the offered advice and negotiate the downed tree in that manner.

After the race I checked with my teammates. Every one of the Northwestern runners had stepped the tree.

Whether the prerace advice had been true or false was not important. Whether I stepped the log or took the path was not important. What was important was to plan to handle that particular obstacle as well as the rest of the course. You do not waste your concentration while racing by making decisions that should have been made in advance.

At one national cross-country championship over a rain-soaked course at the University of Chicago, all the runners in front of me took a wide detour around a large puddle. I cut straight across and caused many of those behind me to do the same because, as they admitted later, "We thought you knew what you were doing." They may have been right, but their *reason* was wrong because I might have been wrong. As it turned out, I don't think it made much difference which way the field negotiated the puddle.

At the 1975 World Masters Track-and Field Championships cross-country, the devilish organizers had routed their course through a stream. I arrived the day before the race, and while jogging over the course made at least a half dozen run-throughs to determine where the footing was best on the stream bed and at what angle to attack it.

I had the approach figured out so exactly that I planned to hit the top of the bluff with my right foot, the bank with my left, a dam with my right, then push off into the water and lift my knees high to avoid being bogged down. One competitor running just ahead of me on the first lap actually stopped when he came to the stream, uncertain what to do. He was obviously shocked by the prospect of jumping into uncharted water. Perhaps he couldn't swim. I never saw him again.

Observers who watched the race from near the stream said I picked up a minimum of 10 yards on almost everybody in the race each of the two times we hit the water. I earned third place and a bronze medal by a margin of only four seconds under the next runner from Finland. I like to think I won that medal by thinking.

Shortcuts

Sometimes it becomes impractical — unless you arrive the day before the race — to examine the entire course on which you plan to compete. The race might be on a single six-mile loop, in which case only the most dedicated 120-mile-per-week zealot will risk warmup over the entire route. If so, the most important thing to remember is that the critical stages in any race are the beginning and the end.

I want to see the first half-mile of any course because I want to know: Can I afford the luxury of a relaxed start, or will I need to get off the line fast to avoid being pinched by runners seeking a single path?

I want to see the last half-mile of any course because I want to know where to begin my final sprint. I don't want to emerge from a woods into a clearing and suddenly see cheering fans standing at the finish line 100 yards away with enough remaining energy to run another mile at the same pace.

To pace myself better, I like to know exactly where I am at all times. Many courses have mileage markers and this helps. Some do not. A map may show some landmarks for checkpoints, although maps frequently are not to scale and are not to be trusted. You can wear a wristwatch in a pinch and use elapsed time as a guide to how much distance you have run

I always examine course maps closely, before and after warm up. If the race is important, I may study a course many weeks in advance if I can get one. Not all courses have maps, and when they are not available you have a right to complain to the race director. Our local high school conference has a rule that the home team must provide a course map in advance of any scheduled meet; I consider this a good rule.

But maps can only hint at terrain, and while the start and finish areas are most important on most courses, this is not always true. An example would be at New Prairie, Indiana, the site of an important invitational high school race that my son Kevin won following my advice.

The first mile of New Prairie is run in a flat, open field with numerous 90-degree turns; then a long straight of maybe 500 yards leading into a narrow, twisting path through the woods. The path continues for maybe a half-mile before reentering the open field and is pretty much single-file running throughout.

Because of this configuration, New Prairie is not a course on which a runner who paces himself properly and likes to come from behind is going to achieve much success. The 500-yard stretch before the path must be negotiated at full speed to permit you to enter the woods ahead of slower runners who may block you. Unless you realize this, you can never achieve success at New Prairie.

Leaders And Followers

Most milers have a tendency to fear the lead like they fear the plague, but cross-country is one of the few running events where leading may be a distinct advantage. It particularly can be an advantage on a course such as New Prairie where there are multiple sharp turns and a runner in a pack is forced to run the turns wide or even to slow his pace. It is also an advantage where there is only one fast line.

It is a disadvantage, of course, on windy days when an opponent is using you to break the wind for him. The tactical gambit to use on runners attempting to draft you is to shift pace, forcing your opponent to go slow then fast when you want him to, or abandon straightline running and run broken field, forcing him to change position if he wants to stay in your draft. The danger is that if you waste energy in one-on-one combat with one runner you may lose ground on the pack.

The drafting runner can sometimes use the other runner to guide him around an unfamiliar course, but that does not always work. Once, while competing with my club in a meet with Valparaiso University, the lead Valpo runner took a wrong turn on his home course, and lead the entire field astray.

It is never wise to trail on a course over rough ground or on one with frequent hazards: because you can't dodge hazards if you can't see them. It is best on such courses to move into a clear position, wind or not.

Where you make your move on a track is dictated only by the ability of opponents and your own ability, but your move in cross-country may be dictated by terrain: a tall hill on which you can break an opponent's spirit by pushing up it, a long straight on which you can surge and leave him, a series of steep downgrades where you can use your hill-running ability to break contact.

The Shoe That Fits

Shoe selection is important to cross-country success. My second son David plays tennis; I notice that the top tennis players often come to matches carrying as many as four rackets under their arms. I'm not sure why, but I suspect it probably is for the same kind of reason that I often appear at cross-country races with three or four pairs of shoes — particularly if I don't know the course. After an examination of the terrain and conditions, I select the pair that offers the best chance of victory that day.

I prefer a light pair of shoes with short spikes, the kind you might wear on an all-weather track. Traction is good on most grass courses, particularly on golf courses, so you don't need long spikes. I might switch to longer spikes on a course that has a lot of soft or loose ground. I go from eighth- to three-eighths-inch spikes, but rarely to five-eighths-inch which are too long for my running stride.

I also might use longer spikes in rain, wet grass, or for sharp turns or steep hills. Long spikes may prevent a fall, but long spikes can be a hindrance if there is mud on the course; mud will clog spikes and add weight to the shoes. Shoes with a smooth plastic plate are preferable to those with rough ridges for the same reasons.

Flat road-running shoes may be preferable if the course includes much running on hard surfaces. I may choose flat shoes if the grass course is paralleled by a hard surface to which I can shift. You can run faster on smooth asphalt than on soft grass, but I would prefer that course designers not require runners to make such choices. Cross-country should be cross-country, with hard surfaces avoided as much as possible.

Flat shoes with ridged or waffle soles usually work better than those with smooth bottoms on cross-country courses. Whether in waffles, spikes, or bare feet, I usually look forward to getting off the road and into the woods each fall.

22

Getting Hurt

Preventing and treating
injuries is a must

If ever there is an award for the most creative running injury of the year—perhaps of all time—it may go to Laura Geiger, a member of the Des Plaines Destiny Striders and postgraduate student at the University of Illinois. Laura went to Florida during spring break and sunburned her feet so badly that she could not put on her running shoes for three days. As far as I know, none of her club, who had spent all winter slogging through snowdrifts, sent sympathy cards.

Once you start to run, it is less a question *if* rather than *when* you will get injured.

Runners get hurt. Injuries go with the franchise. Dr. Steven Subotnick explains why: "Training consists of gradual adaption of the body to stress. When you train you are training your body to accept stress. Too much training leads to too much stress, and too much stress leads to injury. These are overuse or over-stress injuries: runner's knee, shin splints, arch fatigue, pulled muscles, and stress fractures."

"Right Here!"

Most overstress injuries are what John Joyce describes as "right here" injuries. John is an exercise physiologist at the Leaning Tower YMCA northwest of Chicago. He says that when he walks into the locker room one of his joggers frequently will call to him: "Hey, John. Right here!" pointing to some part of the body. "What's this?"

The jogger naturally expects Joyce to diagnose the right-here injury and offer some immediate treatment. John avoids the role of diagnostician, as he should, because he never went to medical school, nor has he made a detailed study of all the right-here's that can cause trouble.

They do this for two reasons. Long distance runners sometimes tend toward parsimony, so if they can obtain a diagnosis or treatment at a free running clinic, they may save themselves the cost of a visit to a doctor's office. Second, they have been conditioned by some people to believe that nothing good will happen to them if they go to a doctor's office.

Three things can happen to you if you go to a doctor's office; only two of them are bad. You can: get cured, not get cured, pay a lot of money. If you are a runner and the first occurs, you probably don't mind the third, but if the combination includes the second and third, you lose your respect for the medical profession.

That apparently happened to Don Higdon, my friend from Ridgewood, New Jersey, who has been plagued by a series of injuries recently. Don mailed me a card labeled "Trust," which included the people an injured runner should consult in descending order from most- to least-trustful:

1. An experienced, long-distance runner.
2. Your own body.
3. George Sheehan.
4. A podiatrist who runs.
5. A podiatrist who doesn't run.
6. A cardiologist who runs.
7. Your spouse.
8. Almost anybody.
9. Idi Amin.
10. A high-priced orthopedic surgeon.

Don Higdon must have had problems with the last on the list.

People who approach John Joyce and me, intuitively or not, seek help from the first on the list: the experienced long-distance runner. We may not be able to help them, but we probably won't hurt them either. Most important, they will not hear "Don't run," the advice they often obtain from nonrunning physicians.

As Dr. Subotnick points out, most stress related injuries occur when runners attempt to move from one level to another too fast. The fitness jogger becomes recreational runner; runner becomes racer. While attempting to move up a level they frequently extend themselves too much and get hurt. The elite runner and mileage freak, meanwhile, constantly tempt disaster because of their excessive mileage. They totter constantly on the brink of collapse in their quest for excellence. Those who remain in this category very long are probably more in tune with their bodies than lower-level runners, so they may maintain their balance.

The runner should drop down one or more levels to allow healing from an injury. But so addictive does regular running become that the mind suffers while the body heals. Runners often find it more difficult to cope with psychological problems of injury than they do with the physical. That's why they don't accept the advice offered by nonrunning doctors who tell them to stop running. They may not even accept such advice from a running doctor. While stationed in Germany with the U.S. Army, I developed mononucleosis after a period of peak training and racing. I was so sick I didn't argue when shipped to the hospital and instructed to lie in bed, but I recovered faster than my doctor expected. At a time when he was prescribing strict bed rest, I would sneak out of my room at 10:00 pm and run on the hospital grounds in pajamas, bathrobe, and Adidas shoes. I didn't run fast. I didn't run far. But I ran.

One of the physicians became suspicious after a week or two of this activity. He began to hear rumors of "the phantom runner," somebody spotted at night running in a bathrobe. I naturally pleaded innocent. The doctor suspiciously eyed my Adidas shoes under the bed, but he did not confiscate them — or put my leg in a cast.

What to Do When Injured

In order of importance, here are ten tips suggesting what you should do if injured while running:

1. *Do nothing.* Your injury may be temporary. Any attempt to intervene or change your normal regimen may be unnecessary. The body has amazing recuperative powers; your injury may heal itself if allowed to do so. Take a couple of days rest. Cut your mileage in half a while to see what happens. Dr. Richard Schuster always advises a prospective patient who calls about an injury: "Wait a week before coming in." On the other hand, there are certain running injuries that may need prompt treatment. If you are lying on the ground and can see splinters

of bone sticking out the side of your leg, you might consider a shout for help!

2. *Ask yourself: why?* Injuries usually occur because of a reason; maybe you can come up with that reason. Last winter I was running along the road wearing, for warmth over my regular sweat suit, a bright red jacket earned for finishing the Maryland Marathon. At the mile mark I began breathing hard and seemed to feel giddy. Asking myself why, I considered some of the reasons. I ate only a small breakfast and skipped lunch because of a dentist's appointment. Maybe it was the effects of that appointment, or maybe the 92 miles I ran in practice the previous week. What was I doing differently? Then I thought about the jacket. I had snapped the topmost fastener and it was pressing against my windpipe, possibly restricting my breathing. After I unsnapped the jacket I was able to continue my nine-mile workout comfortably.

3. *Do something different.* If not doing something different caused your injury, maybe you should do just that in order to cure one. Perhaps all of your workouts have been on unyielding road surfaces and you need to shift to cross-country running on trails or golf courses to ease the strain of pounding. Maybe you have been running only cross-country and your problems come from loose ground, hills, or constant changes in terrain. Running on smooth surfaces may cure you. Runners who train too frequently on the track suffer problems related to both going in circles constantly and the stop-start nature of interval training. Maybe your injuries stem from doing the same thing over and over. A change of pace may be the cure.

4. *Change shoes.* This treatment for an injury is related to method three. Runners often become attached to their favorite pair of running shoes almost in the way that Linus, the character in "Peanuts," is attached to his blanket. They associate their shoes with good times. They are comfortable. It feels good to put them on and go for a run. They are insulted when *Runner's World* fails to rank them near the top in its annual shoe-rating issue. Shoes wear, unfortunately, and when they do may provide not only less protection but may cause your foot to land in an unbalanced position. You must repair those shoes or buy a new pair. At a clinic at the Saginaw Bay Marathon, a female runner approached me and said that she constantly was bothered by blisters. "What different kinds of running shoes do you wear?" I

asked. She said she only owned one. "Buy another pair," was my advice.

5. *Take a placebo.* Considerable medical research indicates that cures sometimes occur because the patient believes in the physician's healing powers. Norman Cousins wrote in *Saturday Review* how he had been cured by what he called "the placebo effect," then was surprised to discover that many physicians agreed that he had cured himself.* Cousins said, "What is most remarkable and gratifying about these letters is the evidence of an open attitude by doctors to new or unconventional approaches to the treatment of serious disease. There was abundant support for the measures that had figured in my own recovery—a well-developed will to live, laughter, and large intravenous doses of sodium ascorbate." I don't necessarily recommend that last reason, but feel that we all can benefit on occasion from a placebo: a medicine given to humor the patient. Your running injury may not improve, but at least it won't give you headaches.

6. *Have Faith.* In other words, heal thyself. Rev. Tony Ahlstrom ran across the United States with his brother Joel and came down with severe tendonitis while going through Colorado. Before starting a 32-mile uphill run one morning out of Glenwood Springs, Tony's foot was so badly swollen he could not lace his shoe. The group with Tony held a prayer meeting that morning, then he began to walk, limping badly. He soon started to move somewhat faster, finally was able to run. He tied his shoe after about a mile. Tony Ahlstrom ran the rest of the way without any further major injuries. You may greet stories about miraculous cures with scepticism, but faith in any treatment you take may be the strongest factor in a cure.

7. *Ask another runner.* If you injured yourself running, you probably were not the first to do so in a similar manner. Talk to your running friends; maybe they had a similar problem and cured themselves, or know somebody who might offer help. Runner-to-runner advice is often the most effective. I rarely suffer from sore achilles tendons; but when I did on one occasion, I received some interesting advice from Gordon Dickson, a Canadian marathoner who suffered chronically from the same problem. Gordie said that runners with sore achilles always test themselves: they reach down to touch the tendon checking for continued soreness, and continuously irritate it, so it never heals. At Gordie's recommendation, I stopped touching the ten-

don; within a week or two, my achilles tendon no longer was sore.

8. *Use common sense.* Maybe if you merely think about a way to cure your problem, you may come up with some simple solution. Some cures are surprisingly simple. My cousin Judy Molinaro runs; one time when I was visiting her house, she mentioned a sore back. She even knew why it was sore. While running in midwinter, snow glare bothered her eyes, so she dropped her head, causing her to lean forward and bother her back. "Why don't you try sunglasses?" I suggested.

9. *Seek medical advice.* Like they say in the aspirin commercials: See a doctor if the pain persists. There is no sense running on gimpy legs and feeling uncomfortable when medical intervention may either cure your injury or permit more comfortable running. The first line of defense against running injuries is a podiatrist. Running injuries are invariably caused because of contact between the foot and the ground; and the foot is the province of the podiatrist. Even if your injury is in the knee or hip, the podiatrist may be the logical person to help you.

Your second best choice would be to consult any physician who runs, because even if your problem is outside his specialty, he may be able to refer you to someone else. For certain injuries, however, you may need specific care. Despite Don Higdon's apprehension, there comes a time when you may need a high-priced orthopedic surgeon.

10. *Stop running.* This is the advice that runners often get from nonrunning doctors, unfortunately, and is one reason why runners treat doctors with healthy skepticism. But sometimes those doctors may be right. Certain people are not meant to run because of their physical makeup. One of my friends is Howard Mudd, a former offensive guard for the San Francisco 49ers. Howard's wife and children run, and since retiring from professional football, he has trimmed his previous playing weight by 30 or 40 pounds; if you saw him today you would wonder how he survived as long as he did in the National Football League. He survived, but had so many knee operations that he must exercise by cycling instead of running. I like to feel that I could teach Howard Mudd to run despite his past injuries, but I'm probably wrong. Some people should not run, although usually not for the reasons given by nonrunning physicians. If a member of the American Medical Joggers Association tells you not to run, I would be inclined to accept that advice.

How to Prevent Injuries

Preventive medicine has become very popular lately and is one reason why many people start running: by becoming physically fit, they hope to prevent medical problems, particularly heart attacks and strokes. That is not the reason why people *continue* to run, and escalate their mileage, but it often is the reason why people *begin* to run. It is ironic that in their zeal to avoid one medical problem (atherosclerosis) they sometimes encounter another one (chondromalacia). There are degrees of danger in medicine and the latter problem, the infamous cartilage softening or "runner's knee," is much less life-threatening than a heart attack. The worst danger is that if you stop running because of the latter you may develop the former.

Means by which you can prevent running injuries are: cancelling your subscription to *Runner's World*, resigning your YMCA membership, turning the other way when another runner approaches during a workout, and changing the subject during a conversation if anybody begins to discuss their or your running. If you can avoid becoming enamored with running as a sport or lifestyle, you will be less likely to want to do more of it. Most running injuries come because we do too much.

Everybody has a limit. Dr. Richard Schuster thinks the limit for many people is 30 miles a week. Only when they begin to push their training beyond that do they acquire foot injuries that bring them limping to his office. But championship runners run endless miles without injury. Bill Rodgers and Frank Shorter train 140 miles a week, and seem not to have limits, but even world champions break down if they push themselves too far. Their limits are much higher than normal individuals, which may be why they are champions.

Stretching

One way to prevent injuries is to stretch.

The main reason is because stretching exercises work. Indirect causes of many injuries are tight muscles. Running—particularly slow running on hard surfaces—tightens muscles. Runners who maintain loose muscles reduce their chance of injury. Stretching is one of the most effective means of loosening muscles. Stretch, Dick, stretch.

We usually did exercises at the beginning of each workout when I ran on my college track team, mainly because the coach so instructed us. Some of the intent was to loosen muscles, but most of the exercises involved calisthenics aimed at strengthening us. As captain, I often led our team in pushups, situps, jumping jacks, and various other exercises; on some occasions even a duck-waddle (walking with our tails nearly dangling on the ground) which I now would no more do than put my hand into a buzz saw.

Strengthening exercises are not necessarily bad, and many runners lift weights (once forbidden) to increase their basic strength. But nobody lifts weights to loosen as well as strengthen muscles.

I frequently tell a story about the track coach whose runners frequently suffered injuries. On one occasion he brought an injured runner to the team doctor, who, having just read an article on stretching advised that the runner begin stretching as one means of loosening his muscles. The coach and runner nodded, then went away.

The doctor encountered the coach two years later and inquired about the team. "I guess those stretching exercises must not have worked," commented the doctor obliquely, "because I never see you or the team anymore."

"On the contrary," countered the coach, "everybody on the team does them. And they never seem to get injured any more."

That story may be apocryphal, but it illustrates what could happen if you add a few minutes of stretching each day to your regimen. Dr. Richard Schuster believes that runners who train in the mornings seem to suffer injuries more frequently than those who train in the afternoon. He suspects that, in their rush to squeeze a workout between sleep and breakfast, they take less time to stretch; and they may be still stiff from getting out of bed.

Stretching is what the name implies. You stretch the muscles by extending them as much as you comfortably can without straining. As an example, assuming you are seated reading this book, raise your hands above your head and try and reach for the ceiling without moving the rest of your body. You have just stretched your arm muscles.

Three things to remember if you get involved in a stretching regimen:

1. *Don't bounce.* Stretching should be done in a static position. If you bounce in an attempt to "improve" your stretch, reaching that extra inch or so that allows you to touch your toes, you defeat the purpose of the stretching exercise.

2. *Don't strain.* You want to stretch to the limits of comfort, but not beyond that limit. Proper stretching is similar to yoga in that you want to play with the edges of tension. According to Robert Anderson, who gave stretching demonstrations at National Running Week: "Looseness and tightness aren't how far you can or can't bend down."

3. *Don't measure yourself.* The object of stretching is not to see how soon you can get into a position where you can touch your toes but rather to become loose. You may become loose without ever touching those toes. People who touch their toes effortlessly may do so because they have very long arms or very short legs.

Dr. Schuster warns: "Most runners stretch too vigorously. The individual who runs is competitive; he gets competitive with himself by stretching. He stretches to beat all fury and tears himself apart."

When Should You Stretch?

Before you run is the most obvious answer. Attempt a few basic stretching exercises after you get dressed but before you head out the door.

But a better time to stretch is at mid-workout, approximately a mile from your door. Runners who do fast training on tracks usually do this. A typical warmup for a track runner is to jog a mile then exercise before any fast running. Those same runners on long distance runs, however, sometimes forget the warmup and simply start to run. They figure that, since they are not running fast, they don't need a normal warmup. They're in a hurry to get on with it; to get out on the road.

Another time to stretch is immediately after you return from your run. You probably don't want to jump into the shower unless you are in a hurry. So take some time while you are recovering to do additional stretching exercises. Apart from helping relieve the tightness caused by a long, hard run, stretching will help you relax.

I stretch at other times of the day simply because it feels good. You rarely encounter my midday stretching exercises in any book. I may clasp my hands and reach high overhead. I may point my feet and curl my toes while sitting on a sofa. While talking with friends I sometimes find myself unconsciously rising on my toes, exercising my arches and ankles. I wonder why people sometimes get seasick while talking to me.

Higdon's Fantastic Four

We have arrived at the point in this chapter when I finally feel obliged to offer you some stretching exercises. I am not going to offer you many because if you become serious you probably should consult any one of many good books that offer stretching exercises. "Light on Yoga" by B. K. S. Iyengar is one such book.

Dr. George Sheehan achieved a certain immortality by developing a series of six exercises: "Sheehan's Magic Six." Having been a comic book fanatic during my youth, I decided to make my attempt at immortality by labeling my stretching exercises, "Higdon's Fantastic Four."

They are not the yoga-based exercises that have become popular with runners. While not ballistic, they involve in-motion stretching to permit stretching several muscles for the price of one. They are designed so they can be accomplished without sitting or lying down. People who live in California and train only on golf courses may not need free-standing exercises, but those of us who live in more northerly climates, and stop to stretch midworkout dislike lying down in snowdrifts. You also can do these exercises without getting your $52 warmup suit dirty.

• **Fantastic Exercise One: The Sun Worshipper.** (Excuse the semidescriptive titles, but I wanted some way to tell one exercise from the other.) Begin by standing with your feet together and flat, your arms at your side. Raise your arms slowly away from your body, gently stretching until they are overhead, your hands cupped like a diver ready to plunge off the cliffs at Acapulco. In the same motion, continue to reach for the ceiling (or sky) with your hands, keeping your heels flat on the floor. Your shoulders should be pressed against your ears at ultimate stretch point.

Hold this position several counts, then bend forward from the waist, maintaining the same hands-over-head position, keeping your legs straight until you are in the classic hang-ten position (ten fingers hanging toward your toes. Notice that I said *toward* your toes, not *touching* your toes). Quit showing off. Every other head in the class is down and can't see your flexibility anyway.

• **Fantastic Exercise Two: The Lighthouse.** Stand with your feet spread, arms on hips. Lean slowly sideways until one elbow is pointing down, the other pointing up. Hold this position several counts, then slowly rotate your body by leaning backward at the waist until the first elbow is up, and the second elbow down on the other side of your body. Hold again. Now rotate back to the first position by leaning forward. Continue rotating for several revolutions, then repeat the exercise from the other direction.

This exercise should be done slowly — as a lighthouse beam rotates — not as a radar scanner.

• **Fantastic Exercise Three: The Gorky Stork.** Stand next to some object such as a tree you can hold unless you have excellent balance. Running partners are acceptable as long as they recognize your intention. Balance on one leg, lifting the back of the other leg from the knee until you can grasp it at the ankle. Gently pull that leg up toward your buttocks, pointing your toe as you do so. Hold that position several counts. Now lift the leg from the groin, moving it sideways until in the position assumed by a trail leg of a hurdler.

The moment you extend to the farthest position in the sideways direction, rotate the leg forward, still holding onto the foot the way a hurdler brings his trail leg forward. When you finish, you should be standing with your raised leg pressed against your chest. Repeat the exercise using the other leg.

• **Fantastic Exercise Four: The Tree Shover.** If you are still standing next to the tree, face it and place your palms against the trunk. This is the classic achilles-stretching exercise that makes runners appear to be trying to push trees, buildings, trucks, and other objects off the top of a cliff. Anything taller than five feet and immovable becomes object of their attention. They usually place both feet together, heels flat, several feet away from the object pushed, which allows them to stretch both achilles tendons at the same time. I prefer to stretch mine one at a time. I lean forward into the tree with one leg back, heel flat, the other leg bent under me, permitting me to get a better stretch. I duck my head between my outstretched arms at the same time, which permits me to stretch and loosen my shoulder muscles. I switch to the other when finished with one leg. I have yet to fell a tree, but I no longer have sore achilles tendons.

For runners who stretch on solitary landscapes with no tall stationary objects nearby Joe Henderson offers a variation on this exercise. He stretches from the classic sprinter's crouch,

similarly pushing backward with one foot, although not necessarily with the heel on the floor.

Stretching While You Run

Joe Henderson recommends that another form of stretching
might be to add speedwork to your training. A runner who
sprints usually gets up on his toes, raises his knees, lengthens his
stride, pumps his arms vigorously, and otherwise submits the
muscles to different ranges of motion than they might otherwise
receive during slow running at a steady pace. Sprinting,
Henderson claims, is another form of stretching. I agree.

To get full value from training, a runner should schedule occasional speed workouts; whether sprints, repeats, fartlek, or
shifts of pace during long runs. Some people suggest formulas
for how much speed training a long distance runner needs. Five
percent sticks in my mind; perhaps it was the Canadian marathoner Jerome Drayton who used that figure while lecturing on
his training methods at National Running Week. I resist such
statistification of training, because the runner is the best judge
of his own needs. One day of speedwork a week should provide
the necessary stretching required for comfortable running and
fast times.

Reading Your Body

Runners must learn to read their own bodies, an expression
elite runners often use to describe the way they monitor their
physical reactions not only in practice but also during competition. By knowing how their bodies react to certain stresses, they
determine when they should slow their pace or when they can
increase it. Extracting every conceivable ounce of energy from
their bodies may be one way that some runners outperform
others.

It also may permit certain runners, wise in the ways of their
bodies, to avoid injuries that might also detract from their performance. Experience teaches them that when they push too
hard, the resulting stress may cause deterioration instead of improvement in their performance. They learn from their training
diaries, instead of becoming slaves to those diaries, by piling up
one high mileage week after another. When a certain situation
or workout causes injury at one stage in their career, they avoid
that situation or workout later, or approach it more gradually
from a different direction.

Runners should be in touch with their bodies, but they do not want to become so fixed on each slight twinge or discomfort that they are unable to run for fear of some disabling injury. Runners should learn how to run up to pain, as long as they do not run *through* pain. "If you begin with stiffness and pain," advises Dr. Subotnick, "and as you run it loosens up, then it is perfectly okay to continue running. If the problem becomes worse as you run, however, then you are only hurting yourself. You should stop, seek proper medical attention, and not run until the situation is reversed."

Remember Dr. George Sheehan: we are all an experiment of one. If you have learned about injury prevention by experience or experimentation—even if it is sprinkling apple cider on your navel while singing your high school fight song—do it! But don't tell anyone, they may think you nuttier than you already are.

Part 6
Running for Everybody

23

Women's Running

Differences, similarities, uniquely female problems

Everybody seems to be running lately, including more and more women. Several of the female members of my family run. And there are constellations of other runners around them.

At an Easter gathering at my cousin Judy's house, there was talk about the bras women wear (or don't wear) while running. I sat at the other end of the room watching *The Wizard of Oz* on television, so paid little attention to their conversation until I heard my wife's comment: "You should talk to Hal. He's been looking into women's bras."

The roar of laughter that immediately followed caused me to temporarily divert my attention from the attempt of the Wicked Witch of the West to incinerate the Scarecrow. I quickly disassociated myself from my wife's sexist statement. It would have been more accurate for my wife to say I was looking into the subject of women's bras. Or researching a chapter on women's running for this book.

With the current militancy of the feminist movement it is easy for men to get in trouble talking about women. At National Running Week in 1977, Dr. Richard Schuster made the statement that since women are different than men, they have more foot injuries—and someone booed him. It wasn't Dr. Schuster's fault that women had wider pelvises, that this causes a slightly different footstrike, which results in more of certain injuries. He simply was reporting the facts.

Running is a very simple sport. The basics that apply to men for the most part also apply to women. Nevertheless, there do exist differences, the most major one perhaps being historical.

The Year Roberta Beat Me

I recall when the first female runner appeared at Boston.* The year was 1966 and, bothered by a leg injury, I had sunk to a low level of conditioning. I entered the Boston Marathon that year anyway to run from the rear and cover the race for the *National Observer*. I stopped somewhere past the Newton hills and eventually wrote my article about the "Loser's Bus," which sweeps the course after most of the runners have passed picking up the drop-outs.

Unbeknownst to most of us at the start, Roberta Gibb, 23 years old from San Diego, stood on the sidelines until the gun went off, then jumped into the race. She wore a black bathing suit and light slacks cut at the knees. Word soon spread on the course of the woman in the race. This caused some resentment—as though a woman had entered the men's locker room and she didn't belong there. Nobody expected her to finish, of course, because women were too weak to run marathons. Everybody knew that. I recall one individual on the Loser's Bus grumbling "If I have to compete against women I think I'll quit!"

Well, of course, he already had. The next day the Boston *Record American* added insult to injury with the headline: BRIDE BEATS 200 MEN IN MARATHON. I don't recall my exact reactions to the prospect of women becoming marathoners, but it was probably indifference. If women wanted to join our races, that seemed all right with me, but I didn't circulate petitions for it. As I usually finished near the front of any race I entered, I did not particularly feel threatened by the prospect of having a woman beat me. Perhaps I had so little respect for the ability of women to run long distance races, I assumed it would never happen. Of course, I was among the 200 men "beaten" that day by Roberta since I dropped out at 22 miles.

Since then, women have proved themselves much more competent athletes than most of us at Boston in 1966 imagined. The fact that women now occasionally finish ahead of me in long

---

* Reportedly a Canadian woman nicknamed "the lady in red" ran Boston in 1951, but 15 years passed before regular participation began.

distance races does not worry me any more than it worries women that a dirty old man of 46 sometimes finishes ahead of them. We're competing in different categories and more often against ourselves than against each other.

Thus, Roberta Gibb started a revolution. The following year at Boston Kathy Switzer appeared on the starting line wearing an official number (having entered herself as K. Switzer to obtain it). Boston Athletic Association official Johnny Semple attempted to reclaim the "illegally obtained" number mid-race, and the resulting photographs of the scuffle, reprinted coast-to-coast, probably did more to further the cause of female marathoning than anything the women could have done themselves. More and more women began to appear at Hopkinton each April. By 1972, the Boston Marathon relented and allowed women to enter officially. In the spring of 1978, I attended the Bonne Bell 10,000-Meter Race for Women in Chicago, which attracted an entry of more than 3,000, the largest women's race ever held in the world—though I suspect that statement will be outdated before this book is published. Women's running is growing that fast.

What impressed me about that race, in which my wife Rose and 15-year-old daughter Laura participated and finished, was that the women seemed to be having such a wonderful time! Sure, some of them looked tired and bedraggled as they crossed the finish line, but that happens to competitors of any sex or age in any race. Within a few minutes after finishing, most of them were bouncing around the cool-down area, laughing, joking, offering each other war stories of how it was out there, their faces shining with the glow of personal accomplishment. "What I enjoyed most," Rose told me, "was coming by the refreshment stations and having men standing on the sidelines handing us water." It was, indeed, a role reversal as was the crowd of mostly men cheering at the finish line.

But shades of Roberta Gibb. In the middle of a pack of women coming toward the finish line I did notice one man running without a number. Perhaps he was running to protest the sexist race, which limited entries to women. Or perhaps he was simply a Sunday jogger who got swept up by the crowd. At least there were no streakers; it was too cold for that.

Women's running has definitely come of age. Within the next decade I predict there will be as many, if not more, women running long distances as men. My only negative concern is that the advent of female runners has made it more difficult for me to go to the toilet. I always used to beat the long lines at the men's toilet by using the women's facilities. Either through fear or habit, most men avoided the women's toilet so I usually had no wait, and there never were any women around anyway. I no longer have that option.

My Running Wife

One afternoon in the spring of 1978 my wife returned from the elementary school where she taught and announced she was going out for a walk. I thought nothing of it, because Rose always liked to walk for exercise. She also enjoyed cycling. Frequently I went biking with her up and down Lake Shore Drive, usually on summer evenings. During our 20 years of married life, she had tried running on several occasions, but never really liked it. I neither encouraged nor discouraged her running, feeling it should be her choice.

One afternoon as she was about to head out the door to walk I said, "I'll go with you." Bothered by a leg injury, I thought some walking might help me recuperate. About a quarter mile away from the house, Rose began to jog at a very slow pace. Surprised, I started to jog behind her. I was afraid to initiate a conversation for fear that if she started talking she would get out of breath. So we ran along together in silence until I finally spoke: "Do you realize you've run a mile?"

"I know," Rose responded.

Another period of silence as we continued at that pace. "That's pretty good," I said.

"I've got something to confess," said Rose. Usually when a woman begins a conversation with her husband in this manner, it is to announce her intention of moving out to live with her lover, but Rose's secret was that instead of going for a walk each evening after school, she had been jogging. "I've been doing up to two miles a day," she announced.

That afternoon we covered nearly four miles, talking most of the way once I discovered that conversation would not adversely affect her wind. A month later, without unnecessary strain, she completed the Bonne Bell 10,000-Meter Race for Women, averaging slightly less than 11:00 per mile, which put her maybe two-thirds of the way back in the pack. She now proudly wears around the house the T-shirt she won with its motto on the back: "Exercise Your Body. Bonne Bell Your Face." She now continues to run about two miles a day, which seems like a comfortable level for her. Sometimes I accompany her either on my easy, second workout of the day or because I still am nursing that injury and want to run slow instead of fast.

I now overhear Rose issuing advice to other women as to how they should start running: "Begin by going out for a walk," she says. "If you feel like you want to jog a little, do so. After a while you will be able to jog more than you walk, but don't try to do too much, too soon."

That is the same, sound, simple advice that I offered at the beginning of this book—for men or for women. Joan Ullyot wrote a book entitled *Women's Running* which was very popular among female runners, but Joan offered nothing revolutionary in that volume. Except for an occasional paragraph here and there, it could just as easily have been written by a man about male running. A number of men runners I know read *Women's Running* and commented that practically everything in it applied to them as well. It was simply a good, basic book on how to begin to run whether you were a male or female—not that Joan intended it as such, but only because there is very little difference between the way men and women run.

Viva La Difference!

There are, however, a few basic differences between the two sexes which probably warrant some discussion.

1. *Physiological differences.* Men are faster than women. Back in paleolithic times, man's role was that of the hunter-gatherer; woman's was that of keeper of the fire. Man had to run after game to supply food for the family, thus evolved as a muscular individual with slender buttocks which permitted him to run fast. Woman had to bear children, thus evolved with a wide pelvis which made the act of childbirth both safer and more comfortable, but limited her running ability.

Joan Ullyot has suggested that because of an ability to convert fat to energy, women may actually be more efficient long distance runners than men and the time may come when female marathoners run as fast as male marathoners. I doubt that will happen unless current evolutionary patterns are reversed, an unlikely occurrence in the immediate future. As more and more women begin to compete in long distance races, the women's marathon record will improve in relation to that of men. (Presently, the best women run approximately one-minute-per-mile slower than the best men over the marathon distance.) But probably the difference will never entirely be bridged because of the basic difference in speed between the two sexes. Women have been competing in sprint races in the Olympics for a half a century, yet their best time over 100 meters lags a full second behind that of the men.

This relative difference in ability, however, is meaningless because women can compete against each other rather than against faster men. Particularly in long distance races each woman can compete against herself, measuring her achievement against her own relative ability.

2. *Psychological differences.* Men are more competitive than women. In primitive times, man developed a more aggressive nature than woman because he often had to compete with other men to obtain food. Paleolithic man also served as protector of the family and often had to defend his home aggressively. Woman was more passive, more accepting. These roles persisted into this century.

In suggesting that women converted fat into energy more efficiently than men, Joan Ullyot was using as evidence the fact that fewer women than men seemed to "hit the wall" at 20 miles. She suspected that once their basic levels of glycogen were used up, they could more successfully metabolize other forms of energy.

More recently some of the top women marathoners have hit the wall. Joan now concedes that maybe they have begun to run the race competitively, performance-oriented, like men. By overpacing and overextending themselves in the early stages of a distance race, they experience the same problems that supposedly more aggressive males faced.

Assuming that women are less aggressive than men, it should be easier for them to become fitness joggers and recreational runners, because they feel less the male-bred obligation to perform, to run fast, to do well. Women are happy to run, which can be a positive factor in their becoming runners. However, I see more and more acceptance on the part of supposedly aggressive males of the role of participatory rather than competitive runner. In this case, there may be less psychological differences between men and women runners than people might suspect.

3. *Sociological differences.* Men have had more athletic advantages than women. Until recently women were neither encouraged nor permitted to compete in sports. The entire focus of most intercollegiate and interscholastic athletic programs was on male sports—a few male sports at that, notably football and basketball. In fact, until a few years ago even male distance runners did not command much respect, so a woman marathoner had two strikes against her. My wife was extremely active and athletic when young, but in college her role, typically, was that of a cheerleader.

During the fall of 1977, I coached the fifth and sixth grade cross-country team at the elementary school where my wife taught. We had both boy and girl teams, competing in separate divisions, but what struck me the first week of practice was how hopelessly out of shape the girls were compared to the boys. At that pre-puberty age there are relatively few physiological differences between girls and boys. If anything, girls mature more quickly and often outsprint boys of the same age. But the girls who appeared for cross-country practice were hopelessly outclassed by their boy counterparts.

The reason was more sociological than physiological. They spent more of their time playing with dolls than playing basketball, thus had no athletic base. Only when it becomes acceptable for girls to play sports as much as boys will females begin to develop their athletic potential.

My wife admits that she did not become a jogger sooner, because there were no other women out on the roads running, except for a few of us hard core road racers. Now with both male and female runners practicing and participating almost everywhere, fewer barriers exist prohibiting women from becoming runners.

Equipment for Women

Bras. My examination of women's bras resulted in no particular revelations. One survey of women runners at a marathon in Minneapolis uncovered the fact that hardly any women wore the same style bra, and most of them were dissatisfied with what they had. Only recently have undergarment manufacturers begun to turn their attention to athletic bras, and I suspect that there will be some false starts before they begin to develop something that a majority of women runners find acceptable.

And they never will develop a product that will suit everybody, because people are different. In choosing running shoes, it depends on the size of your foot; with bras, it depends on the size of your breasts. In the past many women runners ran braless, because the first ones attracted to the sport were often slender and chestless—as was true with the fastest men. Lately people (not merely women) of all shapes and sizes have become runners, so the old standards no longer hold.

Shorts. Here it also is a matter of shopping around, trying on different shorts—both in the stores and during workouts—and finding out what feels more comfortable. Some women runners wear boxer-style track shorts with slits in the side like men either because this style is most comfortable or is most easily available. Some women wear form-fitting tights. Merchandisers now advertise "unisex shorts," so called because they have a built-in pant that can be used either by men or women. I bought such a pair recently, found them uncomfortable, and gave them to my daughter to wear. She didn't like them either. In designing a product supposedly acceptable for everybody, the manufacturer apparently designed one acceptable for nobody.

Shoes. Some women runners' problems are caused by wearing men's running shoes. Men's wide shoes often do not fit. This causes injuries, particularly shin splints. In the past they wore men's shoes because they had no choice. Recently shoe manufacturers have begun to turn more attention to shoes designed specifically for women. The first women's shoes merely had feminine colors, such as pink and lavender, and names you would expect to see on products advertised in *Vogue.* Finally shoe manufacturers have begun to produce shoes with design features suited for women.

Some women still feel more comfortable running in men's shoes. If that is the case with you, do so regardless of color or name.

Uniquely Female Problems

Menstruation. During a college cross-country meet that included a race for women, one of the girl runners on the team had what seemed to be a poor race. Afterwards she stalked away. "What's bothering her today?" the coach commented.

"She's all right," replied one of my son's teammates. "She's just doing her woman's time."

He was implying cavalierly that she was having her period. Some women gain weight, because of the extensive fluid retention, during this time of the month. Other women flow quite heavily and lose excessive amounts of blood. If you fit into these categories, you may want to either limit or eliminate your workouts during your menstrual period, or run easier. However, many women athletes have competed successfully and even won Olympic gold medals while menstruating.

According to Kathy Switzer, who serves as a special promotions manager for Avon Products, exercise reduces any period discomfort. "Cramping is most common in sedentary women," she asserts. She also recommends tampons as the most comfortable protection while running.

One important point worth making, however, is that because of their monthly blood loss, women more often suffer from anemia than men. One out of every four women needs an iron supplement, and this figure could be higher among active female athletes. If in doubt, have a blood test, but iron for women is one of the few supplements that can improve performance. Iron can be taken in pill form.

Birth Control. One woman runner I know commented during a running clinic that she experienced extremely heavy blood loss while using an intrauterine device (IUD) for birth control. When she had the device removed, her blood loss during menstruation returned to normal. This should come as no surprise to anyone who has examined birth control literature on IUDs. Using the pill may be a poor substitute, since by doing so you are tampering with your body chemistry. Using a diaphragm may be the most acceptable means.

Some women runners discover that when they train 50 miles per week their menstrual periods cease, resuming when they decrease their training. This has caused some people to suggest that running may be a form of birth control. Good luck, girls. It may be, but only if the woman uses her athletic skills to run away from men. Any woman who assumes that lack of menstrual cycle will prevent her from becoming pregnant is taking a chance.

Pregnancy. Pregnant women continue to run with no problems. At the National Age Handicap Championships in Michigan City in 1977, Debbie Meier of Indianapolis ran while five months pregnant. She finished the 15-kilometer event in last place, but she finished. At a clinic afterwards I joked about Debbie bringing a new meaning to the term, "out of shape." Probably, I should have said she brought a new meaning to the term, "*in* shape."

Erma Tranter of Park Ridge, Illinois, started to run two miles a day to get in good physical condition after the birth of her first child and continued on this regimen until two days before the delivery of her second child. "I didn't tell my doctor I was running," Erma told me, "because I was afraid he wouldn't approve."

I wouldn't advise a pregnant woman to start running if she has never tried it before, but the woman who continues to run while pregnant probably will have both an easier and a safer delivery, because she is less likely to be overweight and will be in generally better physical condition. But if running while pregnant bothers you, simply stop. You can start running again after the baby is born—provided you can convince your husband to change diapers, but that's another problem.

24

The Young and the Old

Running knows no
age barriers

During a question-and-answer session at a clinic I gave in connection with the Saginaw Bay Marathon, a young girl in the bleachers raised her hand. She wanted to know: "Would you encourage a ten-year-old to run marathons?"

"No," I responded. "I wouldn't encourage a ten-year-old to run marathons." That may not have been what my young questioner wanted to hear, but I immediately balanced the record. "But I also wouldn't discourage a ten-year-old from running marathons either. It depends mostly on what the particular ten-year-old wants to do."

The answer fitted my *laissez-faire* philosophy of running in general. If people, young or old, male or female, want to run they should be allowed to do so. I will support them. I may even encourage them. But I don't go around pulling people away from TV sets and forcing them to get on the road. I like to see runners, but not involuntary runners.

The questioner, as it turned out, was Stormi-Ann Gurtsch, a young runner from central Michigan. Stormi did not plan to run the marathon the next day since she was competing in a five-mile race elsewhere, but she came to hear my lecture. Previously I had encountered her just past the four-mile mark in the National Age Handicap Championships in Chicago. Based on age she and other runners received varying handicaps over runner Garry Bjorklund, who at age 26 was near the ideal age for running 15 kilometers. When I saw Stormi coming toward me on the out-and-back course, she and a younger boy had non-entered runners pacing them. The race sponsors decided to do this to guide them through traffic. At first I considered this an unfair advantage, but Stormi finished so far in front (she won by three minutes), it probably made no difference.

What disturbed me, however, was that the younger boy, when I passed him around eight miles, was crying while he ran. Later, when he crossed the finish line far behind, he still was crying — either from pain or embarrassment. The pacers accompanying him kept cheering him on. His mother stood by the sidelines shouting encouragement. But he kept crying. It seemed an example of a child running not to please himself, but to please adults.

The Little League Parent Syndrome

For children pushy adults are the greatest danger, perhaps the *only* danger, in running. I cannot recall seeing any research showing that long distance running causes permanent damage to the bones or muscles of young children. They may get injured, as anyone who engages in sports may get injured, but at their young age they undoubtedly recuperate faster than someone my age. My gut reaction is that running is good for them, since I believe that running is good for almost everybody.

But I also have been around enough parents to recognize that many of them are frustrated ex- or non-athletes, who sometimes live vicariously through the deeds of their children, achieving the success that they were once denied. I have three teenage children who competed in various sports, and my wife and I frequently saw, at baseball fields or tennis courts, examples of what might be classified as the Little League Parent (*genus Americanus*). The Little League Parent is a father or mother who places excessive pressure on his or her child to excel, who often berates that child for failure, and often screams at everyone involved: children, coaches, officials. Even if that parent does not attend the competition, often the first question asked when the child comes in the door is: "Well, did you win?"

At the other extreme is the parent who doesn't care, who simply allows the child to go to various athletic contests in other peoples' station wagons and does not even bother to ask. A subtle line exists between being "pushy" and being "supportive." There is a similar subtle line between being "indifferent" and being "laid back," the latter being the best term I can come up with for a parent who is willing to allow the child to fulfill his own athletic potential.

With the increased popularity of running, I begin to see more and more Little League Parents (*genus three-stripus*) appearing with their children at long distance races. At least, I suspect them of being Little League Parents. You never can be certain unless you know a family extremely well. On a few occasions I have seen children berated for failure, or overpraised for performing well. I suspect this occurs less in long distance running than in other sports since runners tend to be laid-back people anyway, but running parents whose children run should be aware of the problem.

They need to ask themselves the question: "Is my child running because I want him to, or because *he* wants to?" Should this book fall into the hands of children who run, they probably should ask themselves: "Am I running because *I* want to, or only because I think my parents expect me to?"

When age-group running for children first became popular in the United States a decade or so ago, some of its supporters boasted that runners who start later than age seven or eight would not be able to compete at the upper levels with runners who trained continuously since their youth. That has not occurred, and I am not aware of any age-group champions who yet have achieved Olympic success. In fact, relatively few high school champions later equal the success they had in high school. The individual who hailed the advantages of age-group running had several children who won national championships at early ages, yet by the time they became teenagers stopped competing. This is not to say that he was wrong in encouraging them to participate at an early age, but only in assuming that early participation and success would insure later participation and success. He considered the physiological reasons for success while overlooking the sometimes more important psychological ones. For some individuals, it is enough to be number one once in their lives; then they go on to other interests.

Ideally, as a parent and a runner, I would like to see my children continue to participate in running for many years. Practically, I cannot insure that they will do so. At the present time my oldest son Kevin competes actively as a college freshman; my second son David plays number one singles on his high school tennis team, but also does some running off-season; my daughter Laura gets involved in so many school activities I can't count them, but runs on occasion. Check back with me in another decade or two to see if they continue to run as either competitors or participants.

Dangers of Running for Children

Physiologically, I know of no reasons why young children should not run. Psychologically, problems may arise only if winning or losing receives too much emphasis. Physically, I see potential dangers associated with both training and racing.

Training. Young runners are smaller than adults, thus are less visible—particularly to drivers of automobiles. Everything written in a previous chapter about the dangers runners face from cars can be multiplied several times when it comes to young runners. In addition, children possess less maturity than adults, thus may more likely act careless about where and how they run. Children see distance running as play, which is fine unless you happen to be playing on a highway populated with machines travelling 25 to 55 miles per hour, or more.

For this reason parents probably should be careful where they let their children run in practice. Even a golf course with its soft, velvety surface is a suitable training area only when golfers are not present. One young boy who once ran under my supervision got hit in the head and had to be taken to the hospital because he failed to realize this. Running parents probably will understand this more than nonrunning parents, who, unfortunately, may be much less likely to read this book.

Racing. Traffic also can be a problem in races as well as in practice, particularly if drivers do not expect to see young runners in the race. A recent copy of the *Columbia Track Club Newsletter*, listing the accomplishments of eight-year-old Wesley Paul, who set national age records from 1500 meters to the marathon, also noted that he suffered head lacerations and numerous bruises when struck by a car at the six-mile mark in the 1977 Heart of America Marathon.

Small runners may also suffer collisions with bigger runners. The exuberance of youngsters often exceeds their maturity. At a mid-week race in Ogden Dunes, Indiana, a few years ago, several dozen young runners crowded their way onto the front row of the starting line. As soon as the gun sounded they sprinted the first 50 yards to see who could be first off the line, then immediately slowed while still in the path of older competitors, who had to swerve to miss them. Some of the runners coming up failed to see the kids, and several were knocked down. The next year at the same race I suggested that younger runners start in the back. That didn't help my popularity with them, but at least none got hurt.

The inequality in ability of young runners, women, older runners, and slow runners sometimes causes problems at the starting lines of mass races which now attract fields of more than 5000. People have been trampled to death exiting theatres and sporting events when momentary panic occurred. While I like to think it can't happen in a running race, some danger does exist.

While on occasions, such as handicap races similar to the one described earlier, young runners can compete successfully with older and faster runners, and while they often can participate comfortably in mass happenings and fun runs, they may be best off most of the time competing in races limited to those their own age and ability.

The Growing Legion of Older Runners

As with women and children, practically everything in this book written about training also applies to older runners. Because of their age, older runners may be somewhat more susceptible to certain injuries than younger athletes, or at least will heal more slowly, but because of their maturity and experience they may be less likely to suffer them.

Competition is plentiful for runners over 40, and most major distance races now offer separate prizes for runners not merely in 10-year age categories but often in five-year age categories. In addition, independent competition in track and field is available for masters, or veteran, runners on the international level. The Second World Masters Track and Field Championships held in Gothenberg, Sweden in August, 1977 attracted 2752 competitors from 48 different countries. Numerous similar masters meets and races are held at the national, regional, state, and even local level. There is no need for runners to retire because of old age any more, since they can continue competing right into the grave. Several athletes in the 90 age category competed in the last few world championships. While one of the early worries of those involved in the masters movement was that the participants would be collapsing from heart attacks on the track, there have been very few such incidents. Masters competitors seem remarkably healthy, not only compared to the general public but also compared to athletes of all ages.

People trying to determine the reason for the current running boom—the fact that joggers crowd the roads, that thousands now appear for races—often consider several landmarks in the history of physical fitness in the United States. First was the emphasis on fitness projected after the election of John F. Kennedy as president. Second was the return from New Zealand in the early 1960s of University of Oregon track coach Bill Bowerman, who brought with him Arthur Lydiard's ideas on jogging for everybody. Third was the popularity of the book *Aerobics* by Ken Cooper, and soon after its publication in 1968 the death rate from heart attacks in America turned downward for the first time in history. Fourth was the exposure given Frank Shorter, not merely after his Olympic marathon victory in 1972, but because of the extensive TV coverage given his nearly successful title defense in 1976. All of these factors were partly and concurrently responsible for getting people running. At the same time, *Runner's World* surfaced as the most visible publication offering both tips on how to run and news on people who were doing it. The fact that *Runner's World*'s circulation tripled from 85,000 to 230,000 in the space of a year between 1977 and 1978 was part barometer of the running explosion and part cause of it.

But part of the texture of long distance running, at least at the competitive level, was caused by the increase in numbers of men (and eventually women) over 40 who participated in it. These often were businessmen, secure in their success, their children often grown, individuals who a few decades previously might have channeled their energies and organizational abilities into memberships in Kiwanis, Rotary, Lions, or other service organizations. Instead, these individuals chose to run. After running a while, they became either dissatisfied with the then-existing organization of the sport, or saw how they could improve that organization. They became involved in starting clubs, getting joggers together for workouts, and promoting races. Invariably as I receive invitations to major running races, I find that the prime movers are men who if not yet 40 soon will pass this stage in their lives. At the risk of omitting some obvious leaders in the field of running, they are people such as Dave Pain, Bob Fine, Lee Flaherty, Fred Lebow, Gene Greer, Al

Morrison, Ray Bartel, Wendy Miller, and the list just goes on and on. Often I participate in races they organize but do not run in. They can't compete, because they are too busy seeing that their events function properly. Meanwhile, they are talking about running somebody else's race the following weekend. Once a year they pay their dues by sponsoring a race, and the other 51 weekends they run in the races organized often by other older runners. If the quality of racing and running is better today than it was ten years ago—and I think it is—it is because of the input of such individuals: men and women with experience and maturity.

Dangers of Running for Older People

Consider some of the dangers if you are an older individual and start to run. You might have a heart attack and not get full benefit from your recently purchased lifetime subscription to *Hustler Magazine*. You might collide with a caboose while crossing an Amtrak track at the moment you are experiencing your runner's high. Your wife might run away with a cigar-smoking, crop-duster pilot from Texas while you are out doing your fart-lek. All these bad things, and many even worse ones, may happen to you if you either start to run or continue to do so. If you were worried about such occurrences happening, you never should have bought a copy of this book.

Part 7
Running Hot and Cold

25

Hibernation

How to stay in shape during layoffs

In January 26, 1978, a massive snowstorm combined with near-hurricane-force struck the Midwest, causing drifts 10 to 15 feet deep on many roads including my beloved running course, Lake Shore Drive. Traffic shuddered to a standstill. Several friends got caught at Chicago's O'Hare Field, marooned for three days, unable to bridge the 70 or so miles separating them from home.

Seven weeks later in March, the weather had begun to warm somewhat, although Lake Shore Drive still had snowdrifts higher than my head in certain areas, remnants of the storm. While running I spotted Bill Ludwig, a contractor scheduled to do some remodelling on our house. It was one of my "repair" days, so I had no qualms about stopping mid-workout for conversation. (On another "tear" day with every step measured against the clock, I might have barely managed to wave at Bill.)

After talking briefly about remodelling plans, somehow the conversation moved to my dedication in training, a subject which always impresses others more than it does me. I run because I want to, not because I have to. "You probably didn't get much running done during the blizzard," Bill commented.

I honestly could not remember, so that evening I checked my training diary. "Blizzard!!!" was the notation on Thursday, January 26, 1978, the three exclamation marks indicating the severity of the day's weather. But even while several feet of snow were falling, I managed five miles. The mail failed to get through, no newspaper was delivered, and the garbage would continue to accumulate for another week, but still I ran. If you want to run, you run. Nothing stops you.

But everybody does not possess an equal dedication to running, and as more and more participant runners (as opposed to competitive runners) become involved in the sport, I have become aware of what might previously have been considered an almost heretical neglect of year-round running.

John Laue, for example. John lives in Beverly Shores, a community to the west of Michigan City, right on the boundary of the Dunes National Lakeshore, one of the most enticing running areas in America. Bill Rodgers visited me recently to participate in a running camp I organized, coming a day early, so he said, "to run in the dunes." While planning a ten-mile race in Beverly Shores in the fall of 1977, I came to know John and worked out with him on several occasions. He competed in the mile in high school some ten years previous and only recently returned to running, occasionally racing in competition. He seemed reasonably talented and probably with a year or so of training could break three hours for the marathon, which would have qualified him for Boston, that elusive goal that tempts so many runners.

Several months passed when I didn't see John, then one day I encountered him coming out of the library. More for conversational than any other reason, I inquired: "How's your running coming?"

"I'm not running right now," John said.

A thousand injuries and diseases flashed through my mind: chondromalacia, tendonitis, strained planter fascia, mononucleosis, hepatitis. Which of those dread diseases had struck John Laue.

He explained: "I just don't enjoy running in the winter."

I took two steps backward, certain that any moment that the earth would open beneath his feet. I understand that several thousand miles away in California, clouds formed over Mountain View, but no lightning struck. John Laue enjoyed running, but only on his own terms. If he didn't want to run in cold weather, he would not run. Come spring, John would be back on the trails of Beverly Shores once again.

Groundhogs

John Laue might be described as a Groundhog Runner. Each

fall the groundhog (also known as the woodchuck), fattened from recent eating bouts, curls up in a ball in its underground burrow, nose tucked between hind feet, its tail pulled forward to cover its face. During the winter the groundhog's blood barely circulates. Its teeth do not grow, nor its hair, nor its toenails. Once every six minutes the groundhog takes a solitary breath and its body temperature drops to 38 degrees, its life touching the very boundaries of death. The groundhog remains in this state for anywhere from four to six months, yet reawakens each spring to resume its normal existence.

I understand that every February 2, John Laue dons his New Balance shoes and stumbles out his kitchen door. If he sees his shadow he becomes frightened and does not return to running for at least six more weeks. So goes the legend.

From a physiological standpoint, groundhog runners contribute to their eventual deterioration by their inactivity. Physiologists can measure how rapidly the body loses its training effect. Bob Fitts, an exercise physiologist from Wauwatosa, Wisconsin, suggests that if we stop running, our physical condition will decline rapidly by two weeks. He explains why: "The proteins within our body responsible for facilitating the conversion of food into cellular energy available for work (i.e., muscular contraction, etc.) increase in response to exercise-training. When training stops, the concentration of these proteins decreases rapidly toward pre-training levels. With approximately two weeks of inactivity, half of the exercise-induced increase has been lost, and as a result, our ability to generate energy and do work has also significantly decreased." Fitts suggests that in order to maintain an exercise effort, or stay in shape, people need to train regularly.

Physiologically I agree with what Bob Fitts says, but psychologically not everybody stands as prepared as I am to accept the burden of running over ice and snow when the wind chill dips below zero. Everybody cannot live in Gainesville, Florida, or La Jolla, California. The only alternative then is to hibernate. But how can runners survive as groundhogs? I can suggest several ways:

1. Resume a career as closet jogger. Chapter two of this book suggested how people could ease themselves into the sport of running by practicing in secret at home. But once you step out of your closet and onto the road, that does not prohibit you from returning to a career of running in place. Fifteen minutes a day three days a week will help you maintain at least some of your summer conditioning and ease your *return* to the roads once spring beckons.

2. *Do other exercises at home.* If you don't like jogging in place, obtain an exercycle, which can be purchased for approximately $100. A stand to elevate your bicycle permitting the same activity costs a fraction of that. Alex Ratelle, M.D., a Minneapolis anesthesiologist, cycles in his home sometimes as much as an hour a day and claims it is the secret of why he, at age 53, can run marathons in 2:34. Pick winter as a time to strengthen other parts of your body, either by weightlifting or calisthentics. Try yoga. Such exercises may not prevent your cardiovascular system from deteriorating somewhat, but it at least is better than sitting in front of the TV set.

3. *Become involved in another sport.* Running is not the only fitness activity; it merely is one of the best. Join the YMCA and substitute laps in the pool for miles on the road. Learn to play racquetball or volleyball. While at the Y, take a few laps around the gym floor just to remember what running was like. If snow and ice are what deters your winter running rather than cold air, consider the sport of cross-country skiing. From a point of general conditioning, it probably is superior to running since in addition to cardiovascular benefits it also exercises the upper body. Many competitive runners now use cross country skiing as an alternate conditioning activity.

4. *Run now and then.* Even the coldest winter has days when the sun shines, the air lies still, and the temperature may soar into the 50s and 60s. Be ready for those days so you can enjoy them with a quick run. Don't overdo it, because you will be far from your summer level of conditioning, but you at least can get an occasional jog in this way.

5. *Plan to vacation down south.* Instead of vacationing during the summer, take a mid-winter trip to Florida, Arizona, or California. (If you live in those states, this chapter wasn't meant for you anyway.) Plan to do some running while absorbing the rays of the sun, but avoid getting the bottoms of your feet sunburned.

Sooner or later the temperature will rise, the buds will pop out on the trees, and you can resume your regular running regimen. You will be better prepared to enjoy a summer of running if you don't allow yourself to get too far out of shape.

Maintenance Running

Even competitive runners occasionally go into partial hibernation, restoring their energy so they can resume full training later with more dedication. I began running year-round in 1953 following my graduation from college. For several years prior to that I did no running in either the summer or winter between cross-country and track seasons. It was more from ignorance than any other reason that caused me to take such pre-season breaks. Once I began serious training, however, I have run continuously to the present time with two exceptions: during my bout with mononucleosis in the fall of 1956 and because of a torn cartilage in my knee which caused me to not run during the summer of 1969. (I swam every day, however.)

But though I ran almost daily during this period of nearly a quarter century, I did not always run hard. At certain periods, I limited my running to a mile or two a day. At other times I ran good mileage in practice, but stayed away from competition, sometimes for a period of six months to a year. And during other periods, even though I trained and raced, I did so at a lesser level, being content to finish comfortably in the middle of the pack and not attempt to win or run fast times. This may be one reason why I have been able to survive as a runner for so long: because I controlled my sport, rather than let it control me.

In discussing training methods earlier in this book we talked about the patterns of Bill Bowerman and Ron Gunn: a hard day followed by an easy day, tear followed by repair. The pattern of my running career sometimes has been a tear year followed by a repair year.

If business, family, or other pressures limit your time available for training, you may want to try some form of maintenance running during the middle of the week. I assume you would have more time to get out on the weekend. Fred Wilt formerly advised me on my training when I was trying to make the Olympic team in the marathon in 1964, and I was impressed by a pattern of workout he sometimes used on days when he had a minimum time for running.

He would drive to a nearby track and run eight laps, or two miles. The first mile was a slow warmup jog, then at the start of the fifth lap he would sprint 220 yards, following that with 110 yards jogging. Then 220 sprint, 110 jog again. In this way he covered the second mile on the track, permitting five 220 yard sprints and 110 jogs with an extra 110 cool down at the end. (When I adapted this pattern to my own lifestyle, I deleted the track but ran the workout instead on the road in front of my home. I would jog a mile in one direction, then turn and come back doing fartlek.) This workout could be accomplished in about 15 minutes, and it will *keep* you in shape, although it will not necessarily *get* you in shape. It is the sort of workout you can do it you already have a good background of long distance running and interval training, but merely want to stay in running trim with minimal commitment. I used to call this exercise: Wiltlek.

Probably if Fred jogged to the track instead of drove to it, he could have added a few more miles to his regimen and be able to profit from it longer. One problem with Wiltlek is that sooner or later you reach a point of diminishing returns and need to recondition yourself.

Dr. Sheehan has proposed on occasion that runners consider training only every other day. This fits in with what physiologists tell us about exercise: like uranium, exercise has a half-life. According to Dr. Noel D. Nequin, the half-life of exercise is 60 hours, or two-and-a-half days. It takes that long for the benefit you receive from an extended workout period to wear out, meaning you have to recharge your battery. This suggests that you should retrain every 60 hours, or put in more practical terms, every other day, preferably four days a week.

Sunday: Do an LSD run with friends of at least an hour's duration, maybe more if you have a good background of conditioning.
Monday: Nothing.
Tuesday: Wiltlek. Fifteen minutes of jogging and short sprints. Do this at noon instead of eating a large lunch. Have a quick snack on fruit afterwards.
Wednesday: More nothing.
Thursday: A half hour of easy running. Get up before breakfast to accomplish this. You can lose this extra sleep at least one day a week, or have a light breakfast instead of your usual big one.
Friday: Still more nothing.
Saturday: Forty-five minutes of FCR training. Push a little at the end, but

only if you feel good. Maybe you might want to enter a fun run. Since you are under no pressure to get to work, waste some time jogging before and after.

With such an easy schedule you can combine your running with the other demands of your busy life. During different times of the year, you may want to increase your commitment: train daily, covering more miles so that later you can return to a maintenance level of running.

Diet

When I originally made a chapter outline for "The Beginner's Running Guide," I planned to include a chapter on diet for runners. I included three such chapters in "Fitness After Forty" and later edited another book for World Publications, a compilation of articles by different writers on diet, entitled: "The Complete Diet Guide for Runners and Other Athletes." While finishing "The Beginner's Running Guide," I am looking forward to collaborating with dietitian Joanne Milkereit on: "The Runner's Cook Book." Joanne works for the Hyde Park Co-op, a supermarket on the south side of Chicago, from which she has taken a leave of absence to cook and prepare menus and recipes that would be helpful to runners.

But the more I learn about diet and nutrition, the more I realize that there are very few secrets that can help you run fast. Runners should probably eat more carbohydrates in relation to proteins and fats than does the typical American whose ideal meal of a thick, juicy steak may contribute to heart disease. But surprisingly, when people start to exercise they subconsciously begin to alter their dietary habits. The best words of advice are those of Joanne Milkereit: "Eat a wide variety of lightly processed foods." Joanne believes each runner should tape that message to his or her refrigerator. This is the third book in succession in which I have used that quote, and you probably will see it reappear in future Higdon books on running or diet, because I believe in it.

I also believe that the food faddists are kidding themselves if they believe that eating so-called "natural" foods and ingesting massive amounts of vitamins, minerals, and other dietary supplements will make them run faster than if they follow Joanne's advice. I happen to enjoy certain natural foods, but more for reasons of taste than because I believe they will permit me to cut my marathon time. The May 1978 issue of *Track &*

Field News contained a letter from a reader from California who expressed shock that Bill Rodgers ate pizza, which he labeled as "junk food." The reader recommended a diet of "power foods" such as honey, bee-pollen, carob candy, vitamin E, and ginseng tea. I would be glad to go on a pizza diet for a month while Bill Rodgers ate nothing but the above; at the end of that period I probably would beat him. Far from being junk food, pizza can provide a balanced diet in itself with, in addition to its good pasta base, tomatoes, cheese, mushrooms, and almost anything else you want to toss on it. More later in "The Runner's Cook Book."

But in terms of hibernating from running and going into a diminished maintenance schedule, the runner who wishes to hibernate in winter should consider what this may do not to his cardiovascular condition, but also to his weight. A runner who goes from 30 miles weekly of running to zero burns 3000 less calories a week. If he continues to eat at the same rate, he will gain considerable weight, so that when he emerges from his burrow in spring it will be considerably more difficult to begin running once more. So if you are going to hibernate you probably should not eat. Consider the lesson of the groundhog, who accumulates body fat during the fall so that his metabolism can survive until spring without further nourishment. In short, if you do not plan to run during the winter, do not go out with Bill Rodgers for pizza. He can afford the extra calories, but you cannot.

26

Going All the Way

Reaching the
world-class level

At the sixth annual Podiatric Sports Medicine Seminar, held in Chicago in May of 1978, I shared the podium with George Sheehan and Steven Subotnick. One of Dr. Sheehan's premises, offered at the clinic, was that you do not need to run twice-a-day or even once-a-day, to compete successfully. George seemingly thrives on a schedule (similar to the one offered in the previous chapter) that includes a workout on Tuesday, a workout on Thursday, and a race over the weekend. He told of one friend who runs not a single step in anger or for fitness during the week, then runs 20 miles on Saturday, races on Sunday, and beats him consistently. The inference was that least is best, that possibly if runners did less running they might like it more because they would have more of a *zest* (the word George used) for each individual workout. I agree with that advice—up to a point.

Yet I am an obsessed individual who runs daily, sometimes twice daily, and on certain occasions even *three* times daily. I have seen my share of 100-mile weeks. Steve Subotnick warned the audience against trying to follow my advice: "He's a world-class athlete, and they're not human like us." His point was that the fast marathoners did not necessarily achieve their ability because of doing 100-mile weeks, but were able to *survive* 100-mile weeks because of their ability—so don't try to copy what they do. I agree with that advice—up to a point.

The comments of Sheehan and Subotnick, however, worried

one woman in the audience. She raised her hand to ask a question: "Do you mean we're not supposed to run every day?"

I assured her that it was perfectly all right to take daily workouts. "Run as much as you feel like running," I said, "as long as you enjoy it." As an example I mentioned John Joyce's friend, cited earlier in this book, who averaged 30 miles a day running in the forest preserves even though he had no desire to compete in races. He ran because he enjoyed it, not because he thought it would improve his performance and enable him to qualify for the Olympic team.

Yet people do aspire to run in the Olympics, or to win the Boston Marathon (or even to *qualify* for Boston), or to set personal bests at various distances or in miscellaneous races. They are performance-oriented rather than fitness-oriented and want to squeeze the last ounce of potential out of their body.

This includes, for all his talk about every-other-day workouts, Dr. Sheehan — as you will discover if you ever come into the last 385 yards of a marathon shoulder-to-shoulder with him. I would rather try to outkick Frank Shorter. In the last 100 yards of the 1978 Boston Marathon, Bill Robinson of Washington came up on Frank who then was running in 22nd place. Bill paused, as though unwilling to pass, but Frank waved him past. George Sheehan would not do that. George will do everything but call out the National Guard to prevent you from reaching the line before him. If he happens to be carrying a bottle of beer in his hand (which frequently happens, George believing that beer improves marathon performance), he may even hit you over the head with it. George probably is even more competitive than I am when it comes to long distances.

As for Steve Subotnick, he wants so much to run the marathon faster than three hours (he has done 3:14), but bewails his lack of ability. Steve's problem, however, is less lack of ability than lack of commitment. To achieve this goal he would have to sacrifice time away from his practice or time away from his family, which he does not want to do — an admirable trait I might add. Also, he enjoys running marathons too much, so he will often run three or four in a period of several months. Steve is insane. Never listen to anything he tells you. For anyone to achieve their best, they must be willing to abandon temporary goals that surface-month-to-month, week-to-week, and focus far down the road to a single monumental (and maybe unattainable) goal, which for Steve would be the three-hour marathon.

Of course, this is what the running elite do. As this book is being published in the summer of 1978 there are already not merely several dozen, but probably several hundred, and perhaps even several thousand extremely fast runners focusing their attention on the Olympic marathon to be run several years hence in the summer of 1980. Some of these runners will have been concentrating their planning on that event for several years past, and a few of them may even be looking beyond that goal toward 1984.

Much of the advice in this book has been directed at new runners, people who may never have run before picking it up. The word *beginner* is clearly stated in the title. But at the other end of the scale is the elite runner, the person who not merely wants to run with the best, but want to run faster than the best. But to be included in the elite, you do not necessarily have to be fast, you may only need to be dedicated to performance. The individual who seeks to optimize his talents (as Steve Subotnick might) to break three hours for the marathon, and qualify for Boston, also becomes psychologically or physically part of the running elite. The person over 40 who seeks to go under 3:30 does the same. The person who wants to improve to below 4:00 can be as motivated as the one who merely seeks to *finish* 26 miles 385 yards. Excellence is relative, and the real over-achievers may finish far back in the pack.

Looking Ahead

At various times during the last several decades I have talked to most of the fast American distance runners, as well as many from abroad, and although specific details in their training differ, and trends in training change, three common denominators exist among the people at the top level today: (1) They run 100 miles a week; (2) They train twice a day; and (3) Usually three of their weekly workouts are at race pace or faster.

Some run more and some run less, and Frank Shorter does things slightly different than Bill Rodgers, who may not be running exactly the way Don Kardong or Garry Bjorklund do, but they have much in common. Unless you can come up with some secret training regimen that will revolutionize the sport, you probably need to train like Frank, Bill, Don, and Garry if you want to beat them. And even if you don't expect to beat them, but merely want to maximize your own abilities, you may need to follow their lead.

The fitness jogger, recreational runner, runner, or racer who decides that tomorrow he will embark on a training regimen encompassing the three common denominators listed above, however, is headed for trouble. More specifically, he is headed for Dr. Sheehan, Dr. Subotnick, or one of their peers. By doing too much too soon, you may become a candidate for a coronary (Sheehan) or a leg injury (Subotnick). When this happens, Sheehan will tell you that you ran too much and Subotnick will tell you you should not allow world-class runners to tell you how to train.

True, but world-class runners succeed for reasons beyond the three commonalities already mentioned. Let us consider how we might learn from the world-class athletes.

• **World-class Lesson 1: Establish a Goal.** You never will achieve success unless you determine in advance what success you want to achieve. Remember Sidney Jarrow's advice as quoted in chapter five: "The man who doesn't know where he's going, any road will take him there." When we discussed this point in terms of beginning runners in that chapter, it was in relation to goals set several weeks, or months, in advance.

The elite runner is less concerned with extending distance, having long since proved an ability to run far, but worries more about the time necessary to cover that distance. The focus often is quality rather than quantity. That person also may be achievement-oriented in the sense that victory over other individuals (i.e., a gold medal in the Olympics) may be much more vital than victory over the stopwatch. At the same time, an experienced runner has at least a general idea of how fast he or she must run to achieve that victory. Writing in 1978, I can state with fair certainty that to make the 1980 American Olympic team in the marathon a runner will need to be capable of doing 2:10. Weather, of course, or tactics may cause a slower time in the trials, but considering the current level of American marathoning, it will take at least 2:10— and maybe faster—to finish in the top three at the trials. If I had Olympic ambitions, I would plan my training to achieve that time.

Not even all the elite runners consider themselves capable of winning a gold medal, making the American team, or even qualifying for the American trials (which probably will require a previous sub-2:20 performance for entry). It may be enough to merely come close and maximize their potential. Other slightly less talented runners may ignore the Olympics and focus their efforts on other events in which victory or a maximum performance will be particularly satisfying.

But the important point is that they do have a goal.

• **World-class Lesson 2: Plan Far Ahead.** Once you have a goal and a reasonable idea of what you hope to accomplish, you can plan how to accomplish it. If your goal is to run a sub-2:20 marathon, you know that you need to train yourself to a level of accomplishment where you can average near 5:20 pace for 26 consecutive miles. You need to plan your training not merely to run that fast, but also to run that far.

Occasionally an individual comes along who is tremendously gifted. At the podiatric seminar one of the members of the audience asked a question and during the give-and-take of the answer, I discovered he had been running only nine weeks, but now ran 13 miles every other day. "At a very slow pace," he admitted, but nevertheless that impressed most of us on the podium. Other individuals might train a year or more and not achieve that level.

Similarly, gifted athletes can sometimes double their weekly training mileage from 50 to 100, and their long runs from 10 to 20 with apparent ease. I say "apparently," because often another month or two down the road they suffer some injury because of attempting to do too much too soon.

Less gifted or simply smarter athletes realize they can achieve greater long-range success by gradually increasing the pitch of their training. If they want to go from 50 to 100 miles in weekly mileage, they plan ahead at least six months in advance, which means they need only to increase their weekly training mileage by ten miles each month. That is a monthly increase of only a mile or two each day, permitting the system to adapt gradually, producing less stress, thus less danger of injury.

Speed work can progress in quality at a similar gradual pace. A runner who wants to be able to run an interval workout in 10 x 440 in 60 seconds at the time of maximum competition need not start at that level, but can begin running the quarters at 70-second pace and gradually, every week or two, improve the time by a second or so. Or, approaching from another angle, the runner can begin with three or four 440s and gradually increase the number run. A third variation might be to gradually increase the stress of the interval between each 440, beginning with a 440 walk and eventually jogging the interval at 2:00 pace, and/or cutting the length of the interval. Various formulas can be used to increase the stress of such workouts, although the safest means is to avoid multiple increases, such as improving number, speed, and interval simultaneously. A runner who plans far ahead avoids this trap, which often results in injury.

• **World-class Lesson 3: Develop Your Background.** "Background" might be defined as any nonspecific training that will gradually strengthen the athlete and allow him to compete more successfully later on. The entire theory behind cross-country running for track men is that it permits them to improve their conditioning in the fall so they can run faster in the spring. Of course, many runners found they enjoyed cross-country more than track and reversed the process, utilizing the speed work they did in the spring to prepare them for fall racing. An entire year of competition in cross-country, track, and road races might develop an athlete's background for future years.

The most typical way to develop background, however, is through LSD training at least six months before the regular competitive season. In fact, the training during this period may consist of more SD (slow distance) than L (long). The runner who will be competing intensively once a week at another time of year goes for gentle runs in pleasant surroundings at an aerobic level; that is, not getting out of breath or into oxygen debt. Because part of a runner's ability to compete successfully depends on psychological maturity as well as physiological maturity, the importance of this training may center on its relaxed nature as much as the quality of work done. "Developing background" in some respects can be a euphemism for "taking it easy." This is necessary if the athlete needs to recharge his mental battery to be able to face the stress of difficult training at a later time of the year.

• **World-class Lesson 4: Utilize the Seasons.** In planning ahead, take note of the weather. In the northern part of the country, particularly in the midwest, the winters are difficult. Unless a runner has access to indoor facilities, he may have to cope several months of the year with zero temperatures and snow. This may be a critical problem if the runner plans to be doing 10 x 440 in 60 seconds in January, but not if that same runner is content merely to go out and run gently, run long (to borrow a phrase from Joe Henderson). Most midwest runners do not try to battle the weather, but simply accept it and utilize this time of year for their background training. This may be a massive rationalization on our parts, but I feel that we often emerge stronger because of weather-imposed stress, which in some respects might even be compared to high-altitude training. It is not necessary that running an hour or two at 9:00-10:00 pace on icy roads improves me physically, but only that I *think* it does.

Likewise, when the weather grows hot in the summer, runners in our area sometimes cut their mileage and do more speed work on the track, or slow their pace once again and allow the heat to provide them with the same stress-related workouts the cold did six months before. Obviously, you can best integrate hot and cold weather running into your training if you have followed lessons one and two, establishing a goal and planning ahead.

• **World-class Lesson 5: Never Miss a Day.** If you want to be good, you need to be consistent with your training. Most important, you have to take a professional attitude toward what supposedly is an amateur sport. This means that you cannot let anything interfere with your ability to achieve your daily, and sometimes twice-daily, workout. This does not necessarily mean you have to be less a husband, less a parent, or less a job-holder, but you have to balance those activities with the necessity of your regular training.

Why? Consider Sisyphus. It was the fate of Sisyphus in Greek mythology to push a giant boulder up a steep hill. Whenever Sisyphus paused to catch his breath, however, the boulder rolled down to the bottom of the hill, causing him to begin all over again. This occurred endlessly. Achieving excellence in running is somewhat the same way: If you pause to catch your breath too long the boulder starts slipping.

Someone must have told Ron Hill the legend of Sisyphus, because he never misses a day, never misses a workout. I encountered Ron at a dinner before the start of the New York City Marathon, and he told me that he had not missed a single day's training since 1964! That meant nearly 14 years of continuous, unbroken training, even during times when Ron had such severe injuries that he could limp barely a half mile or so to maintain his string. Not only has Ron Hill not missed a day training, but he has not missed a *workout*, more impressive since, except for the one day a week when he takes a single, extra-long run, Ron runs twice daily. So his feat includes 14 years of 13-workout weeks.

Ron Hill does not boast about his continuous workout streak. He mentioned it matter-of-factly in response to my inquiry about the matter. At the same time, he betrayed an obvious pride in his achievement, as well he should. Although at one stage of his career he attempted to pack in high mileage in the 140-150 miles-per-week range, he found this contributed to too many injuries, so despite his obsession he now averages only 70-80 miles-per-week. He usually runs to and from work, which means he saves both time and money by his routine.

Obsession? Yes, Ron Hill is obsessed with maintaining his string of continuous workouts, as he might readily admit himself. Critics might claim that such excessive dedication to running robs the sport of its game-like quality, but remember: we are not talking in this chapter about fun running. We are talking about "going all the way," the price one needs to pay to extract the final percentile of your ability. Ron Hill's obsession—or "faithfulness" to use a more charitable word—is one reason why he became one of the world's top marathon runners.

- **World-class Lesson 6: Run Twice Daily.** There may be some champion long distance runners who achieve success on single daily workouts, but if so I am not aware of them. There also may be a few who succeed on less than 100 miles a week, but they are the exception rather than the rule. It is almost an axiom that to achieve those seemingly necessary 100-mile weeks, you need to train twice daily.

I can think of two exceptions to the mileage rule. When Craig Virgin was running at the University of Illinois, he averaged *only* 80 miles a week in double workouts and claimed he never had run more than that during his (then young) career. However, he also concentrated on races shorter than 10,000 meters. Craig substituted quality for quantity. Jeff Wells, the Dallas seminary student who finished only two seconds behind Bill Rodgers in the 1978 Boston Marathon reportedly averages *only* 90 miles a week in his training. But Jeff also includes 30-mile training runs in his schedule.

Alex Breckenridge, a member of the 1960 American Olympic team in the marathon, trained *three* times daily, usually about five miles a workout. Most top runners, however, seem content with double workouts.

As to when they take those workouts, the most common pattern is for runners to rise early and take an easy morning run before having breakfast and going to work or school. The second workout later in the afternoon usually serves as the harder (or longer) one. But with the rise of long distance running as almost a professional sport, more and more runners now make the first workout of the day their quality one, running in the late morning. Their afternoon workout may then become the easy one. New Zealand coach Arthur Lydiard recommends this pattern, suggesting that the second workout can be used for recovery, permitting the runner to train hard again the next morning.

Of course, to be able to hold to this training pattern, the runner needs to have the flexibility to run when he wants. Because more and more American runners now operate running-related businesses (Frank Shorter Sporting Goods, Bill Rodgers Running Center), they often are their own bosses and have this flexibility. As a free-lance writer, I establish my own working hours so have been taking hard mid-day workouts for years, particularly during cold winter months when that is the only way to find the sun. Unfortunately, not every runner has the opportunity to run when they want, or even twice a day. But in this chapter we are not talking about "every" runner, only about those who seek excellence at the highest level.

- **World-class Lesson 7: Run Fast Three Times a Week.** Along with the steady, double workouts and the 100-mile weeks, another common demoninator among top runners seems to be speed work at least three times weekly. Frank Shorter claims to run three "interval" workouts a week, although he sometimes classifies a fast race on the weekend as one of those workouts. He also says that most of the other world-class runners he trains with, or talks to, do about the same whether it be around the track, back in the woods, or on the roads. Bill Rodgers admits to only one fast track workout weekly, but he races hard on weekends, and usually gets some fast running in with his regular long runs on the road.

The point is that if you expect to be able to compete at a

certain speed, you need to achieve that speed (and particularly that *rhythm*) several times during the week, particularly as the competitive season grows near. Lydiard has his runners do four to six weeks of anaerobic training (i.e., speed work) immediately before competition. Three seems to be the most common number of weekly speed workouts, which also fits in with the hard/easy pattern which many runners follow.

I suspect also that on at least one day a week you need to train at a faster-than-average speed again, particularly in the last month or so before the important race (or races) for which you are pointing. There are two reasons for this. If you expect to be competitive, you need to develop a fast finishing kick for the end of the race as well as develop the ability to go out fast for tactical reasons. Second, running fast is another form of stretching and may actually help to loosen muscles tightened by long miles on the road.

• **World-class Lesson 8: Don't Be Afraid to Run Slow.** Despite the above advice on fast running, the top runners in the world put in a lot of their mileage at a relative "slow" speed. Of course, slow for Bill Rodgers might be a 6:30 pace, which would be far beyond the ability of many fitness joggers for even one mile. But that would be the equivalent of a three-hour marathoner running at 8:00 to 9:00 pace during workouts.

Occasionally, I will have a slower runner come visit or ask to work out with me, and we will set off on a ten-mile training run along one of my favorite courses. Frequently that slower runner seems to want to move at a much *faster* pace than I want to, so I have to struggle somewhat to keep up with an individual who, if we ran ten miles in a race, might finish anywhere from five to ten minutes behind me. Often this is because that individual feels self-conscious about running with a so-called "faster" runner and extends himself for fear of holding the other back.

And I have been guilty of the same. When my son Kevin comes home from college on the weekend, we often train together. After finishing, we each accuse the other of pushing the pace so as not to slow the other person's training. As runners we should simply relax and run comfortably within our own workout scheme. In the long run, it matters little what you do on any one specific workout than it does the combination of all your workouts over a period of many, many months and even many, many years.

• **World-class Lesson 9: Don't Let Other Runners Rush You.** Steve Subotnick called me from California one day around noon and during our conversation, I commented that I had just finished a 12-mile workout. Steve paused, then announced he was about to go out and run 15 miles. I countered by stating that the 12-miler was only my *first* workout of the day. Steve finally said: "Hell, if I was as fast as you, I wouldn't have to train!"

Runners constantly try to "psych" each other—either by understating or overstating what they do in training. But when runners talk for publication, you always hear about the great workouts, never the bad ones. Magazines such as *Track & Field News* often publish workout schedules of world-class athletes, and usually it is the toughest week that runner ever had in his career—after which he suffered some stress injury. As Marty Liquori commented: "Runners always lie about their training." It is not so much that they lie, but that they simply don't tell all of the truth. You hear about the days when they ran a dozen 440's in 55 seconds, not the ones where they finished the last one in 75 practically on their hands and knees.

Don't believe everything you read in the training books, including this one. And, more important, when you have an opportunity to train with other runners at your competitive level, don't turn the workout into a shootout on Main Street. Save your competitive spirit for the races when it counts. If you know your own capabilities and know that your training is on schedule to achieve your desired goal, it matters little whether someone seems to be obtaining better results by doing something different. You may be able to learn from the successes of others, but don't be trapped by them.

• **World-class Lesson 10: Don't Run with Pain.** When you get injured, seek advice promptly. Notice that I said *when*, not *if*, the assumption being that a person who runs twice daily, covers 100 miles a week, including speed work, and trains near the maximum limit, sooner or later will fall off the tightrope. This may not result in disaster if you act promptly and seek the proper medical attention, either by consulting a podiatrist, an orthopedist, a physiotherapist, or maybe even a psychiatrist. Such treatment may be expensive, but if your primary goal is excellence you should be willing to pay the price, whether in hours of dedication or in whatever it takes to achieve your goal.

Is the Price Worth It?

Many individuals who run for enjoyment may feel disturbed by the message implicit in the lessons of world-class runners. The terms *world-class* or *elite* imply an individual who is singularly obsessed with his own achievement and willing to trample anyone standing in his way of victory. I know people like that, but I also know many others who pursue excellence yet do not lose their own humanity.

For some, the price to be paid for joining the ranks of the elite is too high, not only in terms of effort spent training but also from sacrificing what might be considered a normal life. I suppose everybody has their own idea of normal. Normal in America today may be smoking, overeating, getting drunk, and watching TV six hours a night. Most individuals who get involved in running programs turn their back on that norm, yet they may not be willing to push to the other extreme described in this chapter. More often it is not a matter of their willingness, but the ability to do so. As Arthur Lydiard says, "You can't put five gallons into a four-gallon can." But running—at any level from fitness jogger to elite runner—can be an important part of enjoying life.

A GUIDE FOR ELITE RUNNERS

PHASE ONE

If you find yourself capable of training comfortably at the racing and marathon levels suggested at the ends of earlier chapters, you have enough basic background to move into a more advanced schedule of training and join the running elite. I don't necessarily recommend this, but if you have talent this is how to maximize that talent—or at least help determine your limits. You should already be doing 50-70 miles a week, but to join the running elite you must increase your training mileage 50 to 100%—a minimum of 100 miles a week.

Don't panic, because it may be easier than you think. Most runners at the racer level accomplish such a jump by adding a second daily workout to their regular schedule. For someone training 70 miles a week, adding a second run of four or five miles daily is enough to reach the 100-mile level where all the elite seem to congregate.

But don't go out and do it next week. Advances are best made gradually, and you may want to spend anywhere from six months to a year—*or more*—slowly increasing your workout mileage. Begin, in this first stage, by adding an occasional easy run of two to four miles once or twice a week to your normal training pattern. Find out how your body tolerates the extra stress. Determine the best time of day to take this run, and also the best place to do the workout. For the sake of this schedule, let us assume that you will be taking your easier run in the morning and your harder workouts in the afternoon. Once you feel comfortable with occasional twice daily workouts, move on to Phase Two.

PHASE TWO

Convert immediately into a twice-a-day runner. You already have developed a reasonably good background from previous training schedules, so you should be able to make this change in patterns relatively fast. But while running twice daily, cut the quantity and quality of your normal workout so as not to increase the stress. Don't do much more than you were doing in the final phases of chapters 18 and 19 in terms of mileage. Plan to run seven days a week, however, with double workouts on at least six of those days.

Sunday:	Ten to 15 mile LSD run.
Monday:	AM—Two to three miles easy jogging.
	PM—Three to six miles at a relaxed pace.
Tuesday:	AM—Two to three miles easy jogging.
	PM—Six to ten miles at a steady pace.
Wednesday:	AM—Two to three miles easy jogging.
	PM—Three to six miles at a relaxed pace.
Thursday:	AM—Two to three miles easy jogging.
	PM—Eight to 12 miles FCR.
Friday:	AM—Two to three miles easy jogging.
	PM—Three to six miles at a relaxed pace.
Saturday:	AM—Two to three miles easy jogging.
	PM—Four to eight miles fartlek.

This workout pattern should give you 50-80 miles of running. Begin at the lower mileage and over a period of several months gradually build up to the higher one. When you are able to maintain this amount of training comfortably, move on to Phase Three.

PHASE THREE

Continue your regular twice-daily workout pattern, but steadily increase the mileage you run, as follows:

Sunday:	Fifteen to 20 mile LSD run.
Monday:	AM—Three to six miles easy jogging.
	PM—Five to ten miles at a relaxed pace.
Tuesday:	AM—Five to eight miles steady run.
	PM—Eight to 12 miles steady run, pushing the last few miles.
Wednesday:	AM—Three to six miles easy jogging.
	PM—Five to ten miles at a relaxed pace.

Thursday:	AM—Five to eight miles steady run.
	PM—Ten to 15 miles FCR.
Friday:	AM—Three to six miles easy jogging.
	PM—Five to ten miles at a relaxed pace.
Saturday:	AM—Three to six miles easy jogging.
	PM—Five to ten miles fartlek, or competitive race.

This workout pattern should give you 85-125 miles of running. Gradually build your mileage up over a period of months so that you can regularly average 100 miles or so a week without necessarily worrying about the speed at which you run those miles. If your goal is the 100-mile level, don't feel obligated to cover that many miles *every* week, but over a four-week period the average for those four weeks should be that. When you are able to maintain this high mileage, move on to Phase Four.

PHASE FOUR

Continue your regular twice-daily pattern of workouts. In this phase, you no longer need to increase the *quantity* of your workouts, but concentrate instead on increasing the *quality* of them, particularly by including at least three days of running at faster than race pace. At this level of conditioning, you presumably have become fairly sophisticated and knowledgeable about how fast you are running and what your body can take. Elite runners should worry little about the stopwatch, and don't need a coach standing by the side of the track reciting times except as a form of encouragement. Read your body. Don't be trapped by this schedule. Innovate, shifting from interval work to fartlek to repeats to hill work on your fast days. Train as you feel, but train hard.

Sunday:	AM—Eighteen to 23 mile LSD run.
	PM—One to three miles easy shakedown jog.
Monday:	AM—Three to six miles relaxed running.
	PM—Five to ten miles at a steady pace.
Tuesday:	AM—Five to eight miles steady run.
	PM—Interval training on track. Run at the pace you would run a two-mile race. Jog a short recovery distance between each one. When you think you've run enough, stop.
Wednesday:	AM—Three to six miles easy jogging.
	PM—Eight to 12 mile LSD run.
Thursday:	AM—Five to eight miles steady run.
	PM—Sprint training. Keep distance short enough and repetitions few enough so you can run full speed. For instance: two sets of 10 x 110. Or hill training, springing up the hills at full speed.
Friday:	AM—Three to six miles easy jogging.
	PM—Five to ten miles at a steady pace.

Saturday: AM—Three to six miles relaxed running.

PM—Five to ten miles fartlek, or competitive race.

Once you have reached this final phase, you don't need me giving you advice any more. Other runners will start coming to you for advice on how *they* should train. Continue on with your running career, shifting the mileage and mix of your workouts as you discover what works best for you. As you move from one year to another, remember that the best results usually come from (1) a period of relative relaxation, followed by (2) a period in which you concentrate on quantity, followed by (3) a period where the concentration shifts to quality. As for what to do the week of the most important race of the year, consider the schedule below in Phase Five.

PHASE FIVE

To obtain maximum benefit from your training, you need to ease off just before your most important race of the year. Or you may want to ease off during a period of several weeks when you will be running many important races. Most elite runners taper their training for such races similar to the following schedule.

Sunday: Ten to 15 mile LSD run.

Monday: AM—Three to six miles easy jogging.

PM—Five to ten miles at a relaxed pace.

Tuesday: AM—Three to six miles easy jogging.

PM—Easy interval workout, perhaps half normal difficulty.

Wednesday: Two to four miles easy jogging.

Thursday: Complete rest.

Friday: Easy jogging and walking for whatever distance or time seems comfortable.

Saturday: Win an Olympic gold medal, set a world record, establish a personal best, or simply compete to the best of your abilities.

PHASE SIX

After a maximum performance, or a series of several maximum performances, take anywhere from one to four weeks off from serious running to recharge your batteries. This does not mean you should not run, but rather that you should run at a relaxed pace and whenever it suits your mood. Begin making plans for the next season of running and racing. At the end of this period, you should be hungry again and ready to endure another season of concentrated training toward your next goal.

Index

A

Afternoon running, 83-85
Anderson, Bob, 4
Arm swing, 177-179
Athletic clubs, 212
Athletic supporters, 117-118
Automobiles, *See* Cars

B

Bannister, Roger, 17
Biomechanics of running, 49
Birth control devices
    and running safely, 303
Brands, running shoes, 96-111

C

Camps, running, 213
Carbohydrate—loading, 247-248
Cars
    dealing with, 145-148
Cavanaugh, Peter, 173-174
Children's running
    dangers, 308
    races, 308-309
Clubs, athletic, 212
Coaching
    doing your own, 214
    finding, 211
    running under, 210
Cold
    dressing for, 131-134
    running in, 128-130
Cooper, Dr. Kenneth, 186, 238
Courses, running
    cross-country, 67-70
    roads, 63
    scenic, 64
Cross-country
    courses 67-70

downhill, 272
shortcuts, 276-277
shoes, 278
turns during, 269
uphill, 272

D

Dehydration, 136
Diet, 321-322
Distance practice, 244-245
Doctors, 148-151
Dogs
    dealing with, 142-144
Drayton, Jerome, 4

E

Elite runners
    schedule for 334-337
Exercises
    at home, 318
    before races, 229-230
    stretching, 288-290

F

Fartlek, 191, 194-195
Fast continuous run (FCR), 193-194
Fatigue, fighting, 180-181
Fixx, Jim, 7, 170-172, 197
Foot plant, 94-96, 165, 167
Foot stride, 172-174

G

Girls' running, 309
Glycogen, 92

H

Heat
  racing in, 135
  running in, 134
Henderson, Joe, 11-12, 157, 189

I

Indoor tracks, 32-34, 72-74
  rules, 74-76
  tactics on, 257
Information, exchanging, 6-7
Injuries
  action to take, 281
  changing shoes and, 282
  preventing, 285
  stretching and, 285-287

J

Joggers, *schedule* for 26-28
Jogging
  at home, 25-26
  difference from running, 3-4
Journals, keeping, 215
Juantorena, Alberto, 258

K

Kardong, Don, 1, 47, 55, 325
Kick, finishing, 254-255
Kostrubala, Dr. Thaddeus, 53, 143

L

Levels of running, 197-201
Liquori, Marty, 4, 37
Loading, carbohydrate, 247-248
Long slow distance (LSD),
    192-193, 200, 202, 204-205
Lydiard, Arthur, 37

M

Maintenance running, 319

Marathons
  deciding on running, 238-239
  difficulties of, 240-241
  lifestyle for, 156-158
  preparing for, 246, 326-337
  the wall and, 243
Medical advice
  and injuries, 284
  seeking, 283
Menstruation, 302
Mid-day running, 283
Moore, Kenny, 171
Morning running, 81
Muscles, 38-39

N

Night running, 85
Numbers, race, 227

O

Older runners
  dangers for, 311
  races for, 309-310
Outdoor tracks
  choosing, 71-72
  rules, 74-76

P

Pacing, 255-256
Passing, during races, 259
Physiology of running, 48-49
Pregnancy, 303
Psychology of running, 49-50, 243
Pulse rate, 55

R

Races
  eating and drinking during,
    230-231
  finishing, 232
  going to, 224-225
  numbers in, 227

warmup for, 233
where to start in, 228
Racing
    deciding on, 222-223
Roads, 63
Rodgers, Bill, 4, 13, 16, 39,
    171-172
Running camps, 213
Running courses, 63-70
Running shoes. *See* Shoes, running
Ryun, Jim, 17

S

Schedules
    beginning racers, 233-235
    beginning runners, 43-45
    elite runners, 334-337
    joggers, 26-28
    marathoners, 248-251
Sheehan, Dr. George, 150, 209,
    280-281
Shoes, running
    brand comparison, 96-111
    and injuries, 282
    reasons for, 91-92
    for women, 302
Shorter, Frank, 5, 36, 325
Shorts, running, 118-119
Socks, 114-115
Speedwork, 195-196
Stitches, 41-43
Stretching
    before races, 229-230
    exercises, 288-290
    injury prevention and, 285-287
    when to do, 287
    while running, 290
Stride, 172-174
Subotnick, Dr. Steven, 65,
    169-170, 221, 238, 323

T

Tactics, racing
    boxing as, 264-265
    cross-country, 270-271
    finishing kicks, 254-255
    on hot days, 257
    passing as, 259-263
Technique, 164-167
Tracks. *See* Indoor tracks,
    Outdoor tracks
Training
    patterns for beginners, 203
    two-week pattern, 205
T-shirts, 120-121

V

Vests, 119-120

W

Wall, the (marathon), 243
Warming up, 229
Warmup suits, 116-117
Weather, 128, 216, 317
Weight loss, 55, 216
Wohlhuter, Rick, 129, 258
Women's running
    birth control and, 303
    equipment, 301
    physiological differences, 299
    pregnancy and, 303
    psychological differences, 300
World class running, 326-337
Wristwatches, 121-123

Y

YMCAs, 212
Young runners. *See* Children's
    running

Recommended Reading:

Jog, Run, Race by Joe Henderson. Leads the reader through several new beginnings—from walking to jogging, jogging to running, running to racing. Each beginning has a specific day by day progress guide. Hardback $6.95, Paperback $3.95.

Women's Running by Joan Ullyot, M.D. The first book of its kind to take a serious look at women runners. Tips on diet, clothing, injuries and other problems unique to women. Specific training routines for all levels of abilities. Hardback $5.95, Paperback $3.95.

The Complete Diet Guide: For Runners and Other Athletes, from the Editors of *Runner's World*. How the athlete can use his diet to better advantage is the basis of this book. Areas addressed: Weight control, drinks, fasting, natural vs. processed food, vegetarian diets and more. Hardback $7.95, Paperback $4.95.

Doctor Sheehan on Running, by George Sheehan, M.D. Lively, witty, philosophical, and serious, that's Dr. Sheehan. Provides delightful insight into the world of running and the world of a runner. Packed with good practical information from one of the country's most popular writers on running. Hardback $5.95, Paperback $3.95.

Run Gently, Run Long, by Joe Henderson. Henderson views running as a beautiful pleasant experience. He does not feel that there is any correlation between pain and fitness. He feels that long slow distance (L.S.D.) running can produce optimum training. A beautiful philosophy with many successful users. Paperback $2.95.

Long Run Solution, by Joe Henderson. Henderson devotes this book to the mental rewards of a sport whose popularity is now reaching mammoth proportions. More immediate than the physical benefits, the psychological effects of running are now being explored. Hardback $5.95, Paperback $3.95.

The Running Foot Doctor, by Steven I. Subotnick, D.P.M. Written for the runner rather than the doctor, this book presents the causes and cures of running injuries in more than 25 individual case studies. Hardback $6.95, Paperback $3.95.

Runner's Training Guide, by the Editors of *Runner's World*. An overview of the many training methods in practice today. Looks at the popular systems and the coaches who developed them. Paperback $2.95.

Available in fine bookstores and sport shops, or from:

World Publications, Inc.

Box 366, Dept. A, Mountain View, CA 94042.

Include $.45 shipping and handling for each title (Maximum $2.25).